Energy Law in Colombia

Energy Law in Colombia

Second Edition

Daniel Rincón Rubiano

Luis Ferney Moreno
Milton Montoya Pardo
Adriana Martínez Villegas
Carlos Mantilla McCormick
Luis Pando López
Carlos Forero Jiménez
Daniela Aguilar Abaunza
Juan Felipe Neira
Ana Paola Gutiérrez Rico
Lyndon Winston Jay Huffington

This book was originally published as a monograph in the International Encyclopaedia of Laws/Energy Law.

Founding Editor: Roger Blanpain
General Editor: Frank Hendrickx
Volume Editors: Kurt Deketelaere & Bram Delvaux

Wolters Kluwer

Published by:
Kluwer Law International B.V.
PO Box 316
2400 AH Alphen aan den Rijn
The Netherlands
E-mail: international-sales@wolterskluwer.com
Website: lrus.wolterskluwer.com

Sold and distributed by:
Wolters Kluwer Legal & Regulatory U.S.
7201 McKinney Circle
Frederick, MD 21704
United States of America
E-mail: customer.service@wolterskluwer.com

ISBN 978-94-035-3445-9

e-Book: ISBN 978-94-035-3450-3
web-PDF: ISBN 978-94-035-3451-0

The Authors

Mr Daniel Rincón Rubiano was born in Bogotá, Colombia in 1984. He currently works as senior legal counsel at the DEME Group in Belgium. Prior to that, Mr Rincón Rubiano worked for the Schréder Group and for Enhesa in Brussels, Belgium and for Dentons-Cárdenas & Cárdenas and Deloitte in Bogota, Colombia. Mr Rincón Rubiano obtained his Law degree from Universidad del Rosario, Colombia, in 2006 and completed a postgraduate specialization in Corporate Law at the same university. Mr Rincón Rubiano has an LLM in Energy and Environmental Law from the Katholieke Universiteit of Leuven, Belgium. Daniel is a fellow member of the Sustainability College of Bruges, member of the Ibero-American Association of Energy Law – ASIDE and carries out investigation on international topics for the Department of Mining-Energy Law of the Universidad Externado de Colombia. Mr Rincón Rubiano is the author of Environmental Law in Colombia published by Wolters Kluwer in 2011.

Mr Luis Ferney Moreno is the director of the Department of Mining and Energy Law at the Universidad Externado de Colombia and managing partner of the law firm Moreno Servicios Legales, in Bogota. He graduated as a lawyer from the Universidad Externado, and has a Specialization in Tax Law and an LLM in Economic Law from the University of Louvain, Belgium. Mr Moreno has published a number of books and articles, such as *Household Public Utilities: Perspectives of Economic Law* Prior to joining Moreno Servicios Legales, Mr Moreno worked as auditor for the General Auditing Agency for the National Federation of Coffee Producers, in Brussels, Belgium. He has also performed as national expert in renewable energies for the United Nations for Industrial Development, and legal counsel for regulatory harmonization for Panama and Central America, among other countries. Mr Moreno holds a PhD in Law from Université Catholique de Louvain, Belgium. Mr Moreno has been member of the Senate of Colombia, within which he has worked for the commissions on mining, environmental issues, energy, international affairs and trade.

The Authors

Milton Montoya Pardo obtained his PhD in Law from Universidad Complutense de Madrid and was rated 'Excellent Cum Laude.' He has a Master's in Energy Law from the Energy Institute-YPF Foundation (Instituto Superior de la Energía-ISE – Fundación Repsol YPF), Diploma in Electricity and Gas Regulation from Universidad Externado de Colombia and a lawyer from the same university. He is currently Research Director of the Mining and Energy Law Department at Universidad Externado de Colombia and Professor at the same University of Competition Law in the Energy Sector, Competition Policy, European Energy Law, Renewable Energy Regulation and Research Methodology. He has been a guest lecturer at the University of Dundee, University Carlos III of Madrid and the University of Almería. He is the author of several publications on energy regulation, competition and energy policy. His last book, published by Universidad Externado de Colombia (2012), is called *Merger Control in the European Energy Industry.*

Ms Adriana Martínez Villegas was born in Cartagena de Indias, Colombia, in 22 January 1965. Ms Martínez graduated from Law School at the Javeriana University in Bogota, and completed her postgraduate studies in Corporate Law at the same University. She participated in the drafting of the Colombian Mining Code (Law 685 of 2001) as advisor to the Government. Ms Martínez is currently the President of the Oil and Mines Lawyers Association and lecturer at the Colombian Externado University in Mining Law, Procedural Mining Law and Mining Contracts, in the Oil and Mines Legislation Programme. Adriana Martínez is the head of Martinez-Cordoba & Abogados Asociados, a law firm specialized in Oil and Mines Law with twenty-five years of practice.

Mr Carlos Mantilla McCormick works as a partner in the law firm Martinez, Cordoba & Abogados Asociados in the areas of mining, oil & gas, and environmental law. He practised as lawyer of the Bogotá Chamber of Commerce, adviser of the Bank Superintendence and Manager of the Loteria La Nueve Millonaria Ltda. He has been an Attorney (1992–2006) and Legal Manager (2006–2010) of Occidental de Colombia, Inc. (Colombian branch of Occidental Petroleum Corporation-OXY). Mr Mantilla graduated from the Universidad Externado de Colombia as a Doctor of Law, from Pontificia Universidad Javeriana as a Commercial Law Specialist, from Instituto Universitario de Administracion de Empresas, Universidad Autónoma de Madrid, Spain, as a Master in Business Administration. Carlos has also been Professor at the Universidad Externado de Colombia of Civil and Commercial Law since 1987, Oil and Gas Law since 1998. He received scholarships from Instituto de Cooperación Iberoamericana and Universidad Externado de Colombia. He is a

Member of the Colegio de Abogados de Minas y Petróleos. He is the author of many essays and articles in books and newspapers, and lecturer at diverse national and international congresses, symposiums and conferences.

Mr Luis Pando López is Colombian, Canadian and Spanish citizen, graduated as lawyer from the Universidad del Rosario (Bogota, Colombia), has an LLM from the University of Alberta (Edmon, Canada), LLM in Energy Law from the Instituto Superior de la Energía (Madrid, Spain), and Master's in Regulation and Economics of Public Services from the Unversidad de Barcelona (Barcelona, Spain). His areas of expertise include energy law, public services, competition law and consumer protection. Mr Pando has wide knowledge in the Colombian energy sector, where we has the General Secretary of the Colombian Association of Natural Gas – NATURGAS and has also worked as advisor for several companies in the gas sector. Luis Alejandro also performed as senior lawyer at the Superintendence of Industry and Commerce (SIC) and counsel of the European Union for the implementation of the competition advocacy mechanism. At present, Mr Pando is partner of the law firm Estudio Palacios Lleras S.A.S, member of the Centre of Studies for Competition Law – CEDEC, lecturer and researcher at the Universidad Externado de Colombia, and author of various articles and lectures in matters of energy law, regulation of public services, and competition.

Mr Carlos Forero Jiménez is a Colombian citizen graduated as lawyer from Universidad de los Andes (Bogotá, Colombia). He specialized in International Business Law and Tax Law, has a Master's in Finance from Universidad de los Andes and a teacher at the postgraduate school of Universidad de los Andes and the postgraduate school of Universidad Externado de Colombia of the course 'Foreign Investment Regime and Tax Regime of the Hydrocarbon and Mining Industry'. His areas of expertise are tax advice, tax planning, foreign investment regime, customs law and public policy, specifically focused on the oil & gas sector, mining, commodities trading and maritime and fluvial transport and port infrastructure. He worked as an associate at the firm Brigard & Urrutia for over four years, then as senior associate at the firm Godoy & Hoyos for over three years and since year 2013 he joined Trafigura, a multinational trading corporation in the oil & gas and mining sector around the globe. Currently he is the CFO in Colombia for Trafigura. Some of his publications include: 'Causas y consecuencias de la aplicación de la Convención de Viena sobre compraventa internacional de mercaderías como lex mercatoria'. *Private Law Review, Universidad de los Andes* 2007 and 'Tax Rules for Private Equity Funds in Colombia'. *International Tax Review, World Tax* 2012, p. 149.

The Authors

Ms Daniela Aguilar Abaunza holds a PhD in Law from the University of Waikato, New Zealand, Master's in Energy Law and Policy from the University of Dundee in Scotland, a diploma in Mining and Energy Law from Externado University of Colombia and a lawyer from the same university. She is currently a researcher and lecturer of the Mining and Energy Law Department at Externado University, Colombia, teaching renewable energy regulation, energy decentralization and new technologies in the electricity sector. She is the author of several publications on renewable energy law, prosumers and energy poverty. Currently, works in New Zealand as a project manager of pilot projects for multiple trading relationships in the electricity sector and as consultant for community energy projects.

Mr Juan Felipe Neirais a Colombian citizen graduated with a Law degree from Externado de Colombia University. He also graduated from the Center for Policy and Law in Energy, Petroleum and Mining at the University of Dundee, in the LLM-programme in Petroleum Law and Policy and the MSc-programme in International Oil and Gas Management. He also holds PhD. from the same University, with research in Energy Policy and Sustainable Development. His professional experience has been focused on advising international organizations and private entities, analysis and design of public policies on energy. He has several magazine publications from Latin America and Europe on matters of law and regulation of conventional and unconventional hydrocarbons and energy policy. He is also a professor-researcher in the Department of Energy Mining Law at the Externado de Colombia University and has been a visiting professor at the University of Stirling (Scotland), the Pontificia Universidad Católica del Perú and the University of West Indies (Trinidad and Tobago).

Ms Ana Paola Gutiérrez Rico is a lawyer from the Universidad Externado de Colombia, PhD student of the Universidad de Almeria, in the programme of Economic, Business and Legal Sciences. She is an International Bar Association scholarship holder for Section on Energy, Environment, Natural Resources, and Infrastructure Law – SEERIL. She holds an MBA from the Universidad de Viña del Mar, Chile, a specialist in Administrative Law from the Universidad del Rosario, a member of the Ibero-American Association of Energy Law – ASIDE. She has experience in providing legal advice to public and private entities, especially in public contract law, civil processes and administrative procedures, mining and oil & gas industries, social management of extractive projects, and environmental matters. She is Research Professor of the Department of Energy and Mining Law at the Universidad Externado de Colombia.

Mr Lyndon Winston Jay Huffington is a lawyer from the Universidad Externado de Colombia, holds a Master's in Law and Development from the University of Melbourne, Australia, specialist in Administrative Law and Energy Mining Law from the Externado de Colombia University, a fellow of the Colfuturo Foundation and the International Bar Association, a researcher at the Institute of Studies in Mining, Oil and Energy Regulation, endorsed in category A by the Ministry of Science, Technology and Innovation of Colombia and member of the Ibero-American Association in Energy Law – ASIDE and Professor at the Externado de Colombia University and legal advisor in Public Law.

The Authors

Table of Contents

Table of Contents

List of Abbreviations

ANH	National Agency of Hydrocarbons
ANLA	National Authority of Environmental Licenses
ANM	National Agency of Mining
AOM	Administration, Operation and Maintenance
API	American Petroleum Institute
ASIC	System Trading Administrator
BMC	Bolsa Mercantil de Colombia
BOMT	Build, Operate, Maintain, and Transfer
BTO	Bulletin of Transport by Pipeline
CARs	Autonomous Regional Corporations
CBM	Coal Bed Methane
CHC	Colombian Holding Company
CND	National Dispatch Centre
CNO	National Operation Council
CONPES	National Council of Economic and Social Policy
COP	Colombian Peso
CREG	Regulatory Commission of Gas and Energy
CSA	Cost Sharing Arrangements
DDA	Declaration of Environmental Alternatives
DG	Distributed Generation
DIMAR	General Marine Agency
DNP	National Planning Department
DTT	Double Taxation Treaties
EBSA	Empresa de Energía de Boyaca E.S.P
EIA	Environmental Impact Assessment
EIS	Environmental Impact Study
ECOPETROL	National Oil and Gas Company
E&P	Exploration and Production
ENFICC	Firm Energy for Reliability Charge
GMF	Financial Transactions Tax

List of Abbreviations

GTS	Technical System Operator
HHI	Herfindahl-Hirschman Index
ISA	Interconexión Eléctrica S.A. E.S.P. TP
LDC	Local Distribution Companies
LNG	Liquefied Natural Gas
MASD	Ministry of Environment and Sustainable Development
MCFD	Million Cubic Feet per Day
MEM	Wholesale Energy Market
MME	Ministry of Mines and Energy
MPCD	Available Capacity of Firm Gas for Sale
MST	Maximum Cost of Service
NCRNR	Natural Resources and Protection to the Environment
NGV	Compressed Natural Gas for Vehicles
NOLs	Net Operating Losses
SINAP	National System of Protected Areas
SDL	Local Distribution System
SPNNN	System of National Nature Parks
STR	Regional Transmission System
REE	Equivalent Electrical Efficiency
RES	Non-Conventional Renewable Resources
RUT	Transport Code
SIC	Superintendence of Industry and Commerce
SIN	National Interconnected System
SNT	National Transport System
SSP	Superintendence of Public Services
TEA	Technical Evaluation Agreement
TSO	Transportation System Operators
UPME	Planning Unit for Mining and Energy Sector
UVT	Tax Value Units
VAT	Value Added Tax
WTI	West Texas Intermediate
ZNI	Non-interconnected Zones

Preface

The authors would like to express their gratitude to the Universidad Externado de Colombia, and in particular, the Department of Mining-Energy Law. The Universidad Externado has pioneered academic programmes and research in energy law, yielding important developments in this field. Energy Law in Colombia represents a significant milestone in a country whose steady economic growth has been mainly driven by mining and energy activities.

The Universidad Externado de Colombia has provided the forum, human capital and knowledge grounds to complete this project.

Sincerely,
Daniel Rincón Rubiano

Opinion Disclaimer

This monograph represents the views of the authors and do not reflect the opinions of the entities to which they are affiliated.

Opinion Disclaimer

General Introduction

§1. GEOGRAPHY AND POPULATION

I. Geography

1. The Republic of Colombia is situated at the north-western corner of South America, on the Equatorial line, between the Tropics, bordering the Caribbean Sea between Panama and Venezuela, and bordering the Pacific Ocean, between Panama and Ecuador, and with geographical coordinates 4°N and 72°W.[1] Its territory is crossed by powerful mountain chains that head to the north and are separated by valleys and broad rivers; to the south-east, the territory spreads out over an immense plain forming the Orinoquia region and the Amazon jungle. Three-quarters of the country are located in the northern hemisphere. Colombia is the only country in South America with coastlines on both oceans. It's total boundary length includes the Caribbean Sea on the north, between Panama and Venezuela, 1,600 kilometres (km); north east with Venezuela, 2,219 km; south east with Brazil, 1,645 km; south west with Peru, 1,626 km and Ecuador, 586 km; west with the Pacific Ocean, between Panama and Ecuador, 1,300 km; and north west with Panama, 266 km. Colombian borders have been established by different treaties, including the Suarez – Muñoz Vernaza of 1916 with Ecuador; Lozano – Salomon of 1922, and the Protocol of Rio of 1934, with Peru; Vasquez Cobo – Martins of 1907, and Garcia Ortiz – Mangabeira of 1928, with Brazil; Spanish Arbitration of 1891, Swiss Arbitration of 1922, and Lopes de Mesa – Gil Borges of 1941 with Venezuela; and the Liévano – Boyd of 1976, with Panama.

2. The total area of the territory comprises 1,138,910 km^2, including 1,038,700 km^2 of land, equivalent to twice the size of Texas, and 100,210 km^2 of water. Colombian territorial sea extends to 12 nautical miles (nm), the exclusive economic zone is 200 nm and the continental shelf is 200 miles depth. The territory includes the archipelago of San Andres and Providencia in the Caribbean Sea, and the islands of Malpelo, Gorgona and Gorgonilla in the Pacific Ocean. The government of Nicaragua has claimed sovereign rights over San Andres and Providencia, as well as other islands in the Caribbean Sea. In addition, Colombia has an ongoing dispute on maritime rights over the Gulf of Venezuela.

1. The World Fact Book, Colombia. https://www.cia.gov/library/publications/the-world-factbook/geos/co.htm 29 Sep. 2020.

3. South American terrain presents a variety of geographical areas that shape different reliefs in the continent, such as the Amazon watershed, the Orinoco region, the Marabina space, the Caribbean Sea, the Pacific Ocean, the Guyana region, the Brazilian region, the trapezium of Chaco-Paraná, the Pampa and the Patagonian cone. As part of South America, Colombia participates from five geographical areas that give birth to the country's geographical and climatic conditions, and are known in Colombia as regions. Colombian regions include the Amazon, Caribbean, Pacific, Orinoco and Andean region, and exhibit different characteristics as to topography, hydrography, climate, natural resources and people, which shapes a regional identity, ethnicity, economy and culture. The regional division is only taken into account for geographical and, to a certain extent, environmental management purposes, provided that the main administrative division of Colombia corresponds to nation, departments and municipalities.

4. Being the least populated, the Colombian Amazon region concentrates 30% of the national territory and is wealthy in biodiversity, being home for more than 50,000 different indigenous people dispersed in numerous communities and a multiplicity of species of fauna and flora amid a vast jungle. The Amazon territory is mainly flat, with variations of hills and low plateaus. The main economic activities taking place in this region include forestry, wild species trading and research for pharmaceutical products. Further up in the northeast and bordering Venezuela, the Orinoco River marks the beginning of the Orinoco region. It has an extensive, flat and warm savannas landscape creating a beautiful contrast between the greens of the grassland and the blue of the horizon, covering the surface of low-populated departments such as Arauca, Casanare, Meta and Vichada. Cattle's breeding is the main economic activity of the region and is carried out in the area known as Oriental Plains. In recent years, the discovery of oil fields in Arauca and Casanare has attracted settlers to this region.

5. The Andean region is the industrial region of Colombia occupying 27% of the territory and hosting the main and most populated cities, including Bogota, Medellin, Cali, and Bucaramanga. As the region covers the three mountain ranges, it offers different landscapes such as *paramos*, high plateaus, snowy mountains, volcanoes, valleys, lacunas, springs and mountainous sources of water. In the northern part of the country, we find the Caribbean region with its varied array of ecosystems, such as dry forests in the Guajira peninsula, humid jungle in the gulf of Uraba or the archipelagos and islands of the Caribbean Sea. Although the terrain of the Caribbean region is mainly flat, the highest peaks of the country, Colon y Bolivar, are found in this region at the Sierra Nevada de Santa Marta, where indigenous communities dwell together with endemic species of flora and fauna. Finally, the Pacific region located at the west side of the country, with its wild coastal trip covered with jungle and mangrove swamps, gives origin to one of the most humid climates with annual precipitations of 9,000 mms in areas such as Choco, as well as high temperatures in the whole region. Due to its biodiversity, this area is also known as the Choco-bio and is home of four natural national parks.

6. In general, Colombian climate is tropical and rather homogeneous all year long. Given its location, there is no spring, summer, autumn or winter, but a rainy and dry season that marks changes in weather and ecology. Climatologic conditions also vary according to latitude and altitude factors, which yield temperatures exceeding 23 degrees Celsius (°C) in the coastal zone, the Amazon, Orinoco and the Pacific Region, temperatures ranging between 0°C on top of the Andean Mountains, and 14°C in cities like Bogota. In mountainous regions, the temperature drops 6°C every 1,000 m.

7. Three mountain ranges, known as '*cordilleras*', dominate the Colombian relief. As the Andes enters Colombia at the border with Ecuador at the Nudo de los Pastos, it splits further up north into two branches: the Western and Central cordilleras. From the Central cordillera, a third separates: the Eastern cordillera. The combination of these ridges with the valleys and rivers that travel along the mountains give rise to ecosystems like *paramos*, the Amazon jungle, herbaceous vegetation in Amazon hills, plain savannas, low forests, deserts, wet forests, mangrove swamps, Andean forests, Caribbean savannas, swamps, tropical forests and intervened areas.[2] The Colombian landscape has changed over time in terms of ecosystem reduction and increase in other ecologic units. Initially, a large portion of the territory was covered by jungles and forests, as well as savannas, snowy mountains, wetlands and dry zones, on a lesser scale. Due to natural and anthropogenic causes, the percentage of land occupied by these ecosystems has decreased.

8. Colombia's hydrographic system is formed by five large basins (*vertientes*), which include the Caribbean, Pacific, Orinoco, Amazon and Catatumbo areas. The main rivers rise in the Colombian Massif: the Magdalena, Cauca, Caquetá and Patía, and it is estimated that 1,800 rivers exist in the national territory. Some lacunas located above 2,700 m are considered sacred and magical thanks to the legends and myths that former cultures created to explain the origins of the universe prior to the Spanish arrival.

II. Population

9. Colombian population is a mixture of indigenous ancestors, Spaniard colonizers and African tribes. According to the World Bank, in 2019 Colombia had a population of approximately 50 million. Worldwide, Colombia has the twenty-ninth place of highly populated countries, and the third most populated country in Latin America after Brazil and Mexico. The birth rate is estimated at 14.896 births per 1,000 inhabitants, and the death rate at 5.56 per 1,000 inhabitants. Urban population represents 82% concentrated in three major cities: Bogota, Medellin and Cali. The increasing migration rate has left half of the territory with less than 3% of the population. Only 1% are considered indigenous people according to their traditions and languages.

---

2. Germán Márquez Calle, *Ecosistemas Estratégicos de Colombia.* www.sogeocol.edu.co/documentos /07ecos.pdf, 15 Jul. 2003.

10. The existing ethnic groups are classified in mixed blood, representing 58%; white, 20%; black, 4%; and 1% for mixed black-Amerindian. Concerning economic activities, 48% of the population engages in trade and services; 26% in agriculture, forestry and fishing; 18% in industrial activities; and 8% in other occupations.[3] In terms of age structure, the majority of Colombians is comprised between 15 and 64 years of age representing 66.4% of the population, being 14,292,342 male and 14,717,249 female. The annual population growth rate is estimated at 1.184%.

§2. Legal and Political Structure

11. Constitutional tradition in Colombia dates back to 1810 with the first declaration of independence from the Spanish Crown. After a long process of defining the federal and republican nature of the Colombian State, reflected in the adoption of different state constitutions, in 1886, Colombia defined itself as a national state and adopted the 1886 Constitution, which lasted until 1991. In 1991, amid a bloody national conflict fuelled by drug trafficking, guerrillas, emerging paramilitary groups, proposals to adopt extradition in Colombia, and a growing trend to open internal markets towards globalization, the national Political Constitution of 1991 was enacted.

12. The 1991 Constitution defines Colombia as a social democratic State governed by the rule of law. The political form of Colombia is a unitary republic, decentralized, with autonomy of its territorial entities, such as departments, municipalities, districts and indigenous territories, and with separation of powers in executive, legislative and judicial branches. Colombia is a central State territorially divided into departments and municipalities and/or districts. Departments are considered the main political-administrative and they are responsible before the national government for affairs concerning the department's jurisdiction and the municipalities/districts. Departments can only exercise the executive and legislative powers expressly granted by the Constitution or Law, and must not exceed those powers.

13. The Colombian executive branch is vested in the President, who represents the chief of the State, the Government and the Army. The President is democratically elected by direct vote for a four-year period. The President has the supreme executive power to adopt and promulgate national decrees, and under exceptional situations, he can promulgate laws. The executive branch is integrated by the President, the Vice-President, the Ministries and the directors of Administrative Department. At departmental level the executive branch is represented by the Governor, and at municipal or district level, by the Mayor.

---

3. Universia, *Población de Colombia.* http://internacional.universia.net/latinoamerica/datos-paises/colombia/poblacion.htm.

14. The legislative branch is represented by the Congress of the Republic. The Congress is democratically elected by direct vote for a four-year period, and integrated by two chambers, the Senate and the House of Representatives. The Congress is responsible for approving any amendments to the Constitution, passing and enacting Laws, and enforcing political control on governmental and administrative authorities. The Constitution establishes the cases where the Senate or the Chamber of Representatives have the exclusive competence on a specific matter; for example, the approval of international treaties is exclusive competence of the Senate, whereas the presentation of draft laws concerning taxes is part of the competences of the Chamber of Representatives.

15. The judicial branch of power is represented by the four high courts, the Supreme Court of Justice, the Council of State, the Constitutional Court and the Supreme Council of the Judicature. The Supreme Court of Justice is the court of last resort for settling differences arising from criminal, labour, civil, procedural and commercial litigations, as well as for validating sentences adopted in foreign countries. The Council of State is competent to rule on controversies arising between private parties and the Colombian State, including matters of public procurement, licenses, concessions, administrative sanctions, intellectual property, taxes, elections and State liability. The Council of State also serves as advisory body of the executive branch. The Constitutional Court is the highest court on constitutional matters responsible for ensuring that laws and regulatory instruments do not contravene the Constitution. The Supreme Council of the Judicature is the entity in charge of justice administration in the country and settlement of jurisdiction conflicts. The Justice Chambers of the Special Peace Jurisdiction was created as a result of the Peace Accord between the Government and FARC-EP guerrilla in 2017, and it is in charge of the criminal procedures that resulted from actions related to war before 10 December 2016.

§3. Economic Characteristics

16. The influence of foreign investment has contributed, to a large extent, to Colombia's economic growth. Colombian economy is focused on service activities, accounting for 63%; industry, 18.9%, including textiles, coal, emeralds, cement, food processing, and clothing and footwear; and agriculture, 18%, comprising coffee, cut flowers, bananas, sugar cane, and oilseed. The main Colombian exports are represented by petroleum, coffee, coal, nickel, emeralds, apparel, bananas and cut flowers.

17. The official currency in Colombia is the Colombian Peso (COP). The Gross Domestic Product (GDP) is estimated at USD 323 billion, purchasing power per capita of USD 9,200, and unemployment rate of 9.96%, according to official statistics. The Average Annual Income is USD 1,470, and the estimated population living below poverty line is 46.8%. In comparison with Latin-American countries, Colombia is the fourth-largest economy in the region.[4]

§4. Social and Cultural Characteristics

18. According to the Constitution, Spanish is the official language of Colombia accounting for 80% of Spanish speakers. Languages and dialects spoken by ethnic groups include more than sixty-nine tongues and are enshrined in the Constitution. The Constitution establishes that languages different from Spanish are deemed as official languages in the territories they are spoken; however, the education provided thereof has to be bilingual. The various Spanish expressions, idioms and dialects mark relevant cultural differences among nationals, which are evidenced in our traditions, behaviour, ethnicity and political views.

19. Pursuant to the Constitution, the education system is free in primary school, and to some extent, in secondary and high school. In terms of higher education, Colombia has a wide offer of universities, colleges and high education institutions that are mainly located in Bogota and the main cities. The prices of higher education are considerably different for private and public institutions, which in some cases limits the access of low-income families to high-quality education. The literacy rate is 95%.

20. The former Constitution of 1886 established the Catholic, Apostolic and Roman religion as the official religion for the whole nation. The adoption of the National Constitution of 1991 brought along the protection of the right to free beliefs and practice of own religions, ensuring non-discrimination for religious reasons. It is estimated that 81% of the Colombian population is Roman Catholic, although only 25% are practising Catholics. The second-largest religion is Protestantism with 13.5%, followed by other faiths with 3.4%. Although the separation between the State and the Catholic Church is a principle of Colombian Constitutional Law, the church still plays an important role in shaping laws involving fundamental rights and has influence over national security issues.

§5. Main Energy Concerns

I. Introduction

21. As the major coal exporter of Latin America, considered a net oil exporter since 1986 and having its energy offer largely based on hydro power, Colombia faces serious challenges in the wake of a steady economic growth. The broad array of energy sources and their development costs has demanded an active role from

4. Heritage, *2020 Index of Economic Freedom.* https://www.heritage.org/index/country/colombia.

the State in setting priorities to satisfy internal demand, increase energy coverage, liberalize the market and meet environmental standards. In addition, the government has had to harmonize all the latter by promoting foreign investment in this sector.

22. The country has responded to those challenges in different ways. The series of regulatory instruments issued to make oil and gas sectors more attractive for investment have had an effect on production rise. The gradual privatization of the National Oil and Gas Company (ECOPETROL) has also been seen as an effort to enhance the upstream industry and incentivize investment from the public. Accompanying these initiatives, the State has engaged in protecting electricity, and oil and gas transport infrastructure from terrorist attacks. Despite these achievements, the energy sector is still maturing and will need to draw strategies to cope with existing and future concerns.

23. The oil industry has been targeted by the current government to reach 1 million barrels per day (bbl/d) of production. In 2011, Colombia produced 939.98 bbl/d, increasing by 35% with respect to the production of 2008, but by 2019 the country produced an average of 898.965 bbl/d. Its total oil reserves by 2017 were calculated at 1.8 trillion barrels, with a low expectation of increase due to the slow exploratory activity. In 2018 only sixty-six exploratory wells were drilled.

24. The main destination for oil exports is the United States, which imported 422.000 bbl/d of crude oil and refined products, followed by China and Japan. Today, the country has six major oil pipelines and in 2013, construction was completed on the 230-km pipeline connecting the Araguaney station with the Banadia station through a 42-inch-diameter steel pipeline with a wall thickness of 0.688 inches, the Oleoducto Bicentenario pipeline. Concerning refining capacity, the government has launched plans to expand the refineries of Cartagena and Barrancabermeja and improve their processing capacity. On 21 October 2015, the expansion works of the Cartagena refinery were inaugurated. This expansion increased its refining capacity to 165,000 bbl/d from the previous 75,000 bbl/d.

25. The production of gas was 378 billion cubic feet (Bcf) and consumption was 391.63 (Bcf) in 2018. Reserves are estimated at 3.16 trillion cubic feet (Tcf) in 2020.

26. Colombia has one of the largest open-pit coal mines in the world, in the Guajira Peninsula bordering the Caribbean. Colombia's total coal production was 90 million short tonnes (MMst) in 2019,[5] while consumption stayed at 7.5 MMst in 2018. Coal reserves are calculated in 4,554 MMst, being the largest in South America.

---

5. Knoema, *Colombia – Producción Primaria Total de Carbón.* https://knoema.es/atlas/Colombia/topics/Energ%c3%ada/Carb%c3%b3n/Producci%c3%b3n-Primaria-de-Carb%c3%b3n (February 2021).

27. In 2018, 92.14 MMst with very low ash and sulphur content were exported to Europe, the United States and other South American countries. It is one of the main drivers of Colombian economy, representing 15% of the export earnings. China has expressed great interest in the coal sector, and its desire to finance infrastructure projects to facilitate exports to Asia.

28. Due to its location in the tropical zone and the mountain ranges, the country has a substantial hydropower potential, being second only to Brazil in this area. The installed capacity in 2018 was 17.7 GW, generating 75.04 billion kilowatt hours (BkWh) and consuming 70.20 BkWh. Around 69% of the electricity comes from hydropower and the rest is mainly sourced by thermoelectric plants.

II. Concerns

29. The country has been expressing a concern for security of energy supply throughout the years. Alongside, the State has endeavoured to diversify the energy matrix, with a main focus on liquid fuels and biofuels.[6] Regulations and policy mechanisms have been designed to prepare the country for this challenge by enhancing the entry of new operators, extending the benefits to foreign companies and creating tax incentives. Nonetheless, financial and supply concerns remain in spite of the lack of investment, security risks, service quality and power theft. Although the number of attacks from illegal groups to pipelines and energy infrastructure has remarkably decreased, it is still a challenge for the State to secure such infrastructure.

30. Since a large part of the electricity is generated through hydro power, climatic conditions play a crucial role in the definition of energy policies. The *Fenómeno del Niño,* which is a constant nature-made event, brings along both floods in some parts of the country and long dry seasons in some other. This triggers a considerable impact on the firm capacity of hydro power plants, affecting reliability of the service and higher prices. In this context, gas and coal-fired plants must make up for the lack of hydroelectricity, which then need to have the necessary reserves and installed capacity to cope with the demand.

31. Linked to this concern, the gas production estimations may not be sufficient to attend energy needs in times of the Niño phenomenon. What is more, the bilateral contract of gas export with Venezuela increases pressure on the sufficiency of the existing gas reserves, and the calculations on estimated production. If the answer of the government is to open access to new operators to increase production, as most of the gas is untapped, then clear competition rules must be established. If, on the contrary, the government restricts market access to the current operators, then it will have to set out clear rules to prevent abuse of the dominant position.

6. Ministerio de Minas y Energía, *Memorias al Congreso de la República 2010 -2011.* http://www.upme.gov.co/Upme12/2011/Memorias_Congreso_2010_2011.pdf (March 2011).

32. While promoting expansion of generation capacity, improving reliability, especially in low rain seasons, and avoiding extra costs for users, infrastructure must also be enhanced. Projects like floating storage regasification units, refining facilities expansion and construction of countrywide pipelines are in the list of national priorities. However, it must be clearly determined how such projects will be financed, so that users are not exposed to extraordinary costs.

33. As well as concerns, the energy sector has interesting opportunities. The discovery of coal bed methane in coal reserves has gained growing attention from the government. It is said that some of the largest existing coal mines could contain up to 2.2 Tcf of coal bed methane, which works as natural gas. If this is so, the long-term demand for gas would be covered, and the chances to export gas could be higher.

34. A recurrent concern is energy provision for Non-interconnected Zones (ZNI for its initials in Spanish). ZNI refers to those municipalities or remote areas that are not connected to the national grid, which account for 66% of the national territory. The supply of energy is mainly done by diesel-powered plants, solar panels and small hydropower facilities. 344,000 households belong to the ZNIs, which includes 4 capitals of departments, 54 municipalities, and around 1262 villages or population centres, accounting for 1.44 million inhabitants.[7] The government has put in place funds to promote the installation of conventional and non-conventional energy facilities in these areas.

III. Renewable Energies

35. The country has an important provision of renewable sources of energy, although their development is still premature. Small sources of hydroelectric power have gained access to the grid, whereas solar, wind and other type of energies have been promoted for ZNI. The main challenge is funding and incentives for investments in this sector.

36. In general, financial mechanisms have been developed for the rational and efficient use of energy. Multilateral banks as well as national financial institutions have set up credit lines for innovation, improvement in energy technologies and use of renewables in industrial processes. Nonetheless, the absence of a regulatory framework, political commitment and market incentives has prevented potential investors and developers from using those mechanisms for the development of non-conventional energies.

7. Pipeline B.I., *Segundo informe de consultoría para la definición del contrato de vinculación de operadores para las Zonas no Interconectadas.* http://www.minminas.gov.co/minminas/downloads/UserFiles/File/ENERGIA/sanandres/Informe%20Mecanismos%20Seleccion%20Operadores%20ZNI.pdf, September 2007.

37. In terms of regulation, the government has set targets and the basis for an adequate institutional framework. For example, Resolution 180919 of 2010 was issued to develop the national programme of efficient and rational use of energy and other non-conventional energy sources (*Programa de Uso Racional y Eficiente de la Energía y demás formas de Energía No Convencionales – PROURE*) created by Law 697 of 2001. The PROURE is to be developed by a series of sub-programmes and energy saving targets by 2015 and 2020. The idea of this programme is to reach four main objectives: ensure a timely and full energy supply, promote competitiveness in the Colombian economy, protect consumers, and foster the use of non-conventional energies in a sustainable manner.

38. Additionally, the Indicative Action Plan establishes targets for the share of non-conventional energy sources in the energy supply. For such purpose, the targets are established for the National Interconnected System (SIN), being 3.5% by 2015, and 6.5% by 2020; and for ZNI, being 20% by 2015, and 30% by 2020.

39. The main task remains on how to gear up for short and long-term risks, like the Niño phenomenon or climate change respectively, while increasing energy coverage in ZNIs. In line with that, if the concerns on uninterrupted and secure supply of energy mark the government's priorities, and at the same time, there is a need to diversify the energy basket, then it will be necessary to define how the cost allocation of developing renewables will fit in the investment plan for fossil fuel-based energies.

§6. Basic Principles of Energy Law

40. Generally speaking, the principles underpinning energy law seek to secure the supply of energy to attend to the demands of Colombia's development to the lowest cost possible, including environmental costs. The National Constitution of 1991 has been the vehicle through which principles have been established and further transposed into laws, governmental agencies' authority and regulation. That is not to say that the Constitution has a section compiling the applicable energy principles, but that these are developed along with specific matters, like public utilities or freedom of economic activities. Each sector or source, thus, operates under the constitutional principles that are intrinsically applicable to the activity; for example, the ownership of the State over all underground minerals applicable to the extraction of coal, gas and oil.

41. As mentioned before, the State is the sole owner of all natural non-renewable resources and the subsoil.[8] This principle, whose development started with Law 20 of 1969 declaring the State's property over all mines and hydrocarbons, requires lawmakers to establish the conditions under which such resources can be exploited, and the relationship between the State and the developer. What is

8. Article 332, National Constitution 1991.

more, the constitutional provision already foresees royalties in favour of the State for the extraction of non-renewable resources.[9]

42. According to the existing legal framework, some activities embody public or social interest. Whenever an activity or sector is declared of public or social interest, then other industries, undertakings or rights must relinquish to the national concern, and the State must put in place the necessary to fulfil the public interest. In energy law, this is often the case with activities involving public utilities, such as gas and electricity, for they mean the living conditions of all citizens. For example, the State can expropriate lands whenever they are necessary to develop infrastructure for power generation.

43. Energy activities are regulated by the State. Different from other undertakings, the State has to intervene to correct market failures and ensure the provision of energy-related services. According to constitutional provisions, the State may intervene in the exploitation of natural resources, including non-renewable ones, and public services, among others.[10]

44. In this regard, it is important to note that the State plays a decisive role in the direction of the national economy. On the one hand, freedom of economic activity, private initiative, free competition and freedom of enterprise must be guaranteed, within the limits of fair competition.[11] On the other hand, the State must safeguard the efficient provision of public services to all citizens. Within this framework, both entrepreneurs and government agencies must interact to achieve the ends of the State, as established in the constitution.

45. A more detailed description of the application of energy law principles will be developed in each relevant part.

§7. Historical Background

46. Trying to establish the exact moment when energy law developed in Colombia is a tricky task. It could be argued that the Spanish colonization brought forth the first regulations on energy. In 1384, the Spanish crown declared its property over Colombian mines, and required developers to obtain royal authorization to exploit them. It was not until 1829, having gained our independence, that the Liberator Simon Bolivar enacted the first mining statute.

47. As far in history as coal, and leaving aside the discoveries of oil by pre-Hispanic tribes, the first oil fields were drilled in 1883 in Barrancabermeja, with a daily production of 50 barrels. At the start of the twentieth century, a brand-new refinery was built in Cartagena with a 400-barrel capacity for the processing of

9. Article 360, Constitution.
10. Article 334, Constitution.
11. Article 333, Constitution.

imported crude. This refinery is today one of the government's targets to extend refining capacity in the country. The main contracts for oil exploration and exploitation, then signed under the form of concessions, were put in place in 1905 and were known by the name of the developer: *Concesión de Mares* and *Concesión Barco*. It could be argued, though, that the creation of the national oil company, ECOPETROL, marked a key moment in the history of energy law.[12]

48. Electricity has a remote precedent with Law 113 of 1928 declaring water for electricity of public interest. However, it is only in 1946 when the electric sector takes off with the arrival of the first power plants and the creation of the hydroelectric company, Electroaguas. The first companies, started by private investors, had a view to generate, distribute and market energy within the existing municipalities. It was basically a negotiation between the mayor and local councils with the investor, aimed at setting mechanisms to recover the investment.[13]

49. The historical background of gas has some peculiarities. Seen as natural gas, its development is relatively recent, as the widespread use of this source started in 1986. Thanks to the State-sponsored programme, the number of gas residential and industrial users grew considerably, while triggering the development of pipelines throughout the country. Liquefied natural gas (LNG), though, can be traced back to 1946. This year is commonly referenced as the start point of the LNG industry in Colombia, encompassing the creation of the first LNG distribution companies. Its consumption was predominantly domestic for food cooking and water heating.

50. The start of this century raised concerns on the environmental impact of fossil fuel-based energies and boosted legislation on renewable energies. In Colombia, the use of non-conventional sources was early foreseen in 1974 through environmental legislation and by 1986 there were already governmental agencies responsible for investigating and proposing policies on the matter. It was only in 2001 that the government set out general lines to adopt regulatory measures on renewables. The development of regulation and economic incentives for this sector is an ongoing process, which finds obstacles and opportunities when interacting with traditional sources.

51. From a regulatory point of view, the evolution of energy law can be observed differently. The adoption of the 1991 Constitution sets a new paradigm in the State's role, obligations and rights of citizens, public services, energy security, entrepreneurship and competition. Compared to the laws and decrees adopted on the grounds of the former 1886 Constitution, this novel legal framework integrates all concepts and draws the lines of contact between energy-related activities and taxes,

12. Asociación Colombiana de Ingeniería de Petróleos, *Historia del Petróleo en Colombia*. http://www.alip.org/docs/Historias/breve_historia_petrolera_colombia.pdf.pdf.
13. Ana María Sandoval, *Monografía del sector de electricidad y gas colombiano: condiciones actuales y retos futuros*. https://www.dnp.gov.co/Portals/0/archivos/documentos/DEE/Archivos_Economia/272.pdf (November 2004).

competition, environment, economy and public law. The historical features and details of each sector will be further developed in the corresponding sections of this manuscript.

§8. Role of Government Institutions in the Shaping and Administration of Energy Law and Policy

52. The main governmental agency involved in the energy sector is the Ministry of Mines and Energy (MME). It is responsible for planning, policymaking and general regulation, as well as supervision of electricity. Part of its supervision powers are delegated in the Regulatory Commission of Gas and Energy (Comisión Reguladora de Energía y Gas – Regulatory Commission of Electricity and Gas (CREG)) and Unidad de Planeacion Minero Energética (The Union of Mineral and Energy Planning (UPME)).

53. As the owner of all hydrocarbon reserves, the State partially owns the main oil and gas company: ECOPETROL. Among many other functions, these companies help the State to control the development of hydrocarbons. The National Agency of Hydrocarbons (ANH) and National Agency of Mining (ANM) also play a significant role in the administration of energy resources. Each part of the manuscript will elaborate on the main governmental and public authorities with authority in electricity, gas, oil and coal.

§9. Sources of Energy Law

54. Colombia has a legal system based on the Roman-Germanic tradition of civil law, and establishes a written hierarchical scheme of laws. Within this pyramidal system, the Constitutional law is the highest source of law. International treaties, laws and any other regulatory instruments must be in accordance with constitutional provisions, so they can be part of the Colombian legal framework. The principles and aims of the State are embedded in the Constitution and have a normative value that must be regarded by laws. Concerning energy law, the Constitution establishes the rights, duties, competences and instruments for the exploitation of energy resources, provision of public utilities to citizens, and the level field for competence in this sector.

55. International treaties are part of the sources of environmental law, and are considered as constitutional norms. In general, the incorporation of international treaties in national legislation involves the approval of its text by the government; the submission of the Law Proposal approving the treaty before Congress; the enactment of the Law approving the treaty; a mandatory review of the law's constitutionality by the Constitutional Court; and the issuance of a Decree from the President of the Republic promulgating the treaty.

56. Below the Constitution and International Treaties, the first and broadest regulatory instrument is the Law. Laws are adopted by Congress after completing the corresponding legislative procedures. Laws can have different hierarchies due to the matters they regulate, such as organic laws, frame laws and laws vesting the President with legislative faculties. Energy issues are generally established in laws, such as Law 142 of 1994 on public services, or Law 685 of 2001 approving the Mining Code of 2001.

57. Going lower in the pyramidal legal system, decrees are found after Laws. As part of the regulatory powers given to the President in the Constitution, decrees are adopted by the President of the Republic and have the signature of the Ministry involved in the matter regulated by the decree. In some cases, the decrees can involve the signature of more than one Minister, such as Decree 1530 of 2002 regulating the content of lead in fuels, signed by the Ministry of Environment and the MME. Decrees regulate and develop the content of Laws. Although most of the aspects in energy law are developed via regulations, some general matters are provided for in important decrees, such as Decree 2100 of 2011 providing for mechanisms to ensure the national supply of gas.

Notably, the MME embarked in the compilation of all existing regulations related to the energy sector and produced Decree 1073 of 2015 as a single instrument incorporating laws, decrees and resolutions affecting the industry. This decree does not add, modify or revoke the existing legislation but assembles all piecemeal regulations in a logical order. Decree 1073 of 2015, aimed at facilitating the consultation of energy legislation, and is divided into two books and subsequent chapters: the first book on the structure of the sector, including central and decentralized governmental agencies; and the second, compiling and codifying the regulation on oil, gas, electricity and mining activities. Legislation on the energy sector can then be referenced in two ways: the respective article of the codified piece in Decree 1073 of 2015; or the very law, decree or resolution that adopts such regulation. For example, the provision on the extension of the mining concession contract can be referenced as Article 2.2.4.2.2.3 of Decree 1073 of 2015 or by Article 3 of Decree 943 of 2013.

58. Resolutions are quite an important source of energy regulation. They are regulatory instruments whereby the corresponding Ministry or public entity provides for technical or practical issues contained in the decree. For example, Resolution 181709 of 2003 from MME setting the methodology to determine the price of crude oil, stating that the base is the international crude oil export price. Another example is illustrated by Resolutions 25 and 26 of 1995 from the CREG setting out rules to operate within the SIN.

59. Decisions from the High Courts and opinions rendered by relevant public authorities help understand and interpret the application and enforceability of applicable norms.

60. National development plans are also a source of energy law. Each presidential term the new government prepares a programme and a budget for the upcoming four years and sends it to Congress for approval. The programme, known as the

National Development Plan (NDP), sets out the objectives for the next coming years and the policies, targets, mechanisms, market and command-and-control instruments to attain those objectives. The energy sector is thus affected by regulatory changes and market instruments necessary to develop the elected government's energy policies.

For 2014–2018, Congress enacted Law 1753 of 2015 approving the NDP 'All for a new country'. The main aspects impacting the energy industry and particularly the mining sector included: creation and delimitation of specific mining areas for different objectives, such as formalization of clandestine or artisanal mining; new mining categories according to the size and complexity of the mining operations and matching regulation for each category (large, medium, small mining operations and mining for subsistence); reinforcement of the requirements to apply for mining titles; and bolstering of the existing penalties and enforcement procedure regarding compliance with legal obligations.

For the period 2018–2022, Congress enacted Law 1955 of 2019 approving the NDP 'Pact for Colombia, Pact for Equity'. The main aspects regarding the energy sector include the increase in renewable energy installed capacity from 22.4 MW to 1.500 MW, a more efficient management of energy resources and the increase of oil & gas production, among others.

Part I. Regulatory Framework Concerning Electricity

Introduction

61. Colombia's electricity sector is regulated by Law 142 of 1994, which establishes public services providers, contracts, users' rights and obligations, fees' rules, a competition regime and public utilities' control. The industry is also regulated by Law 143 of 1994 providing guidelines on the wholesale market and setting the rules for each of the activities that make up the electric industry: generation, transmission, distribution and marketing.

62. The CREG is the regulator for this sector. In particular, CREG has issued several decisions that constitute the rules of operation, such as Resolution 24 of 1995, Resolution 25 of 1995, Resolution 70 of 1998, and Resolution 156 of 2011. These operation rules apply only to companies that are part of the SIN.

63. In this industry, two systems operate: the SIN and ZNI, each with its own structural rules. The SIN is a system composed of plant and equipment for the generation, network interconnection and inter-regional networks of transmission and distribution network electrical loads of all users connected to each other.[14] In practice, the SIN is a network that operates in areas of the country that are more densely populated and economically developed.

64. This is because in these regions, the electric power connection to the consumption points is less expensive and more cost-effective. In the electricity market, SIN is divided into the wholesale market, where generators and traders are involved, and the retail market, involving users and traders. In contrast, in ZNI areas, long distances, extreme dispersion and low population density make it an extremely costly interconnection. This explains why some solutions have been created in ZNI areas, such as local power supply. For ZNI, the integration of activities is allowed, the market is only one, there is no wholesale market and they are exempted from operation rules.

14. Article 11, Law 143 of 1994.

65. Henceforth, whenever we refer to the generation, transmission, distribution and marketing, we shall indeed make reference to the rules that apply for companies operating in the SIN network and very marginally, to the rules applicable for the ZNI networks.

Chapter 1. Production and Exploitation

66. Generation and production of electricity[15] is understood as the sum of assets that transform primary energy from a certain resource, should this be water, mineral (coal), fossil fuels (natural gas, fuel oil, diesel) and/or non-conventional sources (wind or solar energy), into electricity. This is achieved through the conversion of rotational mechanical energy present in turbines and delivered at the SIN[16] according to the required technical conditions.

67. The sites where electricity generation systems are located are known as generation centres, and the installed power[17] is defined based on the generation nominal power, which corresponds to the maximum electricity demand that can be satisfied instantly. Consequently, the electricity capacity that is generated in the country is directly related to the installed capacity and the availability of the primary source.

68. Electricity generation is, therefore, just as the other activities of this sector, a public service. It is considered an essential utility, which means that the right to go on strike does not apply and is of public utility, since the civil works involved in public utilities, easements and land expropriations must be guaranteed.

69. According to Article 4 of CREG[18] Resolution 055 of 1994, the generators that connect to the SIN must sell and buy energy, as required by the Wholesale Energy Market (MEM, for its initials in Spanish), and is subject to operating rulings and to the Operation National Council[19] agreements (CNO, for its initials in Spanish).

§1. Activity's Nature

70. Electricity generation is a complimentary activity to a public residential utility.[20] From an economic perspective, it is organized as a free competition activity[21] since it exhibits certain features: users' demand, generators' offer, market freedom

15. Both terms are synonymous and refer to the same process.
16. The National Interconnected System, SIN, is composed of the following elements: plants and generation equipment, interconnection network, regional and inter-regional networks of transmission, distribution networks, and users' electrical charges.
17. Maximum power that a production unit can reach for a specific period.
18. Commission for the Regulation of Electricity and Gas.
19. Article 4, CREG Resolution 055 of 1994: Obligation to get connected to the network: 'All generators that are connected to the National network system will have to make transactions of sale and purchase of the energy they produce or require in the wholesale energy market, and shall be subject to the Rules of Operation and agreements by the National Operation Council (…)'.
20. Article 14.25, Law 142 of 1994. Electricity Public utility service: The electricity transmission from regional transmission networks to the end user's home, including its connection and measurement. This Law shall also apply to the generation, marketing, processing, interconnection and transmission.

of access and withdrawal, as well as technical organisms' intervention in regulation. Besides, electricity is a homogeneous good and there is a certain flow of information.

§2. ENTRY AND WITHDRAWAL IN THE GENERATION ACTIVITY

71. In general terms, there is entry freedom in the electricity generation activity, as long as some conditions are met. Regarding withdrawal there is also freedom, according to some conditions as well, such as notifying this situation and following a procedure in case there is a withdrawal of a generation plant.

I. Generation Business Entry

72. The entry into generation business is free, according to Article 10 of Law 142 of 1993, and Articles 7 and 24 of Law 143 of 1994. The State does not exclude others from entering this business, and there is no public ownership. These are the available options for starting electricity generation in Colombia.

– Own Risk

73. As there is free entry in the electricity generation public utility, the investor assumes the risks inherent to the generation activity, according to Article 85 of Law 143 of 1994.

– Auctions for Reliability Charge

74. The auction consists of selecting one or few investors who commit to meeting Firm Energy obligations. In other words, amounts of energy to produce are allocated, based on the offers made by the participants in the auction.[22] This scheme replaces schemes of Power Purchase Agreements (PPA),[23] BOT and Build, Operate, Maintain, and Transfer (BOMT). These auctions are designed for power plants with centralized dispatch or a power capacity greater than 20 Mega Watts (MW).

– Public and Private Partnership

21. Constitutional Court, Sentence No. C-615 of 2001; Magistrate: Marco Gerardo Monroy Cabra: '(…) Competition: social market economy's structural principle, meant to not only defend the interests of entrepreneurs who interact in the market, but also to protect the public interest, which turns out in the whole community's benefit due to goods and services' higher quality and better prices, that comes as a result of healthy competition. From an objective perspective, it takes the form of superior guidelines or rules under which economic actors should act and that, at all times, must be carefully preserved by the government. (…)'.
22. CREG Resolution 71 of 2006.
23. Power Purchase Agreements, PPA: Where energy is not marketed directly but supply is guaranteed with their plants by a third party, who is responsible for the marketing.

75. According to Law 1508 of 2012, the State, represented by the MME, would be authorized to invite the public initiative or to receive a private initiative to build and operate a power generation project. This figure of association can be translated into a concession contract or a partnership agreement with or without contribution of public resources. To this day, this mechanism has not been used to develop any power generation project.

– Agreements Granting Exclusive Service Areas for ZNI

76. The MME is authorized by Article 114 of Law 1450 of 2011 to establish exclusive service areas and sign contracts with investors in order to provide such electricity activities or services. The Ministry, through a contract which grants an exclusive service area, gives the investor, at his own risk, the right to provide exclusively activities related to the provision of electricity in predetermined areas, corresponding to ZNI areas,[24] in exchange for payment.

77. All generation projects must fulfil certain legal conditions for its entry into operation: (i) power generation projects to be developed in the SNA must be registered before the UPME, regardless of their structuring phase;[25] (ii) obtaining the environmental, water use, and municipal permits. In regards to environmental permits, it is mandatory to obtain an environmental license for the generation project. Regarding the water use permits, these are obtained for the respective studies or a water concession for the generation project construction. The municipal permits refer to land and public space use.

II. Withdrawal from the Market

A. Generator's Withdrawal from the Market

78. When a utility company decides to leave the market it must notify the competent authority to ensure that the service is not interrupted.[26] Article 12 of CREG Resolution 24 confirms that any generator without energy generation obligations may withdraw. Companies in this situation must give further notice to the SSP, the CREG and the System Trading Administrator (ASIC). This recall does not excuse compliance with its obligations in the market. It is clear that Article 11 of CREG Resolution 71 of 2006 does not support the voluntary recall of a generator that is assigned firm obligations unless they transfer these obligations to another generator.

24. Geographical area where the public electricity service is not provided through the national network.
25. UPME Resolutions 520 and 638 of 2007.
26. Article 61, Law 142 of 1994, and Art. 12, CREG Resolution 024 of 1995.

B. Withdrawal of Generation Plants

79. The removal and re-insertion of energy plants is regulated for two types of plants: those with firm energy obligations and those without obligations. The first ones may withdraw and be re-inserted when they have ensured compliance with the firm energy obligation, upon notice to the National Dispatch Centre (CND) and CREG. For those generation plants without firm energy obligations, withdrawal is free.

80. Articles 55, 56 and 57 of Law 143 of 1994 provide that the State may enter into concession contracts when no one is willing to provide that service. A contract award is exceptional in its nature, and only shall take place upon invitation or public summoning.

§3. Power Generator and Wholesale Market Agent

81. The generator must be established as a public utility company. Otherwise, it may opt for one of the mechanisms referred to in Article 15 of Law 142 of 1994. For example, in order to get established as a public service provider, these are the options: authorized organizations or any other legal form. The discussion emerges on whether generator plants of less than 20 MW should or should not adopt any of the forms established by Law 142 of 1994. On this point, we consider that in fact they must be established as utility companies, as authorized organizations or any other figure rather than marginal producers, since the latter can only produce energy for themselves and for their affiliates.

82. Pursuant to Article 11.8 of Law 142 of 1994, generators must report the start of their activities to the CREG and the Superintendence of Public Services (SSP). CREG Resolution 56 of 1994 specifies that the notice of start of activities must include the company's by-laws, the names of the shareholders or owners of more than 10% of shares, initial financial statements and a description of the market to which the company is oriented, and the assets and permits the company has available.

83. Generators wanting to purchase and sell electricity in the wholesale market must register as an agent of the Wholesale Market, in accordance with Article 6 of CREG Resolution 24 of 1995. The requirements for this registration include:

- Filling out the registration form.
- Acknowledging and accepting the contents of CREG Resolution 24 of 1995.
- Submitting a certificate of good standing.
- Signing a mandate agreement.
- Providing guarantees.
- Reporting the location of trade borders.
- Filing certificates of measurement equipment calibration.

84. It is clear that this register is not mandatory for smaller plants generating up to 10 MW, or marginal producers (self-generators and cogenerators). It, thus, must be completed by generation plants ranging from 10 MW to 20 MW when deciding to voluntarily access the central delivery system. For plants with a capacity higher than 20 MW registration is mandatory, since these must be centrally dispatched.

§4. Conventional and Non-conventional Sources for Power Generation

85. Laws 142 and 143 of 1994 are neutral in regards to conventional and non-conventional sources for power generation. With the enactment of Law 1715 of 2014, Non-conventional Renewable Resources (RES) have a special legal treatment with provisions that promote and tend to encourage the integration of such resources.

86. Colombia has chosen to promote the development of RES via a special reduction on income tax, VAT exclusion in the acquisition of goods and services and accelerated depreciation. Lately, other mechanisms used for the promotion of RES include auctions and renewable portfolio standards. The renewable portfolio standard establishes that retailer companies must purchase between 8% and 10% of their energy from conventional sources.[27] To facilitate this obligation, auctions are organized. The last auction was held on 21 October 2019, in which eight projects with a total effective capacity of 1,298.9 MW were awarded, which are distributed as follows: 17.39% corresponding to solar photovoltaic, 82.61% to wind and a total assigned energy of 10.186 MWh-day was obtained. The start date of the electric power supply obligations will be 1 January 2022 and the term of the contracts will be fifteen years.[28]

87. The use of water, conventional source of electricity, in hydropower projects is conditioned to the issuance of a water concession.[29] For thermal generation (coal gas) engaged in electricity sales at the national interconnected network, long-term contracts must be signed to ensure the supply of fuel in a timely manner and with affordable prices, as established by Article 27 of Law 143 of 1994.

27. Law 1955 of 2019, Art. 296.
28. Presidencia De La República De Colombia. Con nueva subasta, Gobierno Nacional superó en más del 50% la meta en energías renovables. (22 Oct. 2019). Available at: https://id.presidencia.gov.co/Paginas/prensa/2019/Con-nueva-subasta-Gobierno-Nacional-supero-en-mas-del-50-la-meta-en-energias-renovables-191022.aspx.
29. Decree 309 of 2000.

§5. Types of Generators

88. Generators are broadly divided between marginal producers and generators providing the energy production public service. The latter in turn can be classified into power generators with plants of less than 20 MW and power generators with plants larger than 20 MW.

I. Marginal Producer

89. According to Article 15 paragraph 15.2, marginal producers are those individuals or companies that produce for themselves public utilities contemplated under Article 16 of Law 142 of 1994. They can also produce free of charge this service to those who are involved with them economically or who can provide these services massively in exchange for remuneration. These marginal producers are not required to be organized as utility companies.

90. Marginal producers are required to comply with environmental and health permits, as well as municipal permits regarding land use, public space, circulation and transit. Additionally, they must comply with the payment of the electricity sector transfers, which must be paid to corporations and municipalities according to Article 45 of Law 99 of 1993.

91. In terms of electricity generation, the following ones have been considered as marginal producers: self-generators and cogenerators. The self-generating activity takes place while connected to the SIN network. These producers are regulated by Law 1215 of 2008 and CREG Resolution 005 of 2010.

II. Generator and Public Service Provider

92. Public service generators are classified into generators with plants under 20 MW and generators with plants greater than 20 MW. This distinction comes from CREG Resolution 55 of 1994, according to which only plants with total effective capacity greater than 20 MW are subject to the centralized dispatch of generation. Plants smaller than 20 MW are not subject to the central dispatch, which excludes them from the Wholesale Market business rules, unless they voluntarily are subject to such regulation.

A. Generators with Plants of up to 10 MW

93. Although plants of up to 10 MW generate and deliver power to the network, they are not required to or have the right to participate in the centralized system, as provided by Article 3 of CREG Resolution 086 of 1996, as amended. Indeed, the norm is categorical in saying that these plants must not have access to a central dispatch and as a consequence, they cannot participate in the wholesale electricity market. On this last point, we consider that it is not that they are not entitled to participate in the wholesale market as such, but that they are limited as they are not allowed to participate in the power exchange, as we shall see shortly when describing to whom they can sell energy.

94. 10 MW generation plants may sell energy to marketers that sell it within the Regulated Market and participate in public biddings. It should be emphasized that since the small generators do not have the right or are required to access the central system, they are not allowed to participate in auctions of firm energy obligations (Reliability charge).

95. Depending on the generation source, 10 MW generators must fulfil certain obligations before building the project. First, thermal plants must hire fuel supply for the long term. In addition, plants generated based on water must have water concession permits. Then again, whatever the source, they must request an environmental license. They also should be equipped with hourly energy measurement equipment. Whenever they connect to the SIN, they have to meet connection conditions. Connections to the National Transmission System (STN) must have prior approval by the UPME.[30] Regional Transmission System (STR) or Local Distribution System (SDL) are governed by Resolution 70 of 1998.

96. Generators have the right to sell energy as follows:[31]

- Sale to a marketer that caters the regulated market when participating in public biddings, which is awarded by price merit.[32]
- Direct sale to a dealer without public bidding. The price is only the energy exchange price in each hour minus COP 1 (USD 1).[33]
- Sale to generators or marketers that allocate this energy to the exclusive demand of unregulated users to freely determined prices.

97. It is important to clarify that in the original version of CREG Resolution 86 of 1996 a generator with plants of up to 10 MW could sell directly to unregulated users. Therefore, an obligation for these generators to have support contracts was established, which today is no longer needed since the Resolution was amended.

30. Resolution 25 of 1995.
31. Article 3, CREG Resolution 86 of 1996 (as amended by Art. 1, CREG Resolution 39 of 2001).
32. CREG Resolution 20 of 1996.
33. CREG Resolution 005 of 2001.

B. Generators with Plants of 10–20 MW

98. These plants generate and place energy in the network. The difference with the above ones is that 10–20 MW plants are able to access the central dispatch system, if they choose to do so, which allows them to participate in the energy exchange. If they voluntarily decide that their plant shall be centrally dispatched, they must abide by the Wholesale Market trade rules contained in CREG Resolution 24 of 1995 and may participate in public auctions of firm energy obligations.

99. However, if they are not subject to the central dispatch system, their energy does not participate in the energy exchange but can be sold as established for plants of less than 10 MW.

100. Generators of more than 10 MW must transfer 6% of their power's gross sales to the electricity sector.[34] Also, if they are dispatched at the power exchange they must pay for every dispatched kilowatt per hour COP 1 (USD 1) to reach the Financial Support Fund for the Electrification of non-interconnected zones (FAZNI).

C. Generators of 20 MW or More

101. Major generators (20 MW or more generation plants) must be submitted to the central dispatch coordinated by the National Dispatch Center.[35] This order is subject to that office is directed to generating plants connected to SIN and with a total effective capacity greater than 20 MW. These power plants can be owned by the generator, and by other agents representing the generator through a mandate or through support contracts.

102. Generators with plants of over 20 MW are involved in the wholesale market by signing energy contracts, or by doing transactions in the energy exchange. As a result, they are subject to the commercial rules of the wholesale market contained in CREG Resolution 24 of 1995, and must register as agents of the wholesale market with the ASIC.

1. Conditions for Construction

103. The construction of these projects requires land negotiations, easements imposition and properties' expropriation in order to start the appropriate labours. Also, it is necessary to obtain environmental rights and undergo prior consultation with ethnic communities and even, based on Decision T 348, 15 May 2012,[36] ensure the affected community's participation in the design and execution of mega projects

34. Article 45, Law 99 of 1993.
35. CREG Resolution 55 of 1994.
36. Constitutional Court, Proceeding No. T-3.331.182. Magistrate: Jorge Ignacio Pretelt Chaljub.

or major infrastructure projects with an impact on the environment, as it is usually the case with the construction of plants larger than 20 MW.

104. Regarding land negotiation, there are no special rules for easements and land expropriation other than the provisions of Law 142 of 1994.

2. Conditions for Network Connection

105. The generator must perform the physical connection to the SIN network. As we had the opportunity to point out in previous sections, the generator that gets connected to the STN must have UPME's prior approval, besides following the provisions of CREG Resolution 25 of 1995, more precisely because of the connection code.

106. Normally, the legal relationship between the generator and the transporter or distributor is established in a contract in which price is not regulated by the CREG, but depends on the free negotiation of the parties. Through this contract, the network operator assigns transport capacity.

III. Self-generators and Cogenerators

A. *Self-generators and Distributed Generation*

107. Law 1715 of 2014 provides a legal framework for the integration of non-conventional renewable energy into the SIN and, in so doing, also regulates different topics related to self-generation, large scale self-generators, small scale self-generators, and distributed generation (DG). The law defines self-generation as the production of energy by a natural or legal person to mainly supply their own needs. In case of an energy surplus, this can be exported to the grid according to regulatory authority terms. Prior to this law, self-generators were not able to sell back any energy surplus to the grid. Law 1715 and further regulations[37] established a distinction between large self-generators (more than 1 MW) and small self-generators (1 MW or less) in terms of access to the grid and access to markets regarding who can buy their energy and the remuneration scheme.[38]

108. Small self-generators have access to simplified procedures and net metering. While large-scale self-generators have longer and stricter procedures, they can sell the energy surplus to a retailer or generator for a price agreed by the parties and

37. Decree 348 of 2017, Art. 1.
38. Daniela Aguilar Abaunza, *The Law for the Emerging Active Role of Electricity Consumers* (University of Waikato 2020).

enter into a back-up contract with the grid operator.[39] Neither small nor large-scale self-generators can participate in the wholesale market and should always be represented by a retailer or generator.[40]

109. The regulation for connection of self-generators has different procedures and requirements depending on the capacity of the DG device, whether it is large (more than 100 kilo Watts (kW)) or small (less than 100 kW).[41] A critical characteristic of the Colombian regulation is that it sets connection limits regarding network availability. In this sense, the regulation by the CREG establishes two connection and injection limits:[42] (i) only 20% of the capacity of the local network can come from DG and (ii) the amount of energy that can be injected per hour cannot be greater than 50% of the daily demand for energy. Both limits are known as 'technical standards' that are checked before proceeding with the connection request.

110. Having checked the network availability (technical standards), the requester continues with the connection procedure. The procedure will be different depending on the size of the DG. For a DG with a capacity of less than 100 kW, the procedure is simplified; in contrast, for larger devices, the procedure will be very similar to the connection of generators to the transmission grid.

111. Also, Resolution CREG 30 of 2018 establishes net-metering in Colombia, which is called 'energy credit' and is the remuneration scheme applicable to small generators (less than 1 MW) using alternative renewable resources.

B. Cogeneration

112. Law 1215 of 2008 establishes a new regulatory framework for cogeneration, which is complemented by CREG Resolution 005 of 2010. Some of the aspects developed in this law are taken from its origins, including CREG Resolution 107 of 1998 (which amended Resolution 085 of 1996) and Law 142 and 143 of 1994.

113. Law 1215 of 2008 defines cogeneration as the combined production of electricity and thermal energy, which is an integral part of the cogenerator's productive activity. The above Law empowers the cogenerator to sell its surplus electricity to energy trading companies. It also empowers the CREG to establish requirements and technical conditions to be met by combined processes to be considered as cogeneration processes, as well as the methodology for the back pay awarded by the National Grid to cogenerators.

---

39. Regulated in Decree 1073 of 2015.
40. Decree 1073 of 2015 (Colombia), Art. 2.2.3.2.4.4.
41. Decree 348 of 2017 (Colombia), Art. 5.
42. Resolution CREG 001 of 2018 (Colombia), Art. 6.

114. CREG Resolution 005 of 2010 establishes technical conditions for Equivalent Electrical Efficiency (REE, after its wording in Spanish) higher than the minimum required, and a minimum production of electricity and heat in the process. It also establishes the measurement system conditions that enable the registration of electricity, heat production, and fuel consumption, to evaluate the REE and the cogenerator's minimum electrical output. Cogenerators, as well as self-generators, must sign a network availability contract with this operator, in order to support this availability. This agreement is governed by the provisions set out in Resolution CREG 082 of 2002 and 097 of 2008. Likewise, cogenerators must enter into a contract with the supplier for the backup power supply as established by Articles 8 and 9 of Resolution 005, 2010.

115. In regards to cogenerators surplus' sales, Article 10 of Resolution 005 establishes three rules.

– Sales of Surplus Energy with Guaranteed Power of Less Than 20 MW

116. The first rule has two options: For the first one, the cogenerator does not have access to the central dispatch so it does not participate in the energy exchange. The same rules that apply to small plants that do not participate in the wholesale market apply for this type of sales, with the only difference that they can sell their energy to a dealer that has access to the regulated market directly without public auctions in order to sell with power exchange prices in each of the delivery times, or sell to the marketer serving the regulated market by participating in public tenders to sell to marketers that use that energy to fulfil the requirements of unregulated users with freely determined prices. In the second option, cogenerators have access to a central dispatch and sell energy according to the guidelines of the previous option.

– Sales of Surplus with Guaranteed Power Equal or Greater Than 20 MW

117. In the second rule, the cogenerator can sell to marketers considering the guidelines, meaning participation in public tenders mentioned in the second choice of the first rule, as long as it is accessible to the central dispatch and that they must participate in the power exchange.

– Sales of Surplus Power Without Performance Guarantee

118. The third rule also has two options: the first option, by not accessing the central dispatch and not participating in the energy exchange, this surplus is sold to marketers serving unregulated users to freely agreed prices. The second option, by accessing the central dispatch and participating in the energy exchange, the offer and settlement price will be the one applicable for inflexible generation.

119. Cogenerators participating in the energy exchange with or without power guarantee must be registered with the trading system. It should also be noted that cogenerators that do not have access to a central dispatch cannot participate in auctions of firm energy obligation (reliability charge).

§6. Generators' Rights and Obligations

I. Rights

120. Generators enjoy two types of rights: personal rights and property rights. Personal rights are covered in the Civil Code and specific regulations, such as Article 42 of Law 143 of 1994 and Annex B of CREG Resolutions 24 of 1995, 116 of 1998, 70 of 1999, and 156 of 2011, among others. Property rights are covered by the Civil Code.

A. Payment Rights

121. Generators are entitled to claim payment from other market participants for the execution of long-term energy contracts and also from the ASIC for the sums owed due to transactions made in the energy exchange.

122. Regarding the first case, the billing, collection and settlement of the energy contract are made directly by the parties and not by the ASIC.[43] The ASIC reports a list of the hourly assigned agreement to contractors for each contract, which serves as a support for the billing process between contractors. Hence, this is one of the reasons for the need to register energy contracts with the ASIC.

123. Regarding the second, the claim for payments owed for transactions made in the energy exchange, the generator must file the invoice and charge it to the ASIC, in accordance with paragraph 2 of Annex B of CREG Resolution 24 of 1995. Billing is made each month and the ASIC must act as director of the wholesale market' players engaged in these transactions in the energy exchange. Annex B applies in its entirety to the billing, collection and settlement in the energy exchange. Complaints about billing and settlement are governed by CREG Resolution 84 of 2007. This one sets the appropriate procedure for complaints and their solution.

B. Right to Request Restriction of Supply

124. In accordance with Article 5 of CREG Resolution 116 of 1998, any generator has the right to ask the ASIC for the limitation of supply for retailers and/or distributors. Resolution 116 of 1998 does not refer to other generating agents, but at

43. Paragraph 1 of Annex B, CREG Resolution 24 of 1995.

all times it refers to a limited supply for retailers and/or distributors. Limiting supply is a progressive programme where the circuits managed by the defaulter get progressively disconnected, excluding disconnectable circuits and other marketer's users.

125. The request to limit supply is grounded on late payment in energy contracts, connection contracts, and payment of charges due to the use of the STR or SDL. Definitely, this administrative mechanism is more effective than a regular debt collection process.

126. This right has undergone several judicial reviews in the Council of State, an action for annulment[44] of CREG Resolution 116 of 1998 and an enforcement action,[45] and finally a protection action in the Constitutional Court. As a result of these rulings the mechanism that limits the supply remains in the electricity sector's law, but cannot be applied to disconnect power to certain establishments which protect the right to life, such as hospitals and prisons.

II. Obligations

127. Generators are subject to statutory obligations for they perform a regulated activity. Most of these obligations include:

- Compliance with operation rules: The network code, the distribution regulation, trade regulation, the rationing Law and XM orders.
- Obligation to submit to the central dispatch coordinated by the CND.
- Generators are required to provide the CND and ASIC in a timely and accurate way the information requested by them in order to perform the central dispatch.
- The bid prices should reflect the variable costs of generation.
- When the CND requires it, generators are required to quote the terms on which they would provide the generation associated services for the SIN operation.
- Generation companies may not discriminate or prefer one person or group in energy transactions in the wholesale market.
- Backup capability: The remuneration of backup capacity for a generator's eligible plant imposes the obligation to maintain and operate that power plant so that it does actually have the ability to provide the available backup.
- Companies that perform marketing and generation activities are required, from their start up time, to establish separate accounts for each one of them.
- Obligations to operate under minimums: (CREG Resolution 100 of 1997 and CREG Resolution 25 of 1995). On this point it is important to note that the Council of State' first section declared that the imposition of such obligation was legal.
- Provision of information on energy generation and demand at intervals and in the manner defined in the Network Code.

44. Council of State, Sentence of 6 Nov. 2001, First Section. Magistrate: Manuel Santiago Urueta.
45. Compliance Action. Ref: Exp. No. ACU 1560. Plaintiff: Electrificadora del Chocó S.A. ESP. Defendant: ISA S.A ESP. Magistrate: Germán Rodríguez Villamizar.

- Provision of financial guarantees as set out in this resolution or advance payments if necessary.
- Generators are obliged to participate in the Power Exchange.
- They must submit to the settlements made by the ASIC for all acts and energy contracts made in the Exchange.
- Making the necessary appropriations for the payments to the Power Exchange.
- Compliance with the payment and clearing systems of the ASIC, to enforce the settlements referred to above.
- Commercial measurement system (CREG Resolution 25 of 1995).
- Compliance with plant removal conditions for firm power plants and non–guaranteed power plants.
- Registration of the energy contract with the ASIC.
- Register trade borders (CREG Resolution 24 of 1995, Resolution 47 of 2000, CREG Resolution 29 of 2001 and CREG Resolution 6 of 2003. Judgment of EC section 1 of the 4 August 2005. CP Maria Claudia Rojas Lasso).
- Other duties regarding the withdrawal of plants with or without firm energy.

§7. Contracts

128. Before describing the contracts signed in the generation business, it is important to mention that the State is involved in certain structural elements of the generation business legal area, such as: type, means, form, content, implementation and termination of each contract. The existing contracts for the electricity industry include:

- Connection Contract.
- Contract of mandate.
- Contracts representing other plants.
- Energy contracts: Article 7 CREG Resolution 24 of 1995 mentions all energy contracts and long-term energy contracts in the Energy Exchange.
- Contract for long-term energy: These are contracts in which generators and marketers freely agree on the terms, amounts, and prices for the purchase and sale of electricity for the long term; they are bilateral contracts. CREG Resolution 23 of 1995 does not provide for a specific contract form but establishes the obligation to register the contract, its minimum content, obligations (execution), the assignment of the contract and the completion of the same.

129. Annex D of CREG Resolution 24 of 1995 establishes the procedure for contract registration. Basically, it comprises the contracts registration periods, establishes the requirements that must be met and sets out deadlines for the ASIC to request clarifications that it deems relevant. The contract should contain at least the following: price, amounts of energy, length and hourly determination of energy. This minimum content must be in writing.

130. In connection with the performance of the contract obligations (implementation), Article 16 of CREG Resolution 24 of 1995 provides two important issues regarding performance: the allocation of contracts, which are finalized in merit order, and the ASIC's role as a third-party intervener or agent acting on behalf of market participants, without responsibility for the compliance of the energy contract's signing parties.

131. As for the assignment of contracts, Article 17 of CREG Resolution 24 of 1995 states that the assignment of the contract must be reported two calendar days prior to the implementation of the assignment.

132. The termination of energy contracts must be notified to the ASIC with a prior notice of seven days. In that case, the Administrator informs the parties about the record of completion. The effect of this report is the cancellation of energy delivery. No provisions are established on the grounds for termination.

133. It is noteworthy that aspects regarding prices, quantities, billing, collection and settlement are governed by the parties' agreements. The ASIC is not involved in this.

134. Energy contracts in the electricity exchange are held by the ASIC, for the sale of electricity by the hour, and the prices, quantities, guarantees, settlement and collection are determined by the provisions of CREG Resolution 24 of 1995. Due to their immediate execution, they are considered purely sale contracts.

135. We can say that they are rather multilateral contracts, because the parties are not identified in these energy transactions. Furthermore, we must recognize that these contracts are purely consensual, as they are held pursuant to wholesale market participants, such as generators, who have signed a mandate agreement with ASIC who manages the energy exchange.

Chapter 2. Transportation

136. Transportation or transmission includes the transport of energy through transmission lines, and the operation, maintenance and expansion of transmission systems, whether national or regional, according to what is provided by CREG Resolution 001 of 1994.

§1. Nature of the Activity

137. From a legal perspective, the national transmission activity is an essential public utility service, pursuant to Article 5 of Law 143 of 1994. The national transmission activity is a natural monopoly where several network owners coexist without competing among them.

138. The transmission activity is regulated as a network or infrastructure activity, and it focuses on the free access of third parties to the network and on the quality of the service. The involvement of transporters in the wholesale market is passive.

§2. Requirements to Become an Electricity Transmission Company

139. The carrier should be established as utility company or choose another way for becoming an electricity provider, as referred to Article 15 of Law 142 of 1994, such as an authorized organization. The operator must give notice of the beginning of its activities to the CREG in accordance with Article 4 of CREG Resolution 56 of 1994, and must also sign an agreement with the billing entity and settle the charges for its network use with the Management and Settlement of Accounts (LAC), which is a dependence of ASIC.

§3. Entry and Withdrawal from the Generation Activity

140. There is no free entry for the transmission activity. The only way to access it is through public tenders organized by the UPME. Regarding the withdrawal, there is no special regulation, but the procedure set by Law 142 of 1994 must be followed.

I. Entry into the Transmission Activity

141. The entrance to the transmission activity is not limited to Law 143 of 1994. This regulation for entry is established in CREG Resolution 022 of 2001, as noted above. Entrance is allowed by selecting an investor through public calls for the network expansion of the STN. The public announcement is made by taking into account the Transmission Expansion Reference prepared by the UPME. As a matter of fact, in public calls, the existing and potential National Transmitters compete for the construction, management, operation and maintenance of the STN expansion projects. It is clear that the existing national transmitters can only grow in the industry through these biddings.

142. The selected investor performs the construction, management, operation and maintenance of the network at its own risk, in accordance with Article 85 of Law 143 of 1994. Those selected shall not act on behalf of the State. Therefore, the same rule states that the assessment of environmental conditions is part of the proponent's responsibility. About this issue, we consider it relevant to have a change of regulations in order to establish that when drafting the selection documents, the environmental conditions should be taken into account. It is not suitable for any power sector project to have investors selected without any previous studies done by the convener, i.e., UPME, on environmental aspects and the impact on communities, especially native ones.

143. In proposals or offers, existing or potential investors must register their expected annual income and the bid security. By presenting this, the selection is aimed at choosing the proposal with the lowest present value of the expected annual revenue for the first twenty-five years of operation, where the investor is paid the investment and Administration, Operation and Maintenance (AOM) costs. After twenty-five years, the investor would receive only AOM costs.

144. The Public-Private Partnership (PPP) addressed by Law 1508 of 2012 is another option to enter the transmission activity. The competent entity to decide on the suitability of any initiative of PPP is the MME. It is also important to emphasize that in case of the absence of interested parties in providing the national transmission service, the MME can offer a concession contract in accordance with Article 55 and the following of Law 143 of 1994.

II. Withdrawal from the Transmission Activity

145. In Colombia, transmitter agents' withdrawal is regulated. The transmitting agent who decides to exit the market must notify the competent authority to ensure that the service is not being interrupted. As previously described, it is not possible to remove the networks. One thing is the removal of the networks and the other is their unavailability. The first situation implies that the networks' owner destroys them, takes them to another place, whereas the unavailability means that the networks are still in operation, but may become unavailable due to maintenance or force majeure. This issue of unavailability is regulated within the transmission's quality of service.

§4. NETWORKS

146. All matters concerning the STN networks are regulated by the Networks Code (CREG Resolution 25 of 1995) through planning, connection and operation codes.

I. Planning

147. The planning code sets the STN's Planning and Development standard to be used by the UPME and transporters. It also defines the procedures for providing the information required by those entities for planning. The planning is done for the short term (three years), medium term (five years) and long term (ten years) through flexible expansion plans that take into account quality, reliability and safety.

148. The proposed projects must be technically and economically feasible and the demand's requirements should be met regarding rational energy use criteria.

II. Connection

149. The connection code seeks to ensure that all network users have the same rights and obligations, and also sets out the requirements to be met by connection carriers. Users of the network include: generators, distributors, unregulated users, STN and STR transporters.

150. Network users' obligations include the payment of the studies conducted by the carrier, compliance with the technical standards of construction, installation and commissioning of the connection, as well as the maintenance duty, as agreed in the connection contract. However, carriers are required to: provide the connection point, meet the technical requirements of the connecting code, conduct studies of the connection request, and execute the connection contract.

151. The connection process starts with the signing of the contract and is completed with the respective connections' start-up. The steps are as follows: an opinion on the connection to STN must be requested to the UPME. Once provided, the connection contract must be signed. The user must prepare designs, calculation reports and specifications for the equipment procurement and the construction of civil works. This must be submitted for approval by the carrier. Once the designs are approved, the equipment must be bought and tested. Also, planning of civil engineering and equipment installation must be informed, as well as the operation' start date. The operation and maintenance must be in accordance with the operation code and the connection contract.

152. It is important to note that, if within four months from the receipt of the request, the carrier and the applicant user have not reached an agreement, the latter may request the CREG to impose the carrier a right of access to the network.

III. Operation

153. This refers to the process in which centrally dispatched generation resources are used to meet demand, meeting the criteria adopted for security, reliability and quality of service. The SIN operation is regulated in the operation code. The operation code is mandatory for generators, transporters, distributors, and traders, besides the National Dispatch Center.

§5. Rights and Obligations

154. Transporters' rights are guaranteed in CREG Resolution 001 of 1994 and obligations are set out in CREG Resolution 25 of 1995.

I. Rights

155. Carriers, just as generators, enjoy real and personal rights. Real rights are guaranteed from the rules of the Civil Code and personal rights are regulated by Article 17 of CREG Resolution 001 of 1994. This article provides that the carriers have the right to be remunerated through fees for network usage and connection charges. The former are prices regulated by the CREG and are settled by the LAC, dependent on ASIC. These charges are regulated and the amount depends on the parties' free negotiation, as established in the contract.

II. Obligations

156. The obligations of the transporter are related to its STN connection and the STN network operation. The connection obligations are established in the connection code and in the contract. For example, the Transporter, with UPME's authorization, must perform technical and economic feasibility studies for any connection request; it must offer the user a connection point with voltage of 220 kV or higher; and meet the minimum technical requirements for existing and or new STN connections and formalize the Connection Agreement.

157. The obligations regarding the transaction have to do primarily with the quality of service, according to CREG Resolution 11 of 2009. It is important to emphasize that the CND is responsible for the requirements on power quality, including frequency and voltage level at the STN. Among the carrier's service quality obligations are:

- Informing the CND of the incidence of any event, within fifteen minutes after its occurrence.
- Ensuring that the length of unavailability of assets used in the service of STN power transmission does not exceed the Maximum Adjusted Annual Hours' Unavailability.

158. It is necessary to add that the network users also have a number of obligations that are contained in Connection Code's Article 4.2 of CREG Resolution 25 of 1995; for example, the carrier must pay the costs incurred by the studies implementation that cause the connection request; meet the technical standards of design, construction, installation, commissioning, operation and maintenance of facilities and equipment, and must meet the conditions set in the Network Code and the specific conditions for each User under the Connection Contract.

§6. Contracts

159. In the activity of national electricity transmission there are mainly two types of contracts: the connection contract and the contract of carriage.

I. Connection Contract

160. The connection contract is signed between a generator, a large consumer and a local distributor, and an STN transporter. The objective is to make a connection to the STN.

161. This type of contract allows for the self-determination of the parties. However, it must follow the minimum rules applicable by the Connection Code, CREG Resolution 002 of 1994 and CREG Resolution 030 of 1996.

162. The procedure for making a connection to the STN can be summarized in three phases: first, application for a transporter connection point; second, study and approval stage, and third, the moment of the contract signature and connection setting-up. No connection fees are paid when the person to be connected is the connection's owner or covers its costs.

163. According to Article 23 of Resolution 001 of 1994, in case the carrier denies access to the connection point, the interested party in the connection may request the CREG an easement to access the network.

II. Contract of Carriage

164. This type of contract is governed by Articles 981 and 1008 of the Code of Commerce. According to this, one party accepts to pay a fee to the other in order for it to carry from one place to another, through a certain medium and within the time allowed, the electricity to be delivered to the final recipient.

165. The contract of carriage is not subject to specific formalities and its execution takes place over time. It involves the operation, maintenance and expansion of energy through national transmission lines and systems. The parties of the power transport contract are the carrier, which provides the transmission service; the generator, as the sender; and the end user as the recipient.

166. The content of the contract is regulated and depends solely on the resolutions issued by the CREG; hence there is no freedom of negotiation for the parties.

167. However, the authors consider the transport contract does not exist, advising that what really exists is an easement for network transmission. However, we actually believe in the existence of a transport contract, regardless of the lack of formalities (i.e., written proof).

Chapter 3. Distribution

§1. Nature of the Activity

168. Although the distribution activity is frequently mentioned, no definitions are provided in Law 142 or 143 of 1994. There is, however, a definition of it in Article 1 of CREG Resolution 24 of 1995, according to which the distribution of electricity 'is the activity of transporting energy through a distribution network at voltages less than or equal to 115 kw'. From this we may establish, first, that it is an activity that allows offering an electricity transmission service, and second, that in the electricity sector this activity does not have a buying and selling purpose.[46]

169. It should be noted that this activity has an important feature: distribution is a natural monopoly. The activities that a dealer can perform are, among others, the connection and transmission of electricity, operation and maintenance of networks, and the suspension of the service.[47] All these activities can be done in the retail electricity market.

170. Distribution is an activity carried out only at local or regional level, with no competition in the market, since there is only one network operator (OR, for its initials in Spanish) and several owners. It is also possible that there may be several network operators that are not in competition, each having its local or regional distribution system.

171. For the purposes of this document we have adopted the following classification: network operators (OR) or distributors and owners. It is important to add that the distribution networks are divided according to the administrative division of Colombia, meaning into thirty-two provinces. CREG Resolution 58 of 2008 follows the provisions of Decree 288 of 2007, which establishes four areas grouping different companies: East, North, Central and West.

172. The CREG has created a system of *comparative competition*, which encourages distribution firms to compete for efficiency gains through a rate formula.[48] There are a total of thirty-two dealers, but, as noted by Fedesarrollo, there are actually only fourteen groups involved in the distribution business. The four main groups by the number of connected users include the state-owned companies, EEPPM, CODENSA, and Union Fenosa.[49]

---

46. Ruben Barreiro, *Derecho de la energía eléctrica* 250–253 (Ábaco de Rodolfo Depalma 2002). This author defines distribution as electricity transport and provisioning.
47. It may be inferred from Art. 1 of CREG Resolution 24 of 1995, by which the commercial aspects of the MEM in the national interconnected system are regulated, which are part of the Operation Regulation, and CREG Resolution 70 of 1998, by which the rules of distribution of electricity were enforced, as part of the rules of operation of the national interconnected system.
48. This system was implemented based on para. 2 of Art. 92 of Law 142 of 1994.
49. Unión Fenosa is now represented BV Gas Natural and Colinversiones.

173. The objectives of the distribution regulation are: fixing service prices, ensuring the service quality and continuity to users, and setting out access rules for transmission.

§2. Requirements to Become a Power Distribution Company

174. The dealer should be established as a utility company or choose a different way of becoming a provider of the services referred to in Article 15 of Law 142 of 1994. The dealer must give notice of the start of its activities to the CREG, in accordance with Article 4 of the CREG Resolution 56 of 1994. Also, the dealer must sign an agreement with the billing and settling manager, with the LAC, and claim the charges for use of the network of STR, according to the CREG Resolution 97 of 2008.

§3. Entering and Leaving the Activity

175. Anyone is allowed to enter the energy distribution business, as long as it applies the distribution charges before the CREG (which is the compensation that it is entitled to charge to others for using the network). Regarding withdrawal, there is no special regulation, it follows the withdrawal procedure regulated by Article 61 of Law 142 of 1994.

I. Entering the Distribution Activity

176. The entrance to the distribution activity has no legal barriers. This is confirmed in Article 28 of Law 142 of 1994 which states: *all companies have the right to construct, operate and modify their networks and facilities to deliver public services.* The investor performs the activity at his own risk, in accordance with the provisions set in Article 85 of Law 143. It is clear that in case that STR networks are not built by the existing dealer, their construction, operation, management and maintenance may be left to free competition.

177. The PPP that is that is referred to in Law 1508 of 2012 is another option to enter the distribution business. The jurisdiction to resolve any PPP initiative would be the municipality for the construction, management, operation and maintenance of SDL networks, and the Province for the regional network. It is important to add that in case there is an absence of available entities providing the distribution service, the province or the municipality may offer a concession contract according to Article 55 and the following ones of Law 143 of 1994.

II. Leaving the Distribution Activity

178. The supplier's exit is regulated in Article 61 of Law 142 of 1994, according to which in case it decides to leave the market, it must warn the competent authority so this one may make sure that the distribution service shall not be interrupted. As previously mentioned, in Colombia, it is not possible to remove the networks.

§4. Networks

179. There are three types of networks in the distribution activity: general purpose, connection, and internal networks.

I. General Purpose Networks

180. General purpose networks may also be known as public networks, since these are used by one or more legal entities or individuals that may be known as network users, according to the definitions set in Numeral 1 of CREG Resolution 70 of 1998. According to Article 14 of Law 142 of 1994, it would also be possible to say these networks that make up the system of public service delivery to the community, from which power supply connections stem, i.e., local networks.

181. General purpose networks can be classified into STR networks and SDL networks. The STR is composed of connection assets to the STN, in addition to the connection set of lines and substations with their associated equipment, operating in the voltage level 4. An STR can belong to one or more Network Operators. The SDL is an electricity transport system that consists of power lines and sub-stations together with associated equipment, operating at voltage levels of 3, 2 and 1, dedicated to service delivery in one or more Trading Markets.

182. General purpose networks are those that are operated, managed and maintained by distributors or network operators, who charge a fee for the use or distribution of energy transport through such networks, which is subject to regulation by the CREG.

II. Connection Networks

183. According to Article 14 of Law 142 of 1994, connection networks conceived as power supply or connections, are derived from the General Purpose Network or a local network to that reach the cut recording device (metre) of the property. It is clear that in the case of apartment buildings or condominiums, the connection or power line reaches the general metre. However, based on Law 675 of 2001, the connection should reach one of the households.

184. The distributor provides the connection service. This service is regulated in CREG Resolutions 003 of 1994, 108 of 1997, 70 of 1998 and 156 of 2011. For the connection service, the dealer charges a one-time connection fee to the network user which is not regulated by the CREG.

III. Internal Networks

185. Article 14 of Law 142 of 1994 defines internal networks as a set of grids, accessories and equipment installed from the metre to the inside of the property. Facilities of such networks are governed by the technical regulation of electric facilities (RETIE, for its initials in Spanish). Distributors generally do not provide this service, for they are contracted with electrical technicians specialized in electrical installations.

§5. Rights and Obligations in the Distribution Activity

186. Both distributor companies and users of the network have rights and obligations. These depend on whether they are distributors of STR or SDL networks.

I. Rights and Obligations of the Distributor Regarding SDL and STR Networks

187. Distributors' rights regarding STR and SDL include the right to claim the charges for use of the network and connection charges, regulated in CREG Resolutions 70 of 1998, 82 of 2002 and 97 of 2008.

188. Charges for STR network use shall be claimed to LAC, a dependency of the Market Experts (XM) entity, which is responsible for its liquidation and collection. While SDL network charges are claimed directly to marketers. The connection charges are claimed to the ones seeking the connection service on both networks.

189. In regards to the obligations of the network operator, the following ones are mentioned.

– Expansion

190. The expansion obligation results in the development and implementation of system's expansion plan. According to CREG Resolution 70 of 1998, the OR is responsible for creating the plan to expand the network of its system. Such development should be done in coordination with expansion plans developed by the UPME. The network operator is obliged to execute the projects included in its system expansion plan. If the OR fails on the proposed expansion of STR or SDL, the interested user or any third party could perform this.

191. It is important to note that CREG Resolution 97 of 2008 provides that where the UPME has identified other STR expansion projects, it must inform the OR for it to express its interest in developing the project. If there is no interest, the project can be executed through free competition, as with STN projects.

192. It is clear that CREG Resolution 70 of 1998 does not set specific penalties for the network operator who fails executing STR or SDL projects included in its expansion plan. Nevertheless, we consider that if the OR's lack of interest affects users, it may be sanctioned by the SSP.

– Connection

193. These obligations refer to technical specifications, conditions, procedures and deadlines required for these connections. If the connection requests come from generators, transmitters or distributors, then the obligations will be regulated by CREG Resolution 70 of 1998. For all other connections requested by users, CREG Resolutions 108 of 1997 and 156 of 2011 apply.

194. If within four months after receipt of a connection request, the operator or distributor has not agreed with the petitioners, the Commission may impose a right of access, which imposes the right to use the network.

– Operation

195. The operation of the connections should be done in a safe, reliable and economically sound way. In addition, information must be provided to the control centres in accordance with the Network Code (CREG Resolution 25 of 1995).

– Quality

196. The quality requirements are two folded: quality of service and power quality. The quality of service for STR networks is regulated in CREG Resolution 97 of 1998. It provides for unavailability, the excluded unavailability and the compensation for exceeding unavailability indicators. Offsets are some discounts that are made to the income of the operator or distributor STR network. This is without prejudice for those affected by an outage, as they may sue for damages. Concerning power quality, there is a current proposal to regulate it in CREG Resolution 65 of 2012.

197. For SDL networks both service quality and quality of power are regulated. The quality of service, according to CREG Resolution 97 of 2008, is an incentive scheme of quality management, which also operates the interruptions and compensation system. Regarding the quality of power, this is regulated in CREG Resolutions 70 of 1998 No. 6, 24 of 2005 and 16 of 2007. Currently there is another resolution in consultation.

– Third-Party Networks

198. The obligations related to the use of third-party assets are regulated in No. 9 of CREG Resolution 70, Article 145 of Law 1151 of 2007 and in CREG Resolution 97 of 2008. Basically, third parties who build networks for general or public use are entitled to be remunerated for the use of their network. CREG Resolution 70 had a formula for compensation, but CREG Resolution 97 of 2008 eliminated it. Today's network owners negotiate with the network operator their economic rights.

199. Finally, we should mention that the network operator or distributor has other obligations, such as environmental liabilities and obligations not to engage in anticompetitive practices.

II. Users of the Network

200. Network users have the right to receive the quality of service and quality of electric power, as well as other rights in the distribution activity. They also have security obligations, which non-compliance may lead to the service suspension (paragraph 4.3.3 CREG Resolution 70 of 1998) and can suspended for them due to a breach of these security obligations (paragraphs 6.2.1.5 and 6.2.2 of CREG Resolution 70). Such obligations have their rationale, because the network user's behaviour can affect the distribution system.

§6. Contracts in the Distribution Activity

201. In the distribution business the following contracts are held: connection contract, network usage contract, extra quality contract (CREG Resolution 97 of 2008) and network backup capacity availability contract (CREG Resolution 82 of 2002 and CREG Resolution 97 of 2008).

§7. Participation Limits in Distribution Business

202. *Vertical Limit:* according to the provisions of Article 74 of Law 143 of 1994, dealers may not be producers at the same time. Nevertheless, the CREG has made a broad interpretation of this article, allowing distribution companies to own up to 25% interest in a power generation company. Additionally, pursuant to Resolution 4 of 1999, a distribution company can own shares in a transport company's capital, as long as it does not exceed 15%.

203. Horizontal limit: according to CREG Resolution 128,[50] a company could not hold more than 25% of the distribution market. This rule was repealed by section 4 of Resolution 1 of 2006. Currently, in Colombia, there is no horizontal limit for growth of the distribution companies.

50. Article 5, CREG Resolution 128 of 1996, which dictates the rules on participation in the activities of generation, distribution and supply of electricity and sets limits on shareholding between companies with complementary activities.

Chapter 4. Consumption and Trade

204. In accordance with the provisions of Article 14.25 of Law 142 of 1994, energy marketing is considered a complementary public service. Article 11 of Law 143 of 1994 defines the trading activity as *the purchase and sale of electricity to end users, regulated or unregulated ones.*[51] We would also add to this definition the sale in the wholesale market, as included by CREG Resolution 156 of 2011.

§1. Nature of the Activity

205. The marketing is unique in that it takes place both in the wholesale and the retail market. In the wholesale market there is a high degree of competition. Meanwhile, the retail market includes both unregulated users (which is a very competitive market) and regulated users (with weak competition level). In theory, the market is considered a competitive activity to the extent that it meets underlying economic conditions, as follows: a large number of traders, the market entry and exit are free,[52] and electricity is a homogeneous good intended for public satisfaction.

206. In practice, the regulation of the energy trade is justified for being an activity with an imperfect competition. This position is supported[53] by the fact that there are a small number of firms in the regional market, as well as a price intervention for regulated users. Also, the government does not obey the limits for market growth, and there is a low level of competitiveness. The aim pursued by regulating energy trade is to preserve and promote the growth of free competition and to prevent the abuse of dominant positions in the market.

207. Energy traders typically develop the following activities: purchase and sale of electricity, metering, billing, sales management, and promotion of efficient and rational use of energy. The trader is responsible for collecting the fees paid by users of the electricity service. In the case of regulated users, this sum is composed of elements **G + T + D + Oc + M** (Generation + Transmission + Distribution + Other costs + Marketing). The unregulated users only negotiate with the marketer both G and M, while T and D are fixed values.

208. There are a total of fifty-seven traders, according to Fedesarrollo,[54] but there are about twenty-one groups in fact; among them are: CODENSA, EEPPM, Unión Fenosa and the National Government.

---

51. Article 1, Law 143 of 1994.
52. In any case, there are preconditions for market access: environmental, sanitary, water use permits, among others.
53. Santiago Urbiztondo & Juan Manuel Rojas, *La Reforma del Sector Eléctrico en Colombia, Breve Análisis y Crítica Constructiva.* http://www.fiel.org/publicaciones/Documentos/DOC85.pdf (October 2005).
54. *Ibid.*

§2. Energy Traders: Requirements

209. Articles 5 and 6 of CREG Resolution 156/2011 establish the following requirements for electrical energy traders:

- Being a utility company or any other type of trader referred to in Article 15 of Law 142 of 1994.
- Carrying the accounting for the trading activity separately from the accounting of other activities performed.
- Defining and publishing contractual conditions for tenders and offers, if the company is subject to regulated users.
- Setting up a 'Requests, Complaints and Resources' office mentioned in Article 153 of Law 142 of 1994, when it intends to supply the service to users.
- Notifying the start of activities to the SSP, CREG and the Solidarity Fund for Subsidies and Income Redistribution of the MME.

210. The marketer can be a company that is dedicated solely to this activity or a retailer that combines this activity with electricity distribution or generation.

§3. Entering and Leaving the Electricity Marketing Activity

211. The entrance to the trading activity inside the SIN is free, provided that the ones that aim to develop this activity do so at their own risk (Article 85 of Law 143 of 1994). The entrance to the trading activity in the ZNI is subject to the decision of the MME. If the Ministry has already granted a contractor for an exclusive service area, then it will not allow the entry for any other interested persons.

212. Withdrawal is also free under certain conditions. They include giving notice of this situation to the competent authority (Municipality) to ensure the service does not get interrupted, according to Article 61 of Law 142 of 1994.

I. Participation in the Wholesale Market

213. According to Article 4 of CREG Resolution 156 of 2011, marketing companies must meet certain requirements in order to participate in the MEM, such as being registered with ASIC. This register allows marketers to buy electricity and sell it in the retail market to users, as well as buying and selling energy in the wholesale market to other participants in the SIN network. The marketer is the only agent in the electricity industry that participates in both the wholesale and the retail market.

214. According to CREG Resolution 24 of 1995, traders can buy or sell either through bilateral contracts or through power exchange contracts. It is clear that when they buy through bilateral contracts they should take into account to which market the energy is delivered to: regulated market users or unregulated market users. If it comes to serving the regulated market, marketers must follow the procedures set in Articles 4 and 5 of CREG Resolution 20, 1996 (as amended by CREG Resolution 67, 2008); for example, performing their electricity purchases through an open call.

II. Participation in the Retail Market

215. The participation of traders in the SIN retail market is regulated by CREG Resolutions 31 of 1997 and 131 of 1998. The first one provides that marketers must serve retail users with rates set under the regime of regulated freedom. The second one states that all non-regulated users should be represented by a marketer in the wholesale market. This means that unregulated users are not agents of the wholesale market, but that they can only be found in the retail market.

§4. Obligations in the Marketing Business

216. Traders' obligations are regulated in CREG Resolution 156 of 2011. They define legal relationships of traders with the market and market players, such as: general conditions, requirements relating to the MEM and STR, obligations with the network operator and other marketers. With respect to users, the requirements are set forth in CREG Resolution 108 of 1997.

217. Users' rights are primarily set forth in Article 9 of Law 143 and Article 3 of CREG Resolution 108 of 1997. Among their rights, users are entitled to receive information, freely choose a provider, metering and have quality of goods and services.

218. The main obligation of users is the payment of services. Non-payment triggers penalties, such as service suspension and outage.

§5. Contracts in the Trading Activity

219. Traders in the wholesale market sign the following types of contracts: agency contract, supply contract, financial contract and contract of purchase and sale of energy in the energy exchange.

220. Supply contracts with unregulated users are regulated by contractual stipulations, the Commercial Code and Law 142 of 1994. These contracts are valid under special conditions. In addition, there are contracts with uniform conditions for regulated users, in which case users agree to the uniform conditions. Although uniform contract conditions exist, special conditions may apply, depending on the users' needs.

Part II. Regulatory Framework Concerning Gas

Introduction

§1. Brief History of Natural Gas in Colombia

221. The activities associated with the natural gas fuel cycle have a relatively short history in the country.[55] In the 1950s gas was classified as a by-product of petroleum production and most of this fuel was burned in the producing wells. However, changes were introduced in 1961 throughout a law that regulated oil exploration – *Ley Regulatoria de Exploración Petrolera de 1961* – which considered gas as an economic resource, regulating its use and restricting flaring to limited quantities.

222. At the beginning of the 1970s, gas started to be used in a moderated way as energy for industrial uses, mainly on the Atlantic Coast. Later on, in 1974, big reserves of gas were discovered in the Chuchupa and Ballena fields located in the Department of La Guajira. The growing tendency of international petroleum prices as well as the increase in oil imports that occurred in that year made natural gas a strategic source of energy, which began to be seen with optimism as a new alternative in the national energy basket.

223. As a consequence of the discoveries of gas in La Guajira, the company Promigas was created in 1974 to promote the interconnection of the pipelines of the Atlantic Coast. The state-owned oil & gas company, ECOPETROL, participated in Promigas with a 42% share of its capital. In 1977 the construction of the main Atlantic Coast Pipeline System began. This system transported gas mainly to the cities of Barranquilla and Cartagena and opened the gate to a massive substitution of high-cost and exported fuels (such as fuel oil) for natural gas. The main beneficiaries of this substitution were the big industries, ECOPETROL and the thermoelectric generators of the Atlantic Coast.

55. The present chapter is based on the research material used for Mr Pando's LLM Thesis for the Faculty of Law of the University of Alberta, and its preparation was developed under the supervision of Professor David N. Percy. However, the contents of this chapter are the creation of the author under his own responsibility and do not compromise any third party or institution.

224. At the same time that the Atlantic Coast Pipeline System was built, several Local Distribution Companies (LDCs) of gas were created, although residential consumption was still very low.[56] At the end of the 1970s, natural gas consumption began in the residential, industrial, thermoelectric and petrochemical sectors. As for the residential sector, consumption started in a massive way in the departments located near to La Guajira fields: Atlántico, Bolívar, Sucre, Córdoba, Santander and Huila.

225. Between 1980 and 1985 gas production and reserves remained constant. In 1986, the first nationwide programme for massive use of natural gas was established in Colombia. This programme was called *Programa de Gas para el Cambio* (Gas for Change) and had as primary objective to substitute high-cost energy mainly in the residential sector. This programme constituted the first energy policy that tried to incorporate natural gas into the domestic energy consumption basket, specifically through two phases: (i) Massive use of gas in the residential and transportation sectors, and (ii) Connection of the gas-producing wells with consumption centres located in the central territories of the country (known as the 'Interior' market).

226. By 1987, the Gas for Change programme had connected 85,000 new users in the whole country: 45,000 in the Atlantic Coast, 34,000 in Bucaramanga and some others in the cities of Neiva, Villavicencio and their neighbouring populations. In that same year the programme arrived to the capital of Colombia – Bogota – with the objective of substituting the traditionally used fuel known as *Cocinol* for gas propane. By the end of 1987, a total of 25,094 users of *Cocinol* had already been substituted for gas in sixty-one neighbourhoods of Bogota. The programme had important achievements at regional level. However, it was an isolated policy that was not framed as an integral national energy policy.

227. In order to solve this situation, in 1991, the National Government adopted a more aggressive programme for the Mass Use of Gas. This programme looked to enlarge the energy supply of the country, which was highly concentrated in hydroelectricity, by incorporating other energy sources such as natural gas. To achieve the above-mentioned objectives, the energy policy-makers recommended the following strategies:

- promoting mass consumption of gas in the main cities of the country;
- fostering private sector participation in the gas industry;
- eliminating price distortions in the energy basket; and
- building a network of pipelines with national coverage.

228. Between 1992 and 1993 new gas reserves were discovered in the fields of Cusiana and Cupiagua, located in the eastern department of Casanare. With these new discoveries the strategies of the gas mass consumption programme needed to be reconsidered. Accordingly, by means of a National Policy Document – National

56. In 1978, gas production was at 146.6 MCFD, where 62.2% of that production was marketed and the rest was re-injected to the wells or flared.

Council of Economic and Social Policy (CONPES) 2646 of 1993 – the national government decided to stimulate the supply and demand of gas and to continue promoting the mass consumption and supply of gas to big industrial consumers and thermoelectric companies.

229. Additionally, CONPES 2646 of 1993 established the foundations for the organization of the regulatory and institutional structure of the natural gas market in Colombia. The adopted politics intended to stimulate freedom of gas prices in the well-head and freedom of prices of other energy substitutes; incentivize the participation of the private sector in the transport of gas through BOMT contracts;[57] and create a state-owned company exclusively dedicated to the transport of Gas, among others. CONPES 2646 of 1993 also established the course of action required to guarantee gas supply, and delegated in ECOPETROL the responsibility of promoting mass consumption of gas in the national territory, directly or by means of contracts for the construction of new pipelines.

230. By 1993, natural gas had a presence in sixty-two municipalities of Colombia and provided service to more than 500,000 users. Nevertheless, natural gas supply was not considered a public utility until 1994, when Law 142 of 1994 was promulgated. This law established a new regime for certain public services connected to household, setting special rules concerning the type of company that provided the service, the way the service had to be provided, the regulatory and control processes, and the regime of consumers' protection. With this legal reform, new institutional and legal tools were created and an overturn was given to the traditional pattern of benefit of public services in Colombia. This reform expressly determined that natural gas distribution was a public service, including related activities, such as production, transportation, and retail.[58]

231. In 1995, under ECOPETROL's leadership, the national gas interconnection between the main locations and consumption centres began. This interconnection started with the construction of more than 2,000 km of pipelines that connected La Guajira wells with the centre and southwest departments of the country and the eastern territories as well.

232. In 1997, a fund called *Fondo de Solidaridad y Redistribución del Ingreso* (Fund of Solidarity and Redistribution of Revenues) was created with the purpose of facilitating access to natural gas for the most-needed socioeconomic population. This fund worked as a cross-subsidy scheme where great consumers (thermoelectric companies, industrial and commercial users) and high-income residential users paid up to a 20% surcharge on their consumption to finance the consumption and connection of poor residential consumers.

57. Build, Operate, Maintain, and Transfer (BOMT).
58. Article 14.28, Law 142 of 1994.

233. That same year, the Colombian Congress promulgated Law 401 of 1997 and ECOPETROL was ordered to unbundle its transport of gas activity from its production and wholesale retail activities. As a consequence, the Colombian Company of Gas – Ecogas – was established, a state-owned transportation company that was a recipient of all ECOPETROL's transportation assets, including pipelines, city gates, gathering facilities, and off course, all of ECOPETROL's former clients. Law 401 of 1997 also created the CNO in charge of establishing the technical rules for the operation of the National Transportation System, and a Special Development Fund,[59] nurtured by mandatory contributions of LDCs and other shippers, with the main objective of financing or co-financing the construction of new transportation and distribution network facilities in geographic areas of the country with high rates of unsatisfied basic needs.

234. With the same purpose of providing gas to lower income locations, between 1997 and 1998 exclusive concession areas for the distribution of gas were granted by the MME to extend the coverage of the service in the Departments of Quindío, Caldas, Risaralda, Valle and Tolima.[60] One year later, in 1999, and with the purpose of promoting mass use of natural gas in the transportation sector, ECOPETROL was ordered to offer special economic conditions (especially discounts and funds) to benefit those who decided to use compressed natural gas for vehicles (NGV).

235. In the first years of the new century, and with the main objective of achieving mass consumption of gas nationwide, the government issued the 2002–2006 National Development Plan. This Plan created beneficial conditions for gas companies to provide gas to smaller municipalities and rural areas. The Plan also acknowledged the great potential for marketing gas internationally, and therefore it defined the conditions under which gas could become exportable.

236. However, due to the fact that ECOPETROL directly controlled and subsidized the prices of liquid fuels competing with natural gas, the mass penetration of gas policy dictated by the government wasn't occurring as well as intended. Accordingly, by means of a National Policy Document – CONPES 3244 of 2003 – the national government identified existing distortions in the energy basket and recommended the termination of ECOPETROL's subsidies to liquid fuels, such as fuel oil and diesel (ACPM).

237. Colombian legislators adopted CONPES's 3244 of 2003 recommendations by means of Law 812 of 2003. Indeed, with the purpose of boosting exploration and increasing the offer of natural gas, as well as achieving higher penetration of gas instead of other fuel substitutes, several articles were included in Law 812 of 2003

59. A fund called 'Fondo Cuota de Fomento'.
60. Article 40, Law 142 of 1994 refers to these '*Areas de Servicio Exclusivo*' or exclusive service areas that can be created to distribute gas in areas of special socio-economic characteristics, primarily locations with a big portion of low-income population and not too many great consumers or industries, normally adjudicated through concession agreements that contain special rules regarding tariffs and expansion plans, after a public bidding process.

which repealed the existing subsidies scheme for gasoline and diesel, liberalized gas reserves for commercial and international exchange, and promoted the development of new transportation infrastructure.

238. Following the rules created in Law 812 of 2003, the MME promulgated two decrees of great importance for the gas industry. In the first place, Decree 3428 of 2003, now repealed, in connection with the international commercial exchange of natural gas and establishing the applicable definitions for the export/import of natural gas. This regulation set the fundamental parameters for the exercise of these activities, and guaranteed the protection of the national interest in terms of supply, access and use of the natural gas resource. Secondly, Decree 3429 of 2003 established rules for the trading of natural gas, looking to protect the market and to assure the benefit of the public service of natural gas.

239. In the same direction, the MME promulgated Decree 802 of 2004, which established rules to promote the consumption of NGV. The regulatory framework on gas was complemented by decrees to increase coverage (Decree 3531 of 2004), regulate the State's participation in the assets, rights and contracts of Ecogas (Decree 1404 of 2005),[61] and set out the rules for high-priority attention when situations of gas restriction or serious emergency occurred (Decree 1484 of 2005).[62] In addition, Decree 2400 of 2006 was promulgated to regulate international interconnections of Natural Gas, and create the conditions for the construction of an international pipeline between Colombia and Venezuela which started operation in 2008.[63]

240. With respect to gas supply, Decree 2687 of 2008[64] set out instruments to guarantee national supply of natural gas. Among those instruments is the establishment of a new procedure for natural gas wholesale retail, which was later regulated by CREG Resolution 095 of 2008.

241. Given the low flexibility of the Colombian gas market and the increasing risk of gas shortages due to climate factors,[65] as well as competition issues related

61. Ecogas was partially privatized and transformed into *Transportadora de Gas del Interior* (TGI CORP. E.S.P.), when in 2006, the *Empresa de Energía de Bogotá* (EEB) bought the majority of their stocks after a public bidding process.
62. According to this Decree, residential users which belong to the regulated market had top priority, and gas exports are the first to be affected in case of gas restrictions. The regulated market is mainly composed by residential and commercial customers with a tariff set by the regulator.
63. Based on Decree 2400 of 2006, the MME issued Resolution 18, 1344 of 2006 authorizing the Colombian Branch of PDVSA (PDVSA S.A.) the construction of an International Interconnection with Venezuela, with 88.5 km of pipeline in the Colombian border starting in the Ballenas station – located in the municipality of Manaure, Guajira – up to point 51 in the geographic limit with Venezuela.
64. This Decree has been modified by several others such as Decree 2730 of 2010, which ordered UPME to draft an indicative expansion plan of the National Transportation System, and to identify new alternatives for gas storage and supply.
65. The presence of a drought season created by a phenomenon typical of the Pacific countries called 'El Niño' creates situations of stress due to higher demand of gas for electricity generation.

to concentration in supply, coordination and vertical integration problems (particularly between supply and transportation), the ANH,[66] the MME,[67] and the CREG[68] carried out a series of studies to identify the problems affecting the gas industry and the possible solutions. After internal debates over the problems affecting the gas upstream supply market and the transportation midstream market, Decree 2100 of 2011 unified the criteria related to measures and instruments to guarantee a full supply of gas, including the establishment of new rules for wholesale retail and gas supply contracts, the import and storage of gas, the construction of an LNG plant, and the promotion of unconventional gas.

242. The comparison of natural gas figures in Colombia from 2016 to 2019 allows us to establish some differences based on the data reported in the Promigas 2020 gas sector report: the proven reserves decreased from 4,024 in 2016 to 3,163 in 2019, the transport infrastructure increased from 7,455 km in 2016 to 7,639 km in 2019.[69]

243. The Law of the National Development Plan 2018–2022, Law 1955 of 2019, places special emphasis on LPG more than on natural gas. However, there is a legal authority given to CREG to define new activities or links in the service provision chain: the return of the natural gas subsidy to irrigation districts[70] and a differential rate for small rural producers, in which the Nation (central government) will cover 50% of the cost of the natural gas for the associations of small farmers.

244. The document 'Consultancy in support of the Energy Transformation Mission in the areas of supply, commercialization, transport, storage, regasification, demand, institutional aspects, and natural gas regulation'[71] of the Transformation Mission establishes two main projects that should be implemented in Colombia. The first one is the Costa Pacifica-National Transport System (SNT) gas pipeline to make viable the pacific regasification infrastructure, and second, the Jobo-Medellín gas pipeline to allow the entry and exit to the gas reserves of Córdoba and Sucre.

---

66. Poyry Energy Consulting, *Recommendations for Further Development of the Colombian Gas Market*, a report commissioned by the National Hydrocarbon Agency (ANH) (Bogota, 2010).
67. Peter Cramton, *Auctioning Long-term Gas Contracts in Colombia*, a paper commissioned by CREG (Bogota, 2008), and Frontier Economics, *Diagnostic of Natural Gas Market Failures in Colombia*, a report commissioned by MME (Bogota, 2010).
68. Harbord, D. & N-H. von der Fehr, *Regulation and Incentives for Investment in the Colombian Gas Transport Network*, a report commissioned by CREG (Bogota, 2010). Also, *Upstream Issues in Colombian Gas Supply*, a report commissioned by CREG (Bogota, 2010).
69. PROMIGAS. Gas Sector Report 2020. http://www.promigas.com/Es/Paginas/Informe%20Sector%202020/Caracterización.aspx.
70. This reference was included in the National Development Plan 2010–2014, then removed from the National Development Plan 2014–2018.
71. https://www.minenergia.gov.co/documents/10192/24166201/2.+El+Rol+del+Gas+en+la+Transformación+Energética.pdf.

245. As indicated in the 2020 gas sector report prepared by Promigas,[72] Colombia currently has the highest historical number of residential users. The coverage of the supply in the last twenty-five years stepped from 12% to 71%. Around 86% of these users belong to the most economically vulnerable population. This is considered to be a positive balance although it is a country with a low level of reserves and lower production. Between 2005 and 2016, residential fuel gas users increased by 51.1%, from 6.6 to 10.2 million users, of which 30% were new LPG users and 70% were new natural gas users. Also, according to the UPME, 90.4% of fuel gas users are located in urban areas and the rest in rural areas.[73]

§2. Regulatory Model Adopted in Colombia

246. The CREG has established a definition for natural gas.[74] The natural gas fuel cycle is basically composed of the following activities: production (which also includes wholesale retail), transportation, distribution, and retail. Accordingly, the Colombian natural gas chain of supply has the following agents:

- Producer – Wholesale Retailer or Gas Marketer: Is the company that produces and extracts natural gas from gas wells to sell it to great consumers, such as industrial users, thermoelectric companies, and LDCs. Currently there are eleven producers in the country.[75]
- Transporter: In Colombia nine pipeline transportation companies operate.[76] They are in charge of moving gas through a number of major pipelines that together form what is known as the SNT.[77] Natural gas is taken from the point of entry to the SNT – located at the production sites – to the city gates,[78] in which gas is

72. PROMIGAS. Informe sector gas 2020. http://www.promigas.com/Es/Paginas/Informe%20Sector%202020/Caracterización.aspx.
73. *Unidad de Planeación Minero Energética. Documento de trabajo del Plan Indicativo de Expansión de Cobertura de Gas Combustible – PIECGC.* http://www1.upme.gov.co/Hidrocarburos/publicaciones/PIECGC-Septiembre-2017.pdf.
74. 'A mixture of gases of great caloric power that was formed throughout the years in the sub-surface of the Earth. The principal component of this mixture is methane. The other components – in small quantities – are mainly other gases such as ethane, carbon dioxide (CO2) and vapour. It can be measured in volume units (cubic meters m^3 or cubic feet ft^3) or energy units (kilowatt hour kWh or caloric units BTU).' http://www.creg.gov.co/html/i_portals/index.php?p_origin=internal&p_name=content&p_id=MI-66&p_options=.
75. Some of these companies are: B.P. Exploration Co. (Colombia) Ltd., B.P. Santiago Oil Company, Chevron Petroleum Company, ECOPETROL, Grupo Petrotesting Colombia S.A., Hocol S.A., Mercantile Colombia Oil and Gas, Pacific Stratus Energy Colombia Ltd., Petrobras Colombia Limited, Petrobras International Braspetro BV and Tepma.
76. Some of the transportation companies operating in Colombia are: Coinobras Gas S.A. E.S.P., Gasoducto del Tolima S.A.E.S.P., Promigas S.A. E.S.P., Promotora de Gases del sur S.A. E.S.P., Sociedad Transportadora de Gas del Oriente S.A. E.S.P., Transportadora Colombiana de Gas S.A. E.S.P, Transportadora de Gas del Interior S.A. E.S.P. y Transportadora de Metano S.A. E.S.P.
77. SNT (Sistema Nacional de Transporte) is defined in CREG Resolution 033 of 1999.
78. City Gate is defined in CREG Resolution 011 of 2003 as the regulatory station from which a distribution system or a transportation sub-system may derive.

injected into the distribution systems[79] of the LDCs. Alternatively, natural gas can be transported directly to great consumers' receiving points (i.e., thermoelectric or industrial companies). Also, transporters can participate in the supply and transportation secondary market.

- LDC and Retailer: It refers to the company that transports gas through a secondary pipeline network known as distribution system, from the city gates to the end users' point of connection. According to Decree 3429 of 2003, LDCs must also conduct the retail activity when its distribution system renders the service to 'regulated clients'. Retail activity to regulated consumers conducted by LDCs includes activities such as installation, collection, and customer support services. LDCs can also participate as retailers in the supply and transportation secondary market.
- Retailer or Marketer: It is the company that purchases or sales gas for profit. Generally speaking, it is a firm that purchases gas to develop its own activities and has the possibility to sell the remaining gas (gas that the company has not used)[80] in the supply and transportation secondary market. In that sense, LDCs and great consumers can also be retailers.
- End Users: They are classified as regulated and non-regulated users.

247. According to Frontier Economics,[81] the Colombian regulatory model adopted for natural gas is known as Wholesale Competition or Competition in Supply, which has the following main characteristics:

- Competition in the activities of production and retail of gas.
- Network activities, such as transport and distribution, are considered regulated activities.
- Open access to third parties' infrastructure (ATR).[82]
- Retail competition limited to large customers.

248. In turn, this model presents three sub-markets: (i) the gas supply market; (ii) the transport of gas; and (iii) the sale of gas to the final user. To be able to coordinate these markets, Colombia's energy regulator has chosen to use the contract-carriage method – instead of the common carrier method.

249. In accordance with the analysis made by Frontier Economics,[83] the following conclusions can be reached about the Colombian natural gas market: (i) the small size of the market hinders competition in production and wholesale retail; (ii) the seasonal pattern of demand originated in the drought conditions created under

79. Distribution System is defined in CREG Resolution 011 of 2003 as a 'pipeline system that transports gas from the city gate or other distribution system to the point of connection to real estate properties, without including its connection and measuring.'
80. This remaining gas is also known as Secondary Available Capacity and/or Gas Supply Rights (*Capacidad Disponible Secundaria y/o Derechos de Suministro de Gas*). CREG Resolution 033 of 1999.
81. Frontier Economics, *Diagnostic of Natural Gas* (22 May 2017).
82. ATR stands for Third Party Access (TPA).
83. *Ibid.*

the climate phenomenon known as 'El Niño', generates a risk of demand and high pressure over long term contracts signed between thermal generators and gas producers, and between shippers and transporters. Given the importance of the consumption of the thermo-electrical industry, this problem affects other shippers; and (iii) the pressure on the fix-term contracts is also increased by the aversion to the gas restrictions of the Colombian authorities. As it is highly likely that the government will intervene in cases of gas rationing, and the recent experience confirms this, the parties do not have enough incentives to knowingly sign complete contracts that won't be honoured in stressful situations.[84]

§3. Geographic Market

250. In Colombia several differences still remain between the Atlantic Coast and the Interior market. It is well known that gas markets tend to develop by regions. This was the case of the Atlantic Coast and the more developed markets of the interior, such as Bucaramanga and Neiva. However, the programme for the mass use of gas along with the construction of pipelines in the interior changed this traditional pattern of industry development. The location of the modern thermoelectric generators followed the electricity demand and the signal of gas transport. Consequently, an important number of generators set their thermoelectric plants in the Mid-Magdalena region, near the Opon gas field, while others located them in the Atlantic Coast near the electricity and gas consumption centres of La Guajira fields.

251. The drastic fall in the electricity demand in 1998–1999 triggered a loss of competiveness for thermoelectric plants. In addition, after the failure occurred in gas supply from the Opon field, the interior transport system received more transportation demand, which reduced the usage of the Ballena-Barranca pipeline system. The interior transport system was able to offer discount for gas at the city gate. As a consequence, demand for the interior transport system increased substantially between 2000 and 2009, particularly in the industrial, residential and NGV sectors. In addition, the increase of NGV demand in the Atlantic Coast reduced the importance of thermoelectrical demand in both regions.

252. Close to 90% of gas production has been developed by geographical regions in the country. There are two submarkets, each with a predominant producer and transporter.[85] The gas produced in La Guajira supplies the Atlantic Coast market. The gas production of the Llanos Orientales is responsible for satisfying the

84. Colombia suffered a thirteen months electricity rationing programme between 1991 and 1992 and more recently suffered gas shortages that triggered the gas rationing programme between 2009 and 2010.
85. Mauricio Santa María, et al. *El Mercado de la Energía Eléctrica en Colombia: características, evolución e impacto sobre otros sectores* (2009).

demand of the markets in the centre of the country. In consequence, the most developed gas markets in the country are on the Atlantic coast and the interior of the country.[86] This situation has created a market with a supply of gas at a competitive cost.

253. In Colombia, considering the concentration of production in two geographic zones (La Guajira and Casanare have around 90%), and the distance between the fields and the main consumption centres, transportation costs creates natural markets for each field; a situation that reduces the possibility of competition in wholesale retail between production sites.[87] Indeed, the transport infrastructure connects the production sites with the principal cities and consumption centres. It is a radial transport system with charges by distance, which allows for a differential production. According to CREG's analysis of gas transportation costs, gas from La Guajira fields is less competitive in interior regions such as Bogota, Boyaca and Santander. Likewise, gas from Casanare (eastern part of Colombia) fields could not compete in the Atlantic Coast region. Competition between fields is more likely to occur in other regions of the country. In any case, competition between gas-producing regions will depend on the degree of congestion of the respective transportation systems.[88]

254. With respect to local distribution, from the geographic perspective, it is a service rendered at a municipal level to both regulated and non-regulated markets. LDCs have a natural monopoly over their distribution system, and in some regions even a legal monopoly has been awarded throughout exclusive service concession areas.

§4. Constitutional and Legal Framework

255. Although the Colombian government has introduced rules for the liberalization and privatization of natural gas markets, including Articles 357–370 of the Constitution of 1991 that apply to public services, as well as the legal regime for public utilities of Law 142 of 1994 applicable to all the natural gas supply chain, government intervention in the natural gas industry continues, usually through regulation.[89] Under Colombian Law, many of the activities related to a continuous and guaranteed supply of natural gas are considered public services, a legal category that involves the State's obligation to satisfy basic public needs of the population, public goods and services.

256. The activities related to the exploration, exploitation, transport, distribution and marketing of natural gas are considered public and essential services. This legal

86. *Ibid.*
87. CREG Document 057 of June 2005.
88. *Ibid.*
89. Luis Pando, *Regulación y Competencia en gas natural: Una visión crítica del mercado colombiano*, in *Regulación de Energía Eléctrica y Gas: Estudio Jurídico y Económico* (Universidad Externado de Colombia, Bogota, December 2010).

concept has important implications in terms of the obligations and duties of the agents developing these activities – especially with residential consumers. It also creates clear boundaries between two equally protected constitutional rights: the public interest, and free market and competition.

257. This mandate is clearly contained in different articles of the 1991 Constitution, which directly or indirectly refers to this State role, including social and economic regulation.[90] According to these constitutional rules, it appears clear that on the one hand, regulation should pursue economic efficiency and operate in a free market framework to assure that goods and services are accessible to all inhabitants independent of their socioeconomic level and their geographical location. However, when the ends of free market enter in conflict with the public interest, the State should intervene to correct this conflict by looking to guarantee the public interest through the suitable mechanism: regulation.

258. In addition to these general rules, the National Constitution contains rules regarding both public services in general and public utilities as a special subcategory. Articles 365–370 establish the basic constitutional framework regarding the provision, regulation and control of public services. In the first place, Article 365 declares that the regular and efficient provision of public services to all inhabitants of the country is a social end of the State. Article 366 establishes the priority of public expenditure for the satisfaction of basic public needs. Finally, Articles 367–370 refer to aspects such as: (i) the requirement of a Law to define matters such as the tariff regime, (ii) the subsidies schemes, (iii) consumer protection and rights, and (iv) the Superintendence of Public Services (SSPD), as a depositary of the presidential function of exerting control over public utilities and the service they render. Finally, according to Law 142 of 1994, the independent regulatory agency in charge of executing this public function for electricity and gas is CREG, and its regulatory function is deeply accompanied by other governmental institutions, such as the SSPD[91] and the Superintendence of Industry and Trade (SIC).[92]

---

90. The principles of competition and government intervention through social and economic regulation are contemplated in Arts 78, 333 and 334 of the Constitution. Article 78 refers to the protection of consumers and the duty of enterprises to provide goods and services of quality and to disclose all relevant information related to the production, import and supply process. Article 333 establishes that the economic activity and private initiative are free, within the limits of the public interest. It also states that free and loyal competition is a basic right that supposes responsibilities, and that enterprises have a social function that implies obligations. Article 334 of the Constitution states that the State is the general manager of the economy, and can intervene in the exploitation of natural resources, in the use of the land, in the production, distribution and consumption of goods, and in the public and private services, to rationalize the economy with the purpose of improving the quality of life of the population, the equal distribution of opportunities and the benefits of development, and for the preservation of a healthy environment.
91. SSPD stands in Spanish for '*Superintendencia de Servicios Públicos Domiciliarios*'. The SSPD is in charge of inspecting, controlling, and reviewing the conduct of Public Service Companies (ESP) Law 142 of 1994 states that all companies rendering domiciliary public services (public utilities) must include the letters ESP in their name, and establishes a special regime for this type of corporations with rules regarding their special subject matter, the functions and composition of the board of directors, and the submission to regulation and control from the government.

259. Decree 1073 of 2015, defined as the Regulatory Decree of the Administrative Sector of Mines and Energy, compiles the norms that were scattered in the national regulation, which includes technical, economic, and regulatory provisions.

92. SIC stands in Spanish for '*Superintendencia de Industria y Comercio*', Colombia's Competition Authority in charge of approving all mergers and acquisitions and investigating abusive market practices, monopolization practices and disloyal competition.

Chapter 1. Production

§1. Overview

260. Natural gas in Colombia has two coexisting property regimes, depending on the conditions of the resource. On the one hand, by constitutional provisions, gas resources located in the sub-surface are property of the State, and the conditions for exploration and exploitation are defined by the ANH. Production or exploitation of gas can be done by ECOPETROL directly or by private investors solely or in association with it. On the other hand, once gas is at the wellhead, it is considered a private good but in some cases subject to price regulation.

261. Due to the ownership regime applicable to hydrocarbons and the prevailing association agreement scheme, ECOPETROL is the leading producer of gas in Colombia, with share in all major production gas fields in Colombia. Chevron, former associate producer with ECOPETROL of La Guajira fields, is the second-largest producer, followed by BP, Total, Tepma, associated producers with ECOPETROL of Casanare fields, and more recently, by Pacific Rubiales with a small share of the market due to the discovery of La Creciente field. In practice, to this date, ECOPETROL and its associates maintain a dominant position in the gas supply market. In 2019, ECOPETROL produced 414 MCF/day. Next on the list is Chevron with 182 MCF/day, Geo production with 85.8 MCF/day, CNE with 59.5 MCF/day, and Hocol with 44 MCF/day.

262. The price of gas is partially unregulated. Due to factors such as concentration in supply and the small size of the market, La Guajira fields still have a regulated price of gas at the wellhead, while prices in other fields and for exports are free.

263. By Article 2.2.2.2.21 of Decree 1073 of 2015,[93] the MME publishes the production declaration made by producers and marketers of natural gas.[94] This declaration is composed of the following parameters: (1) committed production of a producer; (2) total production available for sale; (3) imported quantities available for sale for domestic consumption; (4) operating gas; (5) potential for natural gas production in every particular field.

93. Ministry of Mines and Energy. Decree 1073 of 2015 'Article 2.2.2.2.21. Production statement. Producers and producers-marketers of natural gas will declare to the MME or whomever it determines and based on all the information available at the time of calculation: (i) the PTDV; (ii) the PC duly discriminated according to what is indicated in articles 2.2.2.1.4. and 2.2.2.2.21. of this Decree. Likewise, the producer who is the operator of the field will declare: (i) the PP of each field, and (ii) the percentage of participation of the producers and the State in the production of hydrocarbons of said field or those of integrated exploitation. (…)'.

94. It is a declaration that is presented no later than 31 March of each year or when so determined by the Ministry of Mines and Energy for a period of ten years from the date on which it is prepared.

264. Based on these reports, UPME prepares the technical study for the Natural Gas Supply Plan.[95] The most recent information, certified by natural gas producers and marketers to show the production potential of the country's fields, was analysed, adjusted, and consolidated by the MME and published through Resolution 31329 of 2020,[96] which reflects the production declaration[97]for the period between January 2020 and December 2029.

265. Based on the data published by the Ministry of Mining and Energy[98] and the technical document for the UPME gas supply plan, the national supply is available to meet the demand for the next ten years. The reports also evidence a decline rate of 10.2% average per year. For the next ten years, three basins have 87.7% of the country's total production volume. In consequence, the gas deposits in the east of the country, in the Llanos Orientales 55.5% and the north of Colombia in the Lower Magdalena Valley 22% and La Guajira 10.3%[99] are the most important basins in terms of the volumes declared.

266. From the information reported and analysed by the UPME, there is evidence that the volumes of the Llanos Orientales and La Guajira basins decrease faster than that of the Valle Inferior basins. However, the projection is that from January 2020 to December 2023, in the average month, there will be an additional 48,000 BTU[100] in the offer compared to 2019.

§2. Gas Supply

267. Decree 2687 of 2008 created an auction scheme and established the obligation for producers to openly and transparently declare their 'Available Capacity of Firm Gas for Sale' (MPCD) along with rules for the export and import of gas, and the establishment of a 'Priority of Attention' order in the demand side. After a period of uncertainty about the benefits of the new rules for gas wholesale retail by producers, contained in Decree 2687 of 2008 and CREG Resolution 095 of 2008, the government issued a new set of measures by Decree 2730 of 2010.

95. UPME, *Estudio técnico para el Plan de Abastecimiento de gas natural*, January 2020. https://www1.upme.gov.co/Hidrocarburos/Plan_de_gas_documento_de_consulta.pdf.
96. Ministerio de Minas y Energía. Resolución 31329 de 2020. https://www.minenergia.gov.co/documents/10180//23517//48576-Resolución+31+329++05.06.2020.pdf.
97. Ministry of Mines and Energy. Soporte magnético declaración de producción.
98. Ministry of Mines and Energy. Resolution 31146 of 2019. https://www.minenergia.gov.co/documents/10180//23517//48137-Resoluci%C3%B3n+31+146+del+14+de+junio+de+2019+Declaraci%C3%B3n+de+Producci%C3%B3n+de+Gas+Natural+2019-2028.pdf.
99. UPME, *Estudio técnico para el Plan de Abastecimiento de gas natural*. https://www1.upme.gov.co/Hidrocarburos/Plan_de_gas_documento_de_consulta.pdf.
100. *Ibid.*

268. Decree 2730 of 2010 seeks to strengthen the policy of guaranteeing gas supply for the internal demand, to promote competition and solve the coordination-between-agents problem. Of particular importance are the following: (i) it distinguishes between Major and Minor Fields (production higher or lower than 50 million cubic feet per day (MCFD)) for the purpose of the declaration and offering of production of gas available for sale; (ii) for purposes of reliability and regularity of the service, it introduces the concept of 'strategic storage' as an obligation for agents to maintain minimum quantities of gas in underground storage units, regasification plants, or other storage facilities, and establishes the government's obligation to conduct studies for the construction of a regasification plant; (iii) in order to solve the coordination problem, it creates the Technical System Operator (GTS),[101] an independent agent in charge of guaranteeing the reliability and security of supply, the correct functioning of the transport system, and the administration of the Gas Wholesale Market and the secondary and spot markets; (iv) it also creates gas hubs to coordinate upstream and downstream activities and incentive gas-gas competition between regions and geographic markets; and (v) finally, it introduces new rules to promote gas exports and imports.

269. In addition, Decree 2100 of 2011 reforms the gas sector in order to incentivize the development of the supply and transport infrastructure, obtain new sources of gas, promote the reliability of the gas system and a more efficient use of the supply and transport infrastructure. This Decree aims to stimulate Colombia's self-sufficiency of gas by increasing the activities of exploration and exploitation, promoting gas exports and imports, and fostering unconventional gas exploration and development. In that sense, the Decree establishes freedom of prices for gas exports and imports, subject to the condition that the internal or 'essential demand' of gas is guaranteed.

270. A very important aspect contemplated in Article 6 of Decree 2100 of 2011 is the express obligation for the ANH not to contribute to concentration in gas supply sub-market, when entering into agreements related to the administration or marketing of state-owned gas, and to give priority to that gas to meet the internal demand.

§3. Exploration

271. Petroleum and gas exploration is identical in that the exact nature of the resource can be only established after drilling, which requires contracts for the exploration of hydrocarbons. A fundamental change in the Colombian government

101. 'GTS' stands in Spanish for '*Gestor Técnico del Sistema*'.

Oil & Gas policy occurred with the implementation of a new contractual framework by the ANH,[102] introducing the Exploration and Production (E&P) Agreement and the Technical Evaluation Agreement (TEA). The new scheme looks to promote investment in the hydrocarbons sector by creating a more attractive royalty and tax scheme, and by reducing the State's share in the association agreement[103] from 70% to 50%, while increasing the companies' profit.

272. Under these rules, in 2004 a series of association agreements for the search and maximization of gas reserves were signed: (i) the Tayrona Agreement in the Atlantic Coast Basin; (ii) the Esperanza Agreement in the Low Magdalena Valley Basin; and (iii) La Creciente Agreement in the Low Magdalena Valley Basin. During 2005 a total of thirty-one exploration agreements were signed in the following basins: Los Llanos, Upper and Medium Magdalena Valleys, Catatumbo and Putumayo. In addition, a total of twenty-five TEAs were signed. Continuing this trend and as result of high international oil prices and the changes introduced to the association agreement scheme, in the last years, the number of exploration and TEAs has grown steadily along with foreign investment in exploration.

§4. Contracts

I. Association Agreement

273. This system exists since 1974 and is determined by the legal regime applicable in Colombia to the property of the subsurface and of non-renewable resources, such as oil and gas. ECOPETROL enters into an association agreement with the Oil & Gas company having right to a share of production, bearing no risk of exploration, and also receiving gas or money as royalty during the exploitation of the field. This Joint Operation Agreement (JOA) has changed during the years, particularly regarding royalties and taxes, with the aim to introduce incentives for more exploratory activity.

274. In the analysis of Gas Upstream, a special mention to the association agreement regime must be done, particularly after the legal changes introduced by Decree 1760 of 2003. According to National Policy Document – CONPES 3245 of 2003, the National Planning Department (DNP) – recommended ANH and ECOPETROL to adopt and apply a strategy consisting of extending the duration of the existing association agreements until its economic limit, and establishing conditions to increase production in existing fields. These measures also looked to incentivize

102. Decree 1760 of 2003 unbundled from ECOPETROL the administration of gas reserves property of the State coming from royalties and shares in the exploitation agreement. In that way, ECOPETROL becomes another agent that competes in the upstream business leaving regulatory functions and bidding processes to the ANH.

103. The first contractual scheme for the exploration and exploitation of gas was the concession agreement. Later with the reform of Law 20 of 1969, the new concept of association agreement was introduced, with a term of twenty-seven years, where ECOPETROL had a 40% share of production, and received a royalty of 20% of production paid by the Oil & Gas Company.

hydrocarbons exploration and discover new gas reserves throughout new investments made by the partners under the extension agreement.

275. Under association contracts, production and investment decisions are made jointly by the parties. Hence the producers are not really independent competitors in supply, even if required to market gas independently. Consequently, the degree of market power exercised by ECOPETROL and its partners in the upstream gas supply is a problem that calls for regulatory intervention, particularly in prices.[104]

II. New Contracts

276. Under the new contractual scheme, the ANH assigns areas and enters into E&P and for TEAs through direct contracts, public biddings or competitive open rounds. The new model is a royalty/tax system where the contractor explores and produces with autonomy, at its own cost and risk. It has autonomy and responsibility, and the entitlement to the production, after applying the royalty scheme. If there are additional gains the company must share the profits with the ANH (currently doesn't apply to natural gas). The contractor pays taxes over its revenues according to tax law.

277. The new scheme reduces the State's share from more than 70% to nearly 50%. It also changes the term of the agreements, six years for exploration with possible renewal of up to four years, one to two years for technical evaluation with possible renewal of zero to two years, and twenty-four years for exploitation per field. 100% of production after royalties is for the contractor. In order to sign an agreement, the interested party must demonstrate legal, financial, technical, and operational capacity and obtain approval by the ANH's Board of Directors.

278. With these changes, Colombia has become one of the most attractive countries in the world for Oil & Gas investments. Areas are given in a more efficient and transparent way, through open rounds where interested companies may offer contractual conditions more favourable to them. The administration and follow up of the agreements is made under international standards. As a consequence, the number of contracts has grown and there are more seismic and exploratory activities.

---

104. The Guajira fields are jointly operated by ECOPETROL and Chevron Texaco under an association contract which was extended in 2003 to continue for the life of the field. ECOPETROL's share of production under this contract is 65.6%, and Chevron's is 34.4%. The Cusiana fields are operated by ECOPETROL, BP, and Tepma/Total under five association contracts. ECOPETROL's share is currently 60%, BP's 24.8% and Tepma's 15.2%. From 2010 to 2019, these contracts expire and ECOPETROL will acquire control of the fields.

279. On 8 June 2020, the ANH, through Agreement 004 of 2020,[105] allowed companies with current exploration and production contracts whose cash flow was affected as a result of the market price crisis to pay deferred economic rights for participation in production.

---

105. National Hydrocarbons Agency. Acuerdo 004 de 2020. https://www.anh.gov.co/la-anh/sobre-la-anh/normatividad/Normatividad/ACUERDO%20No.%2004%20DE%2008%20DE%20JUNIO%20DE%202020.pdf.

Chapter 2. Exploitation

280. Gas production and its further marketing are part of the wholesale gas supply sub-market. Wholesale gas supply is understood as gas production that meets the demand of the different sectors, excluding the volumes of gas used for re-injection and for internal needs of the fields. It is also known as gas commercialization or gas marketing developed directly by producers or in association with ECOPETROL.

281. From the legal perspective, gas marketing is considered a 'complementary activity' of gas distribution, and therefore is a public service regulated by Article 14.28 of Law 142 of 1994, subject to CREG's regulations, orders and directives. In addition, CREG Resolution 057 of 1996 defines gas marketing as an activity consisting of the sale and purchase of gas in the wholesale market or destined to end users.

282. However, gas marketing or wholesale gas supply is different from the retail activity or gas supply to small consumers (residential, small commercial and industrial, institutional), which is developed by LDCs.[106] The LDCs charge regulated tariffs to their end users. Even though gas marketing is a competitive activity, due to problems of concentration in production, it is also partially regulated.

283. In general, the rules of private law and the principles of free market and competition apply to prices, contracts and negotiations. Nevertheless, the recent introduction of rules regarding the obligation for producers/marketers to declare and offer the total available production through an auction scheme, as well as CREG's regulation of aspects such as the marketing procedure, the gas supply contract models, and the functions of the GTS, suggests the need for government intervention in the Colombian upstream market to correct the market failures identified in the diagnosis phase.

§1. Production and Supply

284. It is worth noticing that all natural gas sold in Colombia is domestically produced with roughly 90% coming from two main fields: The Guajira fields on the Caribbean coast (Ballena and Chuchupa) and the Cusiana fields in the interior (Cusiana and Cupiagua). Several minor fields account for the remaining 10%.

106. According to CREG Resolution 057 of 1996, the Regulated Users are those with consumption equal or less than 100,000 cubic feet per day. Consumers of more than 100,000 cubic feet per day are Non-Regulated Users.

285. Upstream gas production in Colombia is highly concentrated. The Herfindahl-Hirschman Index (HHI) for gas supply is 4529, and the degree of concentration is set to increase when ECOPETROL acquires complete control over the Cusiana fields by 2019.[107]

286. Numerous regulatory measures relating to gas production and supply have been introduced since the mid-1990s concerning: (i) regulation of prices for Guajira and deregulation of Cusiana;[108] (ii) rules prohibiting the joint marketing of gas;[109] (iii) the definition of 'take-or-pay' and firm contracts, including penalties for breach;[110] (iv) auction procedures to allocate firm gas when demand exceeds supply;[111] (v) declarations of firm and interruptible gas supplies;[112] and (vi) instruments to guarantee supply of gas.[113]

287. An important aspect of production and supply is the obligation for gas producers to submit annual declarations of production to the MME. According to Decree 2687 of 2008 these declarations have to include: (i) the potential production available from each field for a ten-year period and the amount of committed production for each field for the same period; (ii) the total potential production the company offers as non-firm supply (interruptible gas) for a ten year period; and (iii) the amount of the total potential production the company offers as firm supply for a ten year period.[114]

288. In turn, CREG Resolution 95 of 2008 established the procedures for the sale of firm gas supplies declared by gas producers. According to the resolution, firm gas declared available from unregulated fields (those different from La Guajira fields) must be sold via an ascending, simultaneous auction within forty-five days of the declaration, whenever purchase requests from shippers and LDCs exceed available supply. Otherwise, the gas can be sold via bilateral negotiations and contracts.[115] Firm gas from the Guajira field must be sold at a regulated price according to an allocation procedure specified in Article 8 of Decree 2687 of 2008. Any firm gas remaining after this allocation procedure can then be sold according to a procedure defined in Article 7 of CREG Resolution 95 of 2008. Gas supplies declared as 'interruptible' are not subject to any regulations.

---

107. *See* data from Market Analysis, Frontier Economics, and CREG Document 095 of 2005.
108. Guajira price regulation was reviewed in CREG Resolution 187, 2010 to decide whether to deregulate prices or not. Also *see* CREG Resolution 057 of 1996; CREG Resolution 023 of 2000; CREG Resolution 118 of 2005, CREG Resolution 070 of 2006.
109. *See* CREG Resolution 057 of 1996; CREG Resolution 093 of 2006.
110. *See* CREG Resolution 023 of 2000; CREG Resolution 70 of 2005; CREG Resolution 188/2009.
111. *See* CREG Resolution 070 of 2006; CREG Resolution 095/2008.
112. *See* Decrees 2687 of 2008 and 4670 of 2008.
113. *See* Decrees 2730 of 2010 and 2100 of 2011.
114. This should in principle be calculated as the difference between potential production less committed production and the amount declared available as interruptible supplies.
115. *See* David Harbord, *Upstream Issues in Colombian Gas Supply*, a report commissioned by the CREG (Bogota, April 2010).

289. The key reforms recently introduced by Decrees 2730 of 2010 followed by Decree 2100 of 2011 created rules to guarantee the internal supply and also promote exploration and exploitation activities, obliging producers to declare their available production capacity, introducing changes to the operation of transport systems, creating incentives for gas imports and LNG projects, implementing freedom of gas prices for exports, enforcing control over supply contracts, and establishing rules regarding the essential demand and a priority attention order. Overall, these new rules introduce competition in the Colombian natural gas market, especially in production and supply, aiming to solve the low flexibility problem while giving incentives for new investments in all the activities of the natural gas fuel cycle, including new activities such as storage and regasification.

§2. Reserves

290. In the 2020 gas sector report, it is indicated that the country has 54 Tcf of potential gas reserves,[116] equivalent to 130 years of natural gas self-sufficiency.[117] A total of 30 Tcf are located in the offshore reservoirs and 24 Tcf in unconventional reservoirs. This implies an increase of sixteen times the current proven reserves, which are at 3.2 Tcf.[118]

291. The responsible exploitation of unconventional gas fields[119] would allow an increase in the level of reserves to guarantee self-sufficiency for up to 130 years.[120] The investments projected in the ANH call for the four unconventional reservoirs pilot projects represent around USD 100 million each. For the Colombian Petroleum Association – ACP (for its initials in Spanish), if these projects advance to the development phase, the investment could reach USD 5 billion annually, equivalent to 2% of Colombian GDP.[121]

---

116. PROMIGAS. Informe del sector gas 2020 (con cifras de 2019). Publicado el 16 de septiembre de 2020. http://www.promigas.com/Es/Paginas/Informe%20Sector%202020/Informe%20Sector%202019.pdf.
117. Eric Flesch, *presidente de Promigas*. Presentación del Informe del sector gas natural Colombia 2020. 16 de septiembre de 2020. https://youtu.be/XTg-R5Vsel8.
118. PROMIGAS. Informe del sector gas 2020 (con cifras de 2019). Publicado el 17 de septiembre de 2020. http://www.promigas.com/Es/Paginas/Informe%20Sector%202020/Informe%20Sector%202019.pdf.
119. Definition of Decree 328 of 2020. Article 2.2.1.1.1A.1.2 Definitions. Unconventional Reservoir – YNC (for its initials in Spanish): Those that are characterized by having low primary permeability and that must be stimulated to improve mobility and recovery conditions. These include shale oil and gas, tight carbonates, coal bed methane gas, tight sands, and oil sands.
120. Eric Flesch, *presidente de Promigas*. Presentación del Informe del sector gas natural Colombia 2020. 16 de septiembre de 2020. https://youtu.be/XTg-R5Vsel8.
121. FORBES Colombia. 29 Sep. 2020. https://forbes.co/2020/09/29/economia-y-finanzas/fracking-traeria-al-pais-us5-000-millones-al-ano-en-inversion-extranjera/.

292. The Consejo de Estado ruled on 4 September 2020,[122] on the request for precautionary measures presented against Decree 328 of 2020[123] that gives guidelines for the development of Pilot Projects for Integral Research on Non-Conventional Reservoirs of hydrocarbons with the use of the Multistage Hydraulic Fracturing with Horizontal Drilling technique – FH-PH.[124] The court denied the request for a precautionary measure requested by the plaintiffs. This decision does not constitute a prejudice, nor compromise the position of the Office when deciding on the merits of the matter. In consequence, Colombia will be able to continue with the pilot projects for exploration of the unconventional reservoirs.

§3. Prices

293. Historically, CREG has defined two basic schemes for gas prices at the wellhead: (i) regulated price: maximum price at the wellhead for gas fields existent prior to 1995; and (ii) free prices for gas fields discovered after 1995.

294. Gas prices can be both free and regulated, depending on factors such as the size and location of the gas field, the class of gas (conventional or unconventional), the type of demand, and the degree of concentration in the production and supply sub-market. Prices are free for the sale of gas from minor fields (production of less than 50 Mcfd), from unconventional gas fields, and for exports. For major fields (production of more than 50 Mcfd), prices can be free or regulated depending on the field.

295. In unregulated fields, gas prices are set after an auction process. In regulated fields, the gas price is fixed according to a priority order and negotiated at the maximum price at the wellhead. In any case, supply contracts must comply with CREG regulation and use the predefined contractual models in the modality of firm and interruptible.

296. Partial price liberalization was permitted only for the Cusiana-Cupiagua gas fields, with the condition that a gas-treatment plant was constructed by the operators to process associated gas and therefore increase gas production from the Casanare fields. In that sense, CREG Resolution 119 of 2005 established that in case of improvements to the rate of production of these fields during the construction of

122. Consejo de Estado. Sala de lo Contencioso Administrativo. Sección Tercera Subsección C. Consejero ponente: Nicolás Yepes Corrales. 4 de septiembre de 2020. Radicación: 11001-03-26-000-2020-00042-00 (65992). https://imgcdn.larepublica.co/cms/2020/09/04193141/Fallo-Consejo-Estado-sept4-YNC.pdf.

123. The Republic of Colombia. Decree 328 of 2020.

124. The technique used in the extraction of gas or oil in Non-Conventional Reservoirs, such as shales and tight carbonates of low porosity and permeability, through which a fluid composed of water, proppant, and additives at controlled pressures are injected in one or more stages to generate channels that facilitate the flow of fluids from the producing formation to the horizontally drilled well. This technique differs from the techniques used in conventional reservoirs in which hydraulic fracturing is used and in Non-Conventional Reservoirs of methane gas associated with coal beds and tar sands. Decree 328 of 2020 Article 2.2.1.1.1A.1.2 Definitions.

a gas-treatment plant in volumes equal or higher than 180 MPCD, prices were free. CREG Resolution 119 of 2005 also defined a new formula for the determination of the maximum prices at the wellhead for La Guajira and Opon gas fields, and determined free prices for the rest of the production fields.

297. The following is the regulatory treatment for each field:

- La Guajira and Opon field: a regulated maximum price was set by CREG Resolution 119 of 2005, with the purpose to be a reference for the gas supply contracts signed between ECOPETROL and the thermal generators of the central territories of the country.
- Cusiana and Cupiagua fields: the prices for this field were fixed by means of CREG Resolution 050 of 2002. However, as stated above, this maximum price will be free when the production capacity is increased above the 180 MPCD level. This tariff regime should be considered as a regulated-freedom scheme since CREG could always revise the price liberalization if it considers the market conditions have changed affecting competition.
- New Discoveries: prices for new gas discoveries are free without any condition in terms of production capacity or dates. However, as in the previous case, CREG can always revise this situation if minimum conditions of competition are not reached in the natural gas market.

298. Regulation of prices at the wellhead seeks to protect gas customers. Nevertheless, this protection scheme may discourage the required investments in exploration and production, since new discoveries are required to meet the growing demand for natural gas. For example, in the Cusiana-Cupiagua fields, the initial regulatory incentives were considered insufficient, to the point that the gas-treatment plant of Cusiana only began operation in September of 2005, with a four year-old delay with respect to the date initially foreseen. Due to this delay, the interior market (the central part of the country) suffered a gas shortage situation creating limitations for ECOPETROL to assist new clients, particularly in the industrial sector. As a consequence, the gas interconnection project between Colombia and Panama was affected, due to the need to allocate part of La Guajira field's production to assist the interior market of the country.

299. Currently, gas supply contracts from the Guajira field are sold at a regulated price, USD 4.25 per MBTU, using a value estimated in the 1970s and indexed twice a year with the New York fuel oil price.[125]

125. *See* UPME, *Boletín Estadístico de Minas y Energía* 230 (1990–2010).

§4. Import and Regasification

300. Decree 2100 of 2011 defines the activity of importing gas in the country, in particular concerning the LNG industry in Colombia and establishes that the provisions of the CREG for the commercialization of nationally produced gas will apply to imported natural gas destined for the domestic public service.

301. Article 2.2.2.2.34 of Decree 1073 of 2015 determines the freedom of import prices; Article 2.2.2.2.40 stipulates that the agents of regasification infrastructure must allow access to available capacities as long as they contracted capacity and previously agreed contracts are not violated. Access to regasification infrastructure requires the subscription of contracts. The rule of Article 2.2.2.2.41 contains a blank normative reference, indicating that the CREG may implement incentives for the importation of natural gas to guarantee national supply.

302. Colombia has a regasification infrastructure located in the Caribbean, identified as the Cartagena Regasification Plant. The regulation of the infrastructure whose operation is materialized from the regulatory provisions defined by CREG Resolution 062 of 2013 establishes the regulated income for the use of imported gas for energy generation.

303. Resolution 062 of 2013 defines the methodology to establish the regulated entry to a limited group of thermal generators who have imported natural gas as a backup to cover energy generation for supply security purposes following the requirements of the National Dispatch Center.[126] Adjustments were made to the resolution, by CREG Resolution 152 of 2013.[127]

304. CREG Resolution 259 of 2016 establishes a regulated income for the use of imported gas for energy generation and supply security purposes.

305. Currently, the country is advancing on the steps for the construction of an LNG import infrastructure in the Colombian Pacific. CREG Resolution 107 of 2017 established the procedures for the execution of the project within the framework of the natural gas supply plan, adopted by the MME.

The resolution establishes in a general way the contractual procedure for the selection of contractors, and the technical, legal, and economic criteria for the evaluation of the proposals.

306. About the Pacific Regasification infrastructure, CREG Resolution 152 of 2017 delimits the particular procedure for the selection process and the allowed gas market participants. This standard complements the provisions of CREG Resolution 107 of 2017 about the execution of the Pacific gas import infrastructure through an open selection process.[128]

---

126. Energy and Gas Regulatory Commission. Resolución CREG 152 of 2013.
127. Energy and Gas Regulatory Commission. Resolución CREG No. 259 of 2016.
128. Energy and Gas Regulatory Commission. Resolución CREG 152 of 2013.

307. Colombia has a free import, to which the commercialization rules for the import of gas for the provision of public service apply. There is a regulated income, in which access to the activity is free entrepreneurship, but it is materialized through selection processes through public announcement. In practice, there is a robust contractual regime in which infrastructure service contracts intermingle with the importing agent and the thermal generation group.

308. It should be noted that the National Development Plan, Law 1955 of 2019, grants the CREG the faculty to define new agents in the service provision chain, in Article 290.[129]

§5. Market Operator

309. The gas market manager is responsible for collecting and publishing relevant information on the natural gas sector in Colombia. For instance, it reports the amounts of gas that are traded in the market and the prices of the transactions. The operator is in charge of facilitating negotiations for supply and transport, applying the procedures and mechanisms designed by the regulator to guarantee the allocation of the service.[130]

310. Under CREG Resolution 094 of 2014, the Bolsa Mercantil de Colombia – BMC (for its Initials in Spanish) was selected as the operator of the gas market. The CREG Resolution 021 of 2014 defines the expected annual income to be assigned to the market operator. The market operator does not participate in the business, is not an intermediary, nor does it exercise control or sanctioning functions.[131] The CREG Resolution 076 of 2019 determines the services to be provided by the gas market operator and the scope of competences[132]

311. Based on the provisions contained in CREG Resolutions 089 of 2013 and 136 of 2014, CREG defined the coverage mechanisms for the auctions of bimonthly firm supply contracts, long-term contracts, and the auctions of transport capacity in the application of the use it or sell it criteria, under CREG Resolution 065 of 2015.

129. The Republic of Colombia. Law 1955 of 2019.
130. Energy and Gas Regulatory Commission. //www.creg.gov.co/sectores-que-regulamos/gas-natural/gestor-del-mercado-de-gas-natural.
131. Bolsa Mercantil de Colombia. http://www.bmcbec.com.co/nosotros. Consulted on: 7 Dec. 2020.
132. Energy and Gas Regulatory Commission. Resolución CREG 076 de 2019.

Chapter 3. Transportation

§1. National Transport System

312. According to CREG Resolution 001 of 2000, the SNT connects the gas production sites with the principal consumption centres, excluding distribution systems, non-regulated users' connections, international interconnections and storage facilities. The National Pipeline Network is composed by two sub-systems clearly defined in terms of its property, running and operation: the Atlantic Coast Transport System, and the Interior Transport System (CREG Resolution 057 of 1996).[133]

313. As a consequence, Colombia has two large Transportation System Operators (TSOs): Promigas on the Atlantic/Caribbean coast, and *Transportadora de Gas del Interior* (TGI) in the inland part of the country. The Promigas system includes the Ballena-Barranquilla-Cartagena-Jobo network, and is 590 km long with a capacity of 540 GBTUD. The TGI system has two interconnected pipelines networks: the Ballena-Barrancabermeja pipeline which runs for 580 km and has a capacity of 190 GBTUD, and the Cusiana-Bogota-Vasconia-Cali-Neiva pipeline that is 1700 km long with a capacity of 220 GBTUD.

314. Other minor TSOs deliver gas from the TGI system to local markets, such as Medellin and Bucaramanga. More recently, throughout the allocation of resources coming from contributions to the Special Development Fund, created by Law 401 of 1997, new secondary pipelines have been constructed to supply gas to the Cauca department and to interconnect new distribution markets.[134]

315. Currently, through CREG Resolution 185 of 2020, the commercial aspects of the natural gas wholesale market are established, as part of the natural gas operation regulations, related to the commercialization of natural gas transportation capacity. This resolution contains the set of provisions applicable to natural gas transportation capacity negotiations that are carried out in the primary and secondary markets.

316. Resolution 185 of 2020 establishes the following as contract modalities and participants in the primary transport capacity market:

(1) Firm transport contract of quarterly capacities.
(2) Contract of carriage with conditional firmness.
(3) Transport purchase option contract.
(4) Contingency transport contract.

---

133. *See* UPME, *La Cadena del Gas Natural en Colombia* (Bogota, 2005).

134. In the XV Naturgas Annual Congress held in Cartagena on 28 Mar. 2012, the Colombian Ministry of Mines and Minerals announced important achievements such as the growth of the residential demand reaching a total of 6,345,470 end users, the connection of 224,158 new residential and commercial users of natural gas, including 17,697 new users in Cauca due to the successful construction and operation of the secondary pipeline between Pradera-Jamundí-Popayán.

(5) Contract of carriage with interruptions.

317. Resolution 185 of 2020, Title III establishes the commercial aspects of the secondary transport capacity market modalities and minimum requirements of contracts and participants in the secondary market. Chapter I of this resolution establishes the modalities and minimum requirements of contracts and participants in the secondary market.

318. In the secondary market for natural gas transportation capacity, only the following modes of transportation contracts may be agreed:

(1) Firm contract of carriage.
(2) Firm quarterly transportation contract.
(3) Contract of carriage with conditional firmness.
(4) Transport purchase option contract.
(5) Contingency transport contract.
(6) Contract of carriage with interruptions.

§2. REGULATION

319. Transport of gas is considered a complementary activity of the public service of natural gas, and therefore is subject to CREG's regulation. Accordingly, CREG Resolution 057 of 1996 defines the transport activity as the operation, management, maintenance and expansion of the pipeline system, including activities related to storage, compression and measuring. A Transporter or TSO is the person or company that transports gas from the point of entry to the transport system to the point of delivery.

320. Article 5 of CREG Resolution 057 of 1996 establishes unbundling rules to guarantee open access to the SNT and no discrimination or unfair pricing. In particular, this article states that transportation is independent from production, distribution and retail, and that TSOs shall not prefer any shipper, especially those with whom it has an economic interest.

321. The terms and costs of pipeline transportation are regulated by CREG and specified in contracts between pipeline companies and shippers. Shippers include LDCs (which supply gas to the majority of the residential and small commercial sectors), producers, and great consumers of gas. On the Primary Transport Market, TSOs enter into transport and connection agreements with shippers to grant access and capacity to the pipeline system. According to CREG Resolution 001 of 2000 transport contracts can be for firm or interruptible transportation capacity.

322. The market runs through a nomination procedure that consists of the daily request for gas from shippers to the TSO, specifying the quantity of gas to be transported and the points of entry and exit. These requests are the base of the Transport

Programme, and are fundamental to comply with the operational and commercial processes established in the Transport Code (RUT).[135]

323. Regarding prices, CREG has used the following methodologies to establish transport tariffs:

- First tariff period (CREG Resolution 057 of 1996): A system based on distance charges was adopted for the case of pipelines pertaining to the Central Transport System. For the pipelines of the Atlantic Coast Transport System a stamp charge was adopted.
- Second tariff period (CREG Resolution 001 of 2000): Transport charges for each system based on a Long Term Average Costs methodology that sets tariffs according to the existence of firm capacity contracts, the value of transport assets and efficient costs of AOM.

324. Under the current regulation, CREG establishes regulated price caps to pipeline networks for a five-year period, by calculating capacity and volume charges for pipeline segments based on investment costs and demand projections. It calculates average-cost-based capacity and commodity charges for pipeline segments from investment costs, using the WACC[136] methodology and twenty-year demand forecasts. These dual-charges are negotiated between shippers and the transporter, subject to arbitration, and only apply to firm transport capacity agreements. A Utilization Factor is applied to determine whether a particular segment of the pipeline is 'used or usable'. New investments in transport capacity are not controlled by CREG and are paid by applying the applicable tariff or by requesting CREG to set new regulated charges for that investment.

325. Therefore, the total cost of transportation is defined by the sum of charges for the different segments of the pipeline used in the transport of gas by a particular shipper. Maximum variable and fix charges pay for investment expenses, and fix charges pay for AOM expenses.

326. According to the tariff structure defined in CREG Resolution 011 of 2003, transport charges must include taxes and other levies imposed on transporters by law. The expansion of the transport system is based on a 'contract-carriage' regulatory model. This implies that that transport system will develop when the contracts give transporters enough guarantees about the volumes of gas they expect to transport, justifying new investments in infrastructure. This situation has created situations of deficit in firm transportation capacity due to the fact that transporters have not expanded their transport systems because of lack of incentives to build new pipelines.

---

135. RUT stands for Spanish *Reglamento Unico de Transporte.*
136. Weighted Average Cost of Capital.

327. The main characteristic of this tariff methodology is that transport charges are set according to distance, something that resembles what would occur in a competitive market that reflect the actual costs of rendering the service. As a consequence, gas prices are higher if the consumption centres are located at longer distances from the production sites, as it occurs with the markets of Bogota, Medellin and western territories. This methodology made transport capacity negotiations more flexible by introducing the dual-charge concept, which allows the shipper to propose a combination of fix and variable charges that best suits its load curve. In addition, transport tariffs for the central departments have become an arbitration mechanism for gas supply by determining which one of the two principal gas fields of Colombia, La Guajira or Cusiana, is competitive in the centre, southern, and western regions.

328. Finally, the new rules and instruments for gas transportation introduced by the Decree 2730 of 2010 are yet to show whether the problem of coordination between the supply and transport sub-markets, and the problem of the lack of investment in new transport infrastructure problem are solved. In particular, the industry is expecting CREG's regulation of the functions and activities of the new figure of the GTS and the definition by the CNO of the correspondent commercial and operational protocols for the reliable operation of the SNT.[137]

§3. Secondary Market

329. The secondary market is defined by CREG Resolutions 033 and 071 of 1999. This is the market for natural gas and transportation capacity where shippers with secondary available transportation capacity and/or agents with gas supply rights can freely negotiate their contractual rights.

330. Holders of excess firm transportation capacity can sell capacity outright. Thus, there is a 'capacity release market'. Capacity and commodity charges are

137. According to the study conducted by Market Analysis for the CREG regarding the Colombian natural gas transport sector, the following issues related to the transport regulation exist: (i) Most market participants have not requested large-scale changes to the regulatory regime; (ii) Some strongly oppose abrupt changes in a regime in which they are already making large, risky investments; (iii) There have been proposals to adopt a 'reliability charge' & 'common carriage' or 'centralized planning' regime for gas networks similar to the electricity system; (iv) Commodity/capacity charges may not remunerate TSOs' investment costs as intended, especially for gas-fired power plant; (v) Utilization Factor should be changed to reduce the risk of stranded investments; (vi) Commodity charges, average cost prices and other features of the current regime may not be providing adequate location and investment signals;(vii) More transparent and open procedures for allocating firm pipeline contracts; (viii) Relaxation of some vertical integration rules to streamline coordination of new gas field and pipeline developments; and to allow distribution companies to undertake secondary pipeline construction and operation. However, according to the conclusions of the study conducted of Market Analysis for CREG, many of these issues are correctly addressed by the current regulation or have a particular explanation that do not call for major regulatory changes, while some particular aspects such as the implementation of capacity auction schemes and changes to the vertical integration rules do require future changes by the regulator.

negotiated between TSOs and pipeline users, and subject to arbitration. The capacity release market is a way for shippers to change their transportation portfolios. It provides a mechanism to improve transportation flexibility to meet changing gas supply and demand conditions. Because LDCs have traditionally served all consumers in their distribution area, they typically reserve enough capacity to ensure they can meet their obligation even on a day of peak demand. Because of this contracting practice, LDCs tend to have a lower rate of utilization of their capacity than do other shippers.

Chapter 4. Distribution

§1. Distribution and Retail Markets

331. LDCs transport gas through their distribution system from the city gate to end user's connection point. According to Decree 3429 of 2003, LDCs are also retailers when rendering the service to regulated users. Distribution and retail to residential consumers includes related activities, such as customer service, metering, invoicing, and emergency attention.

332. The local distribution market is divided into exclusive and non-exclusive service areas, which are defined by the MME as follows:

- Non-exclusive Service Area: it is the geographic area corresponding to the municipalities and other urban areas in which natural gas is distributed and marketed without a concession contract, therefore allowing for other distributors to provide the service.
- Exclusive Service Area:[138] it is the geographic area corresponding to the municipalities and other urban areas in which natural gas is distributed and marketed with exclusive rights granted to an ESP over this area by means of a concession contract that doesn't allow other distributors to provide the service in the exclusive area.[139]

333. Although these two different types of areas exist, in practice all Colombian municipalities with natural gas distribution have a sole distributor, a situation justified in terms of economic efficiency as provided by CREG Resolution 112 of 2007 that considers natural gas distribution a natural monopoly.[140]

§2. Clients

334. LDCs provide natural gas service to regulated and non-regulated end users, mainly residential, commercial, industrial, and NGV stations. Regulated users have a consumption that is less than 100 KPCD[141] or the equivalent in cubic metres (m^3). Residential consumers, small industrial and commercial consumers fall under this category. Non-regulated users have a consumption that is higher than 100

138. CREG Resolution 051 of 1996.
139. Special concession contracts for natural gas distribution in exclusive service areas. These contracts contain exclusivity clauses and the service is rendered under the conditions of the contract in terms of Price and coverage. Currently six Exclusive Service Areas exist in the regions of Quindio, Caldas, Pereira, Risaralda, Valley Tolima.
140. According to CREG Resolution 112 of 2007, natural gas distribution is a natural monopoly with important economies of scale and in consequence it is efficient for a sole agent to provide the service in each relevant distribution market.
141. KPCD: A Thousand Cubic Meters per Day.

KPCD. Great industrial and commercial consumers, thermoelectric companies and NGV[142] distributors fall under this category.

335. The current regulation allows LDCs to purchase gas by using different schemes, but always, looking for the best supply conditions. Article 100 of CREG Resolution 057 of 1996 clearly determines the way LDCs must purchase gas to serve its market in the best conditions, throughout an open, transparent, equal and competitive process that considers the available sources and gas producers' offer.

336. CREG's regulation also obliges LDCs to have firm supply capacity to meet the demand of the regulated market. With respect to the non-regulated market, prices are set freely in bilateral agreements which may provide for firm or interruptible gas supply.

§3. Price Regulation

337. Bilateral agreements between LDCs and non-regulated users are free and not subject to CREG's regulation. With respect to the regulated market, LDCs are subject to a regulated-freedom tariff scheme.[143]Under this scheme, CREG previously defines the general tariff formulae and each LDC calculates its own tariff and submits it for approval.

338. Once a LDC calculates its particular Maximum Cost of Service (MST) tariff, it must submit the information to CREG for approval. CREG conducts individual tariff proceedings for each LDC and distribution system. In the case of LDCs operating in Exclusive Service Areas, the MST is set forth in the concession contract after a public bidding process.

339. CREG Resolution 057 of 1996 defines the MST formulae as follows: MST=G+T+D+C+Kst. That is to say, the maximum cost of gas (MST) is the sum of the costs of all the activities related to natural gas supply to the end user including a conversion factor (Kst): the cost of gas (G), plus the cost of transport (T), plus the cost of distribution (D) and the cost of retail (C).[144]

340. CREG Resolution 011 of 2003, which amended CREG Resolution 057 of 1996, establishes the general tariff methodology applicable to the distribution and retail activities destined to the regulated market. According to CREG's regulation, each LDC sets a price cap for the service provided to regulated users based on the general criteria defined by CREG. When setting these general criteria CREG considers elements such as the base investment for distribution systems, the cost of capital, AOM, and demand projections.

---

142. GNV stands for '*Gas Natural Vehicular*' which is compressed natural gas used as fuel for vehicles.
143. Article 88, Law 142 of 1994.
144. According to CREG Resolution 057 of 1996, the MST formulae is: MST=G+T+D+C+Kst.

§4. Natural Gas Distribution as a Public Utility

341. As previously stated, the new concept of domiciliary public services or public utilities (*servicios públicos domiciliarios – SPD*)[145] created by the 1991 Constitution and fully regulated by Law 142 of 1994, differs from the traditional conception of public service. Under this new conception, the rules of market and private law preferably apply to these activities instead of the traditional rules of administrative law and public finances.

342. With respect to natural gas, Article 14.28 of Law 142 of 1994 expressly defines natural gas distribution and related activities (production, wholesale retail, transportation, and retail) as a 'domiciliary' public service (a public utility) governed by the special rules contained in Law 142 of 1994 and subject to CREG's regulation. In that sense, natural gas as a public service involves social ends and a public interest for utility companies with both the State and consumers, which includes special corporate rules, licenses and prior approvals, registry and report of information obligations, universal service, and permanent control and inspection from the SSPD.

343. With respect to the regulation of public utilities, Article 73 states that the main objective of the regulatory commissions is to regulate monopolies whenever competition is not in fact possible, and to promote competition among service providers. The regulatory agency looks that operations of the monopolists or the competitors are economically efficient, don't imply abuse of market power, and produce services of quality. For that purpose, the regulatory commissions have administrative functions, half-judicial functions; and regulatory functions.[146]

344. As for the activity of the utility companies and the service they provide, the regulatory commissions may require them to previously demonstrate technical and financial capacity, and exert a strict control over the quality of the service, safety and health issues, customer services and types of contracts, and in general over the commercial relationships between the end user and the company.

345. Accordingly, CREG Resolution 067 of 1995 establishes a Distribution Code that contains technical rules that all LDCs must comply regarding different aspects of the distribution system, the connection to end user installations, quality of the materials used in internal installations, health and safety regulations prior and during the provision of gas, attention of emergency situations, measurement and invoicing, conducting the five-year technical revisions, suspending and reconnecting of the service, and in general, every aspect involved with the operation, administration and maintenance of the distribution network.

145. SPD stands in Spanish for '*Servicio Público Domiciliario*'.
146. For a more complete explanation on the concept of regulation of domiciliary public services *see* Luis Pando, *Solución a los Problemas de la Regulación de los Servicios Públicos Domiciliarios*, Thesis, Facultad de Jurisprudencia, Universidad del Rosario (Bogota, December 1999).

346. A key point regarding regulation of LDCs has to do with open access to the distribution system. Most public utilities have networks with significant characteristics of natural monopoly. Considering that not all portions of the natural gas fuel cycle (supply chain) are open to competition, access to networks and infrastructure, it is considered essential to introduce competition, allowing producers to deliver the service to end users so that the retail activity operates in a liberalized market.

347. Following this free market and pro-competition approach, Law 142 of 1994 has specific rules regarding open access to networks, spin-offs, mergers and acquisitions of utility companies. In addition, it establishes definitions for market power and dominant position, situations of control and linkage between companies, and special definitions of abusive market practices, including those committed against consumers or end users.

348. With respect to competition, Article 14 of Law 142 of 1994 defines the dominant position in the market, which is different to the general rule contained in Decree 2153 of 1992. This rule establishes in first place that a public utility company has a dominant position over all of its customers. Secondly, this rule states that, with respect to the market of the services they provide – and of its close substitutes –, utilities are considered to have a dominant position when they serve more than 25% of the total end users of such market.

349. Accordingly, CREG has developed these special competition rules contained in Law 142 of 1994 and established the following unbundling rules:

- Gas producers may not own more than 25% of gas transport or distribution companies.
- Gas transporters may not own more than 25% of gas production companies or LDCs.
- Gas distributors may not own more than 25% of gas transport companies.
- Gas distributors and retailers must be integrated for the purposes of selling gas to the regulated market (below 0.1 GBTUD).
- Distributors must provide third-party access for shippers selling to non-regulated market.

350. It is important to highlight that Law 142 of 1994 provides that companies created prior to 1994 are exempt from these unbundling rules and may continue to be vertically integrated.[147]

351. There are 41 distribution companies in Colombia, which have been constant since 2017 according to the Report of the Natural Gas Sector in Colombia 2020, which is based on the data reported by the MME. There was an increase of

147. *See* CREG Concept 6587 of 1998 rendered to the SSPD in relation to the scope of the general exception contained in CREG Resolutions 057 of 1996 and 071 of 1998. Also *see* CREG Concept 3-2010-00551 of 2010.

1.8 million users in the last 5 years and there is currently coverage in 751 municipalities, located in 27 departments of Colombia. According to the figures reported on 23 June 2020, there are close to 10,000,000 users.[148]

352. On the occasion of the pandemic caused by COVID-19, the transportation and distribution of natural gas suffered a significant impact, leading to the gas-producing and transporting companies to grant relief to consumers through the temporary renegotiation of contracts with retailers.[149]

148. Ministerio de Minas y Energía y Naturgas. *Colombia Supera El Usuario 10 Millones De Gas Natural.* https://www.youtube.com/watch?v=KmzqViJUXfI.

149. Decreto 437 de 2020, Decreto 517 de 2020, Decreto 798 de 2020, Decreto 581 de 2020, Resolución CREG 035 de 2020, Resolución CREG 048 de 2020 y Resolución CREG 059 de 2020.

Chapter 5. Consumption

§1. Gas Demand

353. The demand for gas in Colombia falls into four main categories: residential and commercial, industrial, electricity generation, and natural gas for vehicles. It is mainly located on the Atlantic/Caribbean coast (34%) and in the Interior (52%). The main consumption points are located in the major urban centres (e.g., Bogotá, Cali, Barranquilla, and Medellín among others) and at gas-fired power plants and refineries sites. These plants are located in the northern part of the country near Barranquilla, and in the central region near Barrancabermeja.

354. The demand for gas in Colombia is made up by regions (North Coast and Interior of the Country) and by sectors: domiciliary or residential, commercial, industrial, thermoelectric, petrochemical, transportation (NGV), and the refinery.[150] There is an expectation of an increase in national consumption as a consequence of the development and implementation of thermoelectricity generation projects and the greater installed capacity, as well as the expectations of improvements in the mass public transport sector.[151]

355. The market is not concentrated on the demand side. The market HHI's for the years 2008–2010 are 793, 931 and 914, respectively. The vast majority of Colombia's gas is sold via firm contracts with durations from three to five years, although some contracts are longer. Current gas contracts are mostly take-or-pay with a high minimum percentage of 'take' over the month or year.

356. According to data of the UPME, for the year 2010, the total demand of gas in Colombia was of 860 Mcfd. The thermoelectric and industrial sectors, accounting for 34% and 28% respectively, are by far the largest consumers of natural gas in Colombia. Residential and commercial users account for about 17%; refinery 12%; NGV 8%; and petrochemical accounts for the remaining 1%.

357. Natural Gas has become one of Colombia's most important energy sources, passing from 5.7% of total energy consumption in 1990 to 16.4% in 2009. However, as the demand grows, particularly in the industrial, NGV and residential sectors, some voices have questioned whether the existing gas reserves are enough to meet the demand in the mid-term. According to MME's Communication 18054 of 29 December 2009, the R/P factor of reference for the year 2009 was of seven years of proven reserves. Notwithstanding, Colombia has the potential to double its gas reserves with unconventional sources such as Coal Bed Methane (CBM) and shale gas that can account for up to 4 TPC additional reserves.

150. Unidad de Planeación Minero Energética (UPME) Balance de Gas Natural en Colombia 2015–2023, Febrero de 2015.

151. Unidad de Planeación Minero Energética (UPME), *Estudio Técnico Para El Plan De Abastecimiento De Gas Natural*, Enero de 2020.

358. UPME's demand projections in its high scenario indicate that by mid-2017, the total consumption of gas will be 1.100 Mcfd, rising up to 1.200 Mcfd in 2020, exceeding the ceiling of 1.500 Mcfd in 2028.

359. Finally, during the drought period of 'El Niño', natural gas consumption reaches its peak of demand due to the fact that thermoelectric plants require more gas to operate and produce electricity. To avoid default – especially in the residential market – under stress situations, the government has established a priority attention order in cases of gas shortages.

360. For the first six months of 2019, natural gas consumption had a general decrease of 2.55% compared to the same period of 2018. This decrease in national consumption was explained by the negative growth of sectors such as industrial and thermoelectric. But from the analysis by each sector, for 2019, sectors such as residential (2.23%) and commercial (7.31%) and transportation (compressors, 2.21%) showed positive growth. The growth in these sectors is due to the 4.8% increase in service coverage for residential and 5.29% for commercial. Other market sectors such as the refinery, with 0.92% has become in the first half of 2019, the second-largest consumer.

361. According to the UPME studies in the context of average production and average consumption, the supply and demand of the gas sector will have equilibrium until February 2024.[152] The projections in the domiciliary and commercial sectors pointed to growth consistent with the increase in the number of subscribers. Growth in demand of around 1.5% is forecast from 2024 for the transport sector.

362. However, due to the pandemic caused by COVID-19 and according to information from the Natural Gas Market Operator, the BMC,[153] average gas consumption had a 29% reduction in the period from March to May 2020, versus consumption from January to March 2020.[154]

§2. Total Connections

363. According to UPME data, there are more than 10,072,089 million connected users of gas, of which more than 98.1%, that is, 9,881,800 are residential or

152. Unidad de Planeación Minero Energética (UPME) Balance de Gas Natural en Colombia 2017, Octubre de 2017.
153. Bolsa Mercantil de Colombia. Andrés Pesca vicepresidente de Mercados Energéticos en Portafolio. Mayo 27 de 2020. 'La mayor reducción se ve reflejada en el consumo de gas natural vehicular (-53%) seguido de las refinerías (-30%) y el sector industrial (-25%)'. https://www.portafolio.co/economia/por-coronavirus-cae-demanda-de-gas-natural-541200.
154. Unidad de Planeación Minero Energética (UPME), *Estudio Técnico Para El Plan De Abastecimiento De Gas Natural*, Enero de 2020.

domiciliary users, commercial users are 184,510 (1.8%), and industrial 5,779 (0.1%)[155] Also, Colombia exceeded 600,000 vehicles converted in 2019.[156]

364. The connections of the gas networks are represented in the participation of 85% of the Colombians from level one, two, and three of income. The national average of effective coverage in twenty-seven departments of Colombia is equivalent to more than 10 million users.[157]

§3. Growth in Residential and NGV Sectors

365. Since the Mass Use of Gas programme began, both the NGV and the residential sectors have presented the highest rates of new connections, demonstrating the benefits of natural gas for purposes such as heating, air conditioning, cooking, and transportation. In the NGV sector, reality exceeded expectations, passing from 18,369 vehicles converted to natural gas in 2002 to 324,515 converted vehicles in December, 2010.[158] During the period between January and July of 2010 an average of 1,580 vehicles converted to gas each month.

366. The policy of vehicle conversion to natural gas received considerable tax incentives. It consists of a Value Added Tax (VAT) exemption for the import of the conversion kit, and has developed along with the construction of natural gas station services or points of natural gas service in existing stations. The Ministry of Environment also assigned an import quota of 100 hybrids, electric and natural gas-powered vehicles for 2010.[159]

367. From the figures reported by the Natural Gas Sector Report 2019, 20 years,[160] it is observed that Colombia has more than 800 refuelling stations and there are more than 600,000 vehicles converted to NGV. Compared with previous years, in the last 10 years there has been an increase in its use as a consequence of the incentives in cargo transport and public transport. In addition, NGV had proven to be a less polluting alternative to oil and diesel, as well as a more reliable and profitable alternative to the electric vehicles on long trips. However, considering the general markets after the COVID-19 pandemic and it's economic impacts, its growth stopped.

---

155. Ministerio de minas y energía, *Cobertura Del Servicio De Gas Natural – II Trimestre De 2020.* https://www.minenergia.gov.co/documents/10192/24212253/COBERTURA+GN+2-2020.pdf.
156. La Republica, Usuarios con gas natural crecieron 5.2% en 2019 tras alcanzar cerca de 10 millones. https://www.larepublica.co/economia/usuarios-de-gas-natural-crecieron-52-en-2019-tras-alcanzar-los-10-millones-3013892.
157. Ministerio de Minas y Energía y Naturgas. *Colombia Supera El Usuario 10 Millones De Gas Natural.* https://www.youtube.com/watch?v=KmzqViJUXfI.
158. UPME, *Boletín Estadístico de Minas y Energía*, p. 218.
159. UPME, *La Cadena del Gas Natural, supra.*
160. PROMIGAS. Informe del sector gas natural 2019, 20 años. http://www.promigas.com/Es/Paginas/Informe_sector_gas_20_edicion.aspx.

Part III. Regulatory Framework Concerning Petrol

Chapter 1. Exploitation

§1. Legal System

368. Colombia has a Roman-German legal system based on the law, as its main source. The State is organized as a democracy with the political constitution as the highest law. The regulatory system includes laws and regulations as the foundation of all the administrative structure of the State, the power and competencies of its three branches – legislative, executive, and judiciary – and the rights and duties of the citizens.

369. The Political Constitution states:

> Article 1: 'Colombia is a legal social state organized in the form of a unitary republic, decentralized, with the autonomy of its territorial units, democratic, participatory and pluralistic, based on respect of human dignity, on the work and solidarity of the individuals who belong to it, and the predominance of the general interest.'
>
> Article 4: 'The Constitution is the supreme law. In all cases of incompatibility between the Constitution and the law or any other legislation or regulation, the constitutional provisions will apply.'

370. The legal system underlying the activities of the oil industry has its foundations in constitutional provisions. They are integrated by principles and rules that allow the State to develop industrial and commercial activities integrating the oil chain. The main constitutional provisions include:

- The subsoil is part of the national territory. 'The state is the owner of the subsoil and of the natural, non-renewable resources, without prejudice to the rights acquired and established in accordance with prior laws.'[161]

161. Article 332, Constitution.

- The law shall determine the conditions for the exploitation of all non-renewable natural resources (minerals). A financial compensation, considered a royalty, shall be paid in favour of the State notwithstanding any other right or compensation.[162]
- The law shall determine the distribution, objectives, purposes, administration, execution, control, efficient use and destination of the income from non-renewable resources, and state the conditions for the share of its benefits. This set of income, assignments, entities, procedures and regulations make up the General System of Royalties.[163]
- There is freedom for all economic activities and private initiatives. Free economic competition is a universal right which implies responsibilities. Companies have a social function which implies obligations. The direction of the economy is in charge of the State who shall intervene by mandate of the law in the exploitation of natural resources.[164]
- Private property and all other rights acquired pursuant to civil law, shall be guaranteed. The said rights cannot be ignored, nor shall they be harmed by subsequent laws. When the enforcement of a law issued by reasons of public or social interest creates conflict between the rights of the citizens and the needs recognized in such law, the private interest shall yield to the public or social interest. There may be expropriation through judicial sentence, and previous compensation, by reasons of public or social interests defined by lawmakers. Said indemnity shall be established by taking into consideration the interests of the community and of the affected party. In those cases determined by the legislator, said expropriation may be carried out administratively subject to subsequent contentious-administrative action, including even the price.[165]
- Public services are inherent to the social purposes of the State. It is the duty of the state to make sure they are rendered efficiently to all inhabitants in the national territories. Public services may be rendered by the State directly or indirectly by organized communities or by the citizens (Article 365 of the Political Constitution).
- In this respect, the Constitutional Court has been tasked to determine whether oil-related activities, namely production, refining, transport and distribution, are considered public services. The matter at stake being that the Labour Code forbids strikes in public services. The Court's opinion has been divided on this respect, as on the one hand, it recognizes that such activities are not an essential public service and therefore workers' right to strike in this sector cannot be restricted; and on the other, the Court has failed to declare the provision's unconstitutionality. The main development from the Constitutional Court's rulings on the matter is that the right to strike is protected insofar as a minimum standard of service is guaranteed so as not to disproportionally affect consumers' rights.[166]

---

162. Article 360, Constitution.
163. Article 361, Constitution.
164. Article 332, Constitution.
165. Article 58, Constitution.
166. Constitutional Court. Sentence No. C-796 of 30 Oct. 2014. Magistrate: Jorge Ignacio Pretelt Chaljub.

- The exploitation of natural resources within Indian territories shall be done without impairment of the cultural, social and economic integrity of the indigenous communities. In decisions adopted in regard to such exploitation, the government shall encourage participation of representatives of such communities.[167] (Articles 334 and 365 of the Political Constitution).
- The State shall plan for the handling and use of the natural resources so as to guarantee its sustainable development, conservation, replenishment or substitution. Besides, the State shall prevent the causes of environmental damage and impose sanctions, as well as compensatory measures for damages caused.[168]

371. In general, the norms are issued in statutes by State entities given specific competencies granted by the Political Constitution or the law. Such statutes have a hierarchy imposing the duty of compliance with the legal and constitutional principles. There is a control of constitutionality and legality for every norm enacted by State entities in accordance to the constitutional hierarchy.

§2. Regulatory Framework of Hydrocarbons: History

372. The first norms about the hydrocarbon's industry were applied at the beginning of the twentieth century using the Mines Law and the Fiscal Regime. It was Law 37 of 1931 the first Hydrocarbon's Law that contained systematic rules about this industry. The Hydrocarbon Law was modified in different occasions to introduce new topics, including Decree 1056 of 1953, Law 10 of 1961, Law 20 of 1969, Decree 2310 of 1974 and Decree 1760 of 2003.

373. The existing regulatory framework on hydrocarbon's exploration and exploitation/production (E&P) is contained in the Petroleum Code,[169] which establishes the provisions applicable to all hydrocarbon mixtures found in the earth, regardless of their physical state. It is applicable to substances that compose the crude oil, that come with it, or that derive from it.

374. The Petroleum Code has been reviewed to introduce new topics, such as technical changes, E&P contracts, and State entities that administer the hydrocarbons. Most of the changes have been issued while guaranteeing that situations governed by past laws keep their legal standing. As a consequence, the applicable law for a specific industrial activity depends on the origin of the right to explore and exploit, and the law that was applicable at the moment when such rights were acquired. The origin of the right can be found in the law; in a governmental or judicial decision based on the law; or in any of the types of contracts executed by governmental agencies.

---

167. Articles 334 and 365, Constitution.
168. Article 80, Constitution.
169. Decree 1056 of 1953.

375. In addition, there are some regulations applicable to E&P works and the main actors involved enacted by diverse type of governmental entities, depending on the matter and the faculties of these entities. For example, the technical regulation about exploration and exploitation works was issued by the MME through Resolution 181495 of 2009.

§3. Administrative Structure of the State

376. There are three government entities directly related with activities of the petroleum industry: the MME; the ANH and ECOPETROL. In general, the first one is in charge of designing the policies on petroleum. The ANH is responsible for the administration of the exploration and production areas, and ECOPETROL has been assigned commercial and industrial functions.

I. Ministry of Mines and Energy

377. Concerning the hydrocarbon sector, the Ministry has the following functions:[170]

- Planning, adoption, direction, and coordination of national policy on exploration, exploitation, transportation, refinery, processing, enhancement, transformation and distribution of minerals, hydrocarbons and biofuels.
- Enactment of regulations for the sector on exploration, exploitation, transportation, refining, distribution, processing, enhancement, marketing and export of non-renewable natural resources and biofuels.
- Regulation of crude transportation through oil pipelines.
- Adoption of expansion plans for the coverage and supply of combustible gas.
- Auditing the exploration and exploitation of the reservoirs, directly or through the entity delegated for the purpose.
- Defining prices and fees for gasoline, diesel fuel, biofuels, and mixtures of the above-mentioned fuels.
- Reviewing and adopting the Expansion Plan for the pipeline network, and the Continuity Plan where the objectives, principles, criteria and strategies shall be defined as necessary to ensure the availability and supply of liquid combustibles, sub products, biofuels and others in the national market in a regular and continuous way.

II. National Oil Company: ECOPETROL

378. ECOPETROL was created by the Colombian Oil Company in 1951 as an effort to fulfil the needs of the country's refineries, and with the largest capabilities to develop commercial and industrial activities related to the oil chain. The law gave

170. Decree 381 of 2012.

ECOPETROL the right to receive the areas declared as national reserve, so that these areas were not subject to normal contracting regimes but to direct exploration, exploitation and administration, or in association with national or foreign private capital.

379. Between 1974 and 2003, ECOPETROL was the administrator of the areas for the exploration and exploitation of hydrocarbons in the country. In order to achieve this, it signed association contracts with private operators, besides carrying out direct operation activities. At present and after different amendments, ECOPETROL S.A became a mixed-ownership company, partially owned by the Colombian government. Its board of directors is integrated by members appointed by the government, and by private investors.

380. As the main function, ECOPETROL must supervise all kind of business related to any commercial and industrial activities on exploration, exploitation, refining, transportation, distribution and marketing of hydrocarbons, its derivatives and by-products, as well as develop subsidiary or complementary operations. ECOPETROL may carry out research, development and marketing of conventional and alternative energy sources; the production, mixture, storage, transportation and marketing of oxygenating compounds and biofuels; the operation of ports and any and/or all related activities for the development of the previously mentioned. It is ruled by private law rules on corporate affairs, contracts, and businesses. As a public entity, it must follow certain rules related to administrative controls and it is supervised by public entities.

381. Currently, ECOPETROL is working in the country and overseas, directly and through subsidiaries. The company is the largest in Colombia and is also considered the fourth-largest oil company in Latin America, with investments in Brazil, Peru and the United States. In some cases ECOPETROL participates in E&P and transportation projects as operator or as capital investor. One of its latest projects is as joint venture with Occidental Petroleum Corp, for the development of unconventional hydrocarbons in the Permian Basin in Texas. Its shares are registered in the New York Stock Exchange (NYSE: EC) and Colombian Stock Exchange with more than six hundred thousand shareholders.

III. National Hydrocarbon Agency

382. The ANH was created in 2003 from the split of ECOPETROL. It is the duty of the ANH to integrally manage all hydrocarbon reserves and resources belonging to the State; to promote the optimal and sustainable use of hydrocarbons and to contribute to the national energetic security. The following are its main duties:[171]

- Design, promote, negotiate, sign and manage all contracts and agreements for the exploration and exploitation of hydrocarbons property of the State, except those

171. Decree 1760 of 2003; Decree 4137 of 2011; and Decree 714 of 2012.

association contracts signed by ECOPETROL up to 31 December 2003. The ANH must also follow up all obligations stated on those contracts.
- Assign the areas for exploration and/or exploitation subject to the contracting models and types that the ANH adopts for the purpose.
- Support the MME in the formulation of the government policy in the matter of hydrocarbons; in the making of the sector plans and in the fulfilment of the corresponding objectives.
- Establish in the exploration and exploitation contracts the terms and conditions under which the contracting companies shall develop their programmes for the benefit of the communities located in the area of influence of those contracts.
- Support the MME and all other authorities interested in matters relating to the communities, the environment and the safety of the area of influence of hydrocarbon projects.
- Set hydrocarbons prices so as to have a benchmark for royalties.
- Collect, settle and transfer all royalties and monetary compensation from hydrocarbon exploitation to the nation.
- Set the volumes of production of oil concessions that the exploiters must sell for internal refining.
- Set the mandatory sell price for crude oil from concessions, earmarked for processing or use in the country and the natural gas effectively used as raw material in the petrochemical industrial processes.

383. The ANH has played a decisive role in steadying the national oil and gas industry after the oil crisis of 2014. Based on its legal duty of carrying out the necessary actions to satisfy hydrocarbon's demand and ensuring internal supply and energy sufficiency, the ANH issued Accord 2 of 2015 setting out regulatory measures to tackle low oil prices and increased hydrocarbon exploration and production, which were later repealed by Accord 2 of 2017.

384. In 2017 the ANH issued Accord 2 of 2017 as the oil and gas main contracts regulation. It defines the principles and rules, the areas that could be awarded by the ANH as well as its classification, the standards and requirements for interested parties, the regulation on working programmes, types of contracts as well as its main elements, type of bidding and contracting process and special conditions for the development of unconventional hydrocarbons, among other key elements of the sector.

385. In 2020 the ANH issued Accords 2 and 4 establishing specific measures to respond to the price and demand crisis created by the COVID-19 Pandemic, including measures on:

- Delayed payment of the share of production obligation, until a certain level of market oil price was achieved.
- Flexibility on deadlines and schedules for compliance with work programmes and other obligations established under the E&P Contract.

– The possibility to allocate funds from the Programme in Benefit of Communities to attend urgent health needs from the town where oil operations were taking place.

§4. Subsoil: Property Rights and Legal Regime

386. Hydrocarbons are owned by the State and can only be exploited by ECOPETROL and/or by individuals upon a contract, according to the law.

387. In order for individuals to have rights on the subsoil, they must have registered their titles before 22 December 1969. Valid titles certify that oil reservoirs have been discovered.[172] The existence of a discovered hydrocarbon reservoir is established when the rock containing hydrocarbons is reached through drilling or similar equipment and the corresponding fluid tests demonstrate so, and it behaves as an independent unit of production and properties.

388. The exploitation of private property hydrocarbons implies a series of obligations for the title holders, such as tax duties and compliance with technical development requirements for industrial activities. In fact, the possibility to get decision from governmental authorities constituting private rights is a very difficult task to interested applicants, due to the law requirements. Some judicial decisions from the highest courts have ratified the difficulty in getting private rights on hydrocarbons.

172. Article 1, Law 97 of 1993.

Chapter 2. Production

389. In Colombia there have been three consecutive contractual systems for hydrocarbons E&P by virtue of their nature, of the contracting State entity and of the applicable regime.

§1. CONTRACT MODELS

I. Old Concessions

390. The first system appeared at the beginning of the twentieth century, known as concession contracts signed by today's MME. These contracts were initially ruled by Fiscal Codes and later by special laws issued for oil activities, compiled in the existing Petroleum Code, which are considered public law. Under the concessions contract model, the operations' risk, cost and control are undertaken by the concessionaire. The production belongs to the concessionaire. It must pay to the State a surface rental fee, during the exploration stage, and royalties, which are established as a percentage of the production during the exploitation stage.

391. From the beginning, the exploration term was five years, which could be extended for six years, and the exploitation term thirty years, which was extendable for ten years. After an amendment in 1961, the exploration term was three years with extension of up to three years. New contracts ceased being signed in 1974, when the MME was no longer administrator of the areas. At present, there is only one standing contract from this system.

II. Association Contract

392. The second contract system is the Association Contracts (*Contratos de asociación*), a private contract ruled by Civil Law between the contractor and ECOPETROL. Although, this was not the only type of contract signed by ECOPETROL, it was the most widely used.[173]

393. During the exploratory stage, operations' risk, cost and control are solely undertaken by the contractor. At the exploitation stage, the risks, costs and control are jointly undertaken by ECOPETROL and the contractor, through the figure of Association. This Association does not constitute a partnership or a legal entity different from the parties, but a contractual relationship managed by an Executive Committee composed of the two contracting parties. The activities established by the Executive Committee are to be carried out by the operator, which is generally the contractor.

173. Besides the Association Contracts, there are Joint Risk Contracts, Special Contracts and Joint Venture.

394. The producers, contractors and ECOPETROL must pay a percentage of the production as royalties. Production is distributed between the two contracting parties in function of the share of each party. In some cases, operational costs and the distribution of production varies according to a profitability factor, called 'R' Factor.

395. The term for the exploration phase is six years, and twenty-two for the exploitation period. New contracts ceased being signed in 2004, when ECOPETROL was no longer the administrator of hydrocarbon areas. By 2019, there were fifty-seven contracts of this type in force. Some Association contracts were extended in the Exploitation term for the remaining economic life of the reservoir.

III. ANH Contract

396. The third system refers to contracts signed by the ANH and includes two types: hydrocarbon exploration and production (E&P Contract), and technical evaluation contracts (TEA Contract). These contracts are regulated by public law.

A. E&P

397. Exploration and Production contracts share the feature of being concession contracts, meaning that during the exploration stage the operations' risk, cost and control are borne by the contractor. The obligation to pay a percentage of the production as royalties is created to the charge of the contractor. The ANH receives earmarked economic rights for the use of the subsoil; for technology transfer; for its production share; for high prices and for the extension of the exploitation period.

398. The term of the exploration period is six years and the exploitation period is twenty-four years. In 2012, there were 361 exploration and production contracts in force. There are specific terms and conditions for E&P Contracts that grant rights on non-conventional hydrocarbons, which will be described later.

B. TEA

399. TEA Contracts have the purpose of obtaining technical evaluation in a specific area, but they do not grant exploiting rights. These contracts do not generate production rights but create rights of conversion into an E&P Contract. The contractor has to perform an exploratory programme and payment of economic rights earmarked for the use of the subsoil in favour of ANH. The TEA contractor is entitled to the conversion by means of an offer to perform an exploratory programme. In case that any third party present an offer and the TEA contractor match such offer, the ANH has to grant the E&P contact to the TEA contractor. TEA Contract term is thirty-six months. In 2012, there were twenty-four contracts in force.[174]

400. All these three types of contracts are regulated by Colombian law and are subject to the jurisdiction of Colombian courts, specifically Administrative-law courts.[175] In Concession and ANH contracts, factual or technical controversies between the parties and the government shall be solved through the decision of experts. The experts are appointed, one by the government; another one by the interested party, and the third by common agreement between the already appointed experts. In the ANH contracts, legal disputes are settled through arbitration. In some specific cases, ECOPETROL and the contractor have stipulated an arbitration procedure to solve some controversies.

401. E&P Contracts for non-renewable resources, as well as those concerning marketing and all other commercial and industrial activities intrinsic of the State entities and within their competencies for these matters, are regulated by special legislation and not by the Administrative Contracting Statute, which regulates all public procurement contracts. Government entities empowered to carry out the said activities determine in their internal by-laws, the selection procedure for contractors; the exceptional clauses that may be negotiated, and the procedure to be followed. Those procedures adopted by the above-mentioned entities expand on the duties of objective selection, and the principles of transparency, economy and responsibility.[176]

C. CEPI

402. The ANH, through Accord 06 of 2020, established the Special Contract for Investigation Projects, as the contractual tool that allows private parties to develop an investigation and scientific project for the development of unconventional hydrocarbons, as defined in Decree 3004 of 2012.

403. This new figure is part of the kind of special contracts, as defined in Acord 02 of 2017. Its main purpose is to perform an activity that provides information to the contractor and to the Colombian Government, on the use of hydraulic fracturing for exploration of oil and gas. This special contract establishes new obligations on the private party, in addition to the traditional obligations defined on an E&P Contract, such as an additional share of the total investment that needs to be spent by the contractor on needs identified by the local community. It also includes local content obligations and creates new transparency obligations that allow real-time sharing of information on the development of the project with the community, the

174. *Ibid.*
175. Article 10, Petroleum Code (Law 1437 of 2011).
176. Articles 13, 76 and 15, Law 80 of 1993; Art. 81, Law 489 of 1998; 'Acuerdo' from the ANH Board of Directors ('BoA Resolution') 04 of 2012.

authorities and the public in general. It also offers an option for contracting parties that wish to develop a commercial project in unconventional hydrocarbons, where the CEPI had taken place after that project is concluded, as well as the possibility to recognize any investment made in the Investigation Project as complying with past obligations that had not been fulfilled by the contractor in previous contacts or, future obligations derived from the CEPI on a further commercial development.

§2. Management of Hydrocarbon Areas

404. The criteria for the management and assignment of areas and the contractors' selection process are ruled by the ANH through Contracting Regulations. The ANH sets limits for the areas and makes a land map including the assigned areas, the reserved ones and those available.

405. Selection procedures for contractors can include: open competition; closed competition (competitors are invited to the process by ANH) and of direct assignment (this type of selection procedure has been suspended for several years and not used in practice). The open competition contracting process involves stages such as the formal opening act; the publication of reference terms; the open or close call to proponents, as may be appropriate; the validation of proponents; the evaluation of proposals and the granting or assignment of areas. For the qualification of proponents, it is necessary to validate the legal, economic, financial, technical, operational and environmental capabilities as well as those relating corporate social responsibility of the applicant.[177]

§3. Economic Effects of Hydrocarbon Activities

I. Foreign Exchange and Exchange Rights

406. Foreign capital investment in Colombia is regulated in the Country's Foreign Investments Statute.[178] As a general rule, all foreign companies willing to do businesses in Colombia must follow the provisions established in the exchange regime. The conditions for an overseas operation to be recognized as foreign investment include: (i) that the investor is not a resident in Colombia; (ii) the capital contribution shall be effectively destined for such investment and (iii) such contribution must correspond to the investment models established in the norm.

407. In order for the foreign company (the contractor) to obtain exchange rights, it must register its investment with the National Bank (*Banco de la República*).[179] Exchange rights refer to the possibility to: reinvest or capitalize the amounts with the right to wire them abroad; and send the profits of such investments overseas in

177. BoA Resolution 04 of 2012 of the ANH.
178. Decree 2080 of 2000 replacing CONPES Resolution 51 of 91.
179. Decree 2080 of 2000.

currency readily convertible, and any other sums derived from the sale of the company's assets, liquidation or capital reduction.[180]

408. The so-called exchange market[181] integrates all the currencies that must be mandatorily channelled through the exchange brokers or through clearing accounts. The main operations concerning the exchange market include imports and exports, direct foreign investment, and international operations carried out with the profits associated with said foreign investment, as well as with foreign debt operations.

409. There are two separate regimes for foreign capital investments, a general regime and a special one. The special regime is applicable to foreign branches engaged in hydrocarbon exploration and exploitation activities, or in the exclusive supply of technical services to the hydrocarbon sector. The exchange regime does not allow the Colombian branch to acquire external loans. Under the special exchange regime, the working capital supplied by the home office to its branch in Colombia, called supplementary investment to the assigned capital, is considered a common operation and not a capital contribution and, therefore, not subject to the payment of presumed income tax to the capital.[182]

II. Payments and Economic Obligations

410. In ANH contracts, during the exploration phase, the contractor undertakes the obligation to periodically pay certain amounts per surface unit, called economic rights for subsoil use, and, except in the TEA Contract, a right of technology transfer earmarked to a training fund for staff members of the ANH.

411. In the exploitation stage of the E&P Contracts the contractor must pay (i) economic rights for subsoil use, per production unit, (ii) economic rights due to high prices, (iii) economic rights as a percentage of production share, (iv) economic rights as a percentage of production share during the extension of the production term and (v) other economic rights, such as training, institutional strengthening and technology transfer.

For example, economic rights on E&P Contracts for the use of subsoil in 2021 have been established by the ANH in Circular 03 of 27 January 2021, according to the contract phase and size of the area. The following amounts are due per exploration phase and per hectare:

---

180. Banco de la República, *La Economía Petrolera en Colombia*, in *Borradores de economía* 692 (Bogota, 2012).
181. Laws 9 of 1991 and Law 31 of 1992.
182. Banco de la República, 'Economía Petrolera'.

Size of the Contract Area	*First 100,000 Hectares*		*Each Hectare in Addition to First 100,000*	
Phase Duration	*Less or Equal Than Eighteen Months (USD)*	*More Than Eighteen Months (USD)*	*Less or Equal Than Eighteen Months (USD)*	*More Than Eighteen Months (USD)*
Within polygons A and B	2.87	3.83	3.83	5.73
Outside polygons A and B	1.91	2.87	2.87	3.83
Offshore	0.96			

III. Royalties

412. There is the obligation of payment of royalties as compensation for the use of a natural resource belonging to the State. This obligation is established in the law, not in the contract, and is based on the fees established pursuant to the nature of the resource, the resource quality; location of the area and the average daily production volume. The general fee for light and semi-light quality of oil, more than 15 degrees (15° American Petroleum Institute – API) is established in a scale ranging from 8% to 25% depending on the monthly average of daily production. For heavy hydrocarbons from an API gravity equal to or less than 15 degrees (15° API), royalties will be of the seventy-five percent (75%) of the royalty applied for light and semi-light hydrocarbons. For gas production, royalty is 80% of the oil fee, when it is onshore or offshore less than 1,000-feet depth; or 60% of the oil fee, if it is offshore more than 1,000-feet depth.[183]

IV. Taxes

413. Additionally, investors have the obligation to pay taxes, rates and contributions for economic activities. Among such taxes, it can be mentioned income tax over a taxable income or for presumptive income. There are certain incentives for hydrocarbon activities in specific situations: exploration periods when there is no production; losses from hydrocarbon activities; donations, and research and development. The following are indirect taxes: VAT/IVA, import tax (not applicable to

183. Law 141of 1994 and Law 756 of 2002.

exports); stamp tax in some regions; tax to records; taxes to stock shares and taxes to financial operations. Permanently imported goods and services must pay customs tariffs and IVA for imported goods.[184]

§4. Expropriation, Right of Way and Unitization

414. The petroleum industry is considered of public interest in the phases of exploration, exploitation, refining, transportation and distribution. Therefore, the Ministry may order expropriations needed for the development of the industry.[185]

415. After the expropriations have been ordered by the Ministry, a legal process must be executed via Court of Justice to determine the compensation. The ruling also establishes the date when the expropriated party must hand out the property rights to the State, which are normally real estate rights. Areas bordering or adjacent to oil exploitation projects may be subject to the creation of a reserve zone, which prevents the authority from granting rights to third parties in nearby areas, or negotiating or expropriating right holders in these areas. The pieces of land within such areas may be managed by a public entity manager of areas for oil exploration and exploitation.[186]

416. When oil operators require the use of privately owned land for the development of its industrial activities, such plots of land may be subject to legal rights of way. Such rights of way are set up through direct negotiation between the oil operator and the owner, according to procedures established by law. In case an agreement is not reached, the assessment of damage and the delivery of the real estate can be requested to a Municipal Civil Court.[187]

417. In case an oil field is located in two or more areas whose owners are different and it is not possible to reach 'unitization agreement', or generates disputes among them, a cooperative or joint exploitation plan must be established.[188]

§5. Good Operating Practices

418. There is a technical regime on conventional hydrocarbon exploration and exploitation issued by the MME[189] aimed at maximizing its final recovery and avoid waste. Said regime includes norms relative to the duty of applying national and international standards and technical standards; techniques for the execution of exploratory activities; the duty to give information to the Ministry; applying good

184. Banco de la República, 'Economía Petrolera'.
185. Article 4, Petroleum Code.
186. Articles 123–130, Law 418 of 1997.
187. Law 1274 of 2009.
188. Article 31, Petroleum Code, and Clauses in the E&P Contracts.
189. Resolution 181495 of 2009 from the MME.

industry practices to identify emergency situations and putting in place contingency plans and to restore the area and comply with the payment of salaries, rights of way and rentals.

419. The technical regime regulates drilling, including the duty to obtain the necessary authorizations; informing the start up so that the Ministry verifies technical conditions; minimum distances between wells; as well as the execution pursuant to the approved programme and the reports to the Ministry. Also, it regulates the closure of wells, the casing to be used, the prohibition to close open-pit wells, the obligation to carry log books, the way to execute tests and physic-chemical analysis, the obligation to take core samples; the suspension of wells and the way to carry out plugging and abandonment. The duty to obtain authorization to extended production tests is regulated. As for the exploitation period, it regulates the authorization for its start, the official measurement, the control of reservoirs, the classification of reservoirs and wells, the rates of production, the pressure tests of reservoirs and the pressure maintenance activities, the approval of the unified exploitation plans, of the enhanced recovery projects and its stoppage, of the projects for water disposal, and gas burning; the duty of avoiding gas waste. Last, but not least, such technical regime includes provisions about the dismantling of constructions and facilities, the periodic reports that must be delivered to the Ministry and the penalties that may be imposed for infringements to the regulations.

420. Operators must comply with the requirements to classify, record and value the reserves, property of the Nation, as well as send the necessary information.[190]

421. There are norms binding all hydrocarbons exploiters to sell their product by earmarking it to refine by-products for internal consumption. The ANH can determine the volumes of production that the exploiters must sell for refining in the country and set the corresponding prices.[191] The MME establishes the methodology[192] to determine the price of crude oil, stating that the base is the international crude oil export price, FOB at Colombian Port, applying the International Benchmark Price, which in this case is West Texas Intermediate (WTI).

422. As far as gas is concerned, there is also the obligation to sell it when it is used as staple for petrochemical industrial processes. In these cases, the ANH must set the volumes to be sold and their prices.[193]

§6. Social and Environmental Regime for Hydrocarbon Operations

423. Colombia has in place a set of standards that encompasses the National Contingency Plan against spills of hydrocarbons, its by-products and other harmful

190. Decree 727 of 2007 and Resolution 494 of 2009.
191. Article 4, Decree 4137 of 2011.
192. MME Resolution 181709 of 2003.
193. Article 4, Decree 4137 of 2011.

substances in the sea, river and lake waters. This Plan has the purpose to coordinate efforts for the prevention, control and tackling of the effects of hydrocarbon spills by the private and public sectors.[194]

424. Affected communities must be granted participation in the analysis of project impacts in order to decide about the granting of environmental permits. Minority communities such as indigenous, Afro-Americans, ROM (*'etnia gitana'*) and San Andrés island's population must be consulted in advance of the administrative decision granting exploration rights, whenever its presence in the area is demonstrated.

§7. Hydrocarbons Regime in Non-conventional Reservoirs

I. Background

425. The exploration and production of hydrocarbons deposited in non-conventional reservoirs and off-shore fields is timidly regulated in Decree 1616 of 2014, which incorporates technical standards and make them enforceable. Such reservoirs including tight, methane gas on coal deposits, shale oil and gas, and bituminous sands were established by a technical regime enacted by the MME.[195] Some norms contain mechanisms to promote the assurance of natural gas supply, including incentives to production coming from non-conventional reservoirs.[196] In addition, the Organic Law on the General Royalty System establishes a more convenient fee for non-conventional reservoirs, consisting of 60% of the percentage of the share of the royalties equivalent to the exploitation of conventional crude oil.[197]

426. The MME has updated its glossary to bring it in line with the new concepts emerging from non-conventional reservoirs and offshore related activities, by means of Resolution 40048 of 2015.

II. Contracting Model

427. The ANH included in the 2012 Colombian Round (*Ronda Colombia 2012*) prospective areas for non-conventional reservoirs and, in the minutes of the exploration and production contracts, the possibility of exploring and exploiting such resources. However, it excluded the Methane Gas on Coal Deposits (GMDC) and those existing in bituminous sands, since they would be subject to a further round.

428. The contract minutes are the same used for conventional hydrocarbons with special terms for non-conventional ones, including longer exploratory term (nine

194. Decrees 2190 of 1995 and 321 of 1999.
195. Resolution 180742 of 2012 from MME.
196. Decrees 2730 of 2010 and 2100 of 2011.
197. Article 14, s. 1, Law 1530 of 2012.

years in three phases of thirty-six months each); no vestment of the areas; a programme called Exploratory Confirmation is included to confirm the existence of the reservoir with the drilling of, at least, four exploratory wells; and the design of a recording programme of well stimulation and completion. The exploratory programme that must be presented by the contractor to the study of the ANH must include the drilling of two exploratory wells instead of only one well A3, which is mandatory for conventional reservoirs. A base price of USD 81 was set for the application of economic right of high prices, showing a lower burden for the investor compared to the same right in conventional reservoirs.

429. The term for informing the discovery of the reservoir is not given by the well completion, as in the conventional ones, but by a series of facts including the completion of several horizontal wells and to have gone into the fracturing phase with specific technical conditions as to distance and specific tests of each reservoir. For the extension of the production period, the contractor must prove the drilling of, at least, four development wells during each previous calendar year and must accept the delivery of an additional 5% of production in favour of the ANH.

430. Regarding coexistence of mines of petroleum operations in the same area, the model establishes the obligation of the interested contractor in making his best effort and to use all diligence and technical and operational capacity to sign one or several operation agreements under the terms of the resolution from the MME.[198] In the absence of such agreement, hydrocarbon-related activities carried out by the concessionaire are suspended, while the agreement is negotiated and decided.

431. Through the Decree 3004 of 2013 and Resolution 90341 of 2014, the government issued the general and technical regulation for unconventional hydrocarbons. This regulation was the result of a long process of preparation of a strict and thorough set of rules that identified measures to decrease risks associated with this subsector, such as the need to establish higher standards for the construction and integrity of wells for the protection of underground aquifers, the use and disposal of water and produced water or the formula of fracturing fluid.

In 2016 a lawsuit that aimed for the annulment of the above-mentioned regulation, based on the lack of consideration of the precautionary principle, was admitted by the Council of State. On 8 November 2018, the high court emitted an injunction that suspended those rules, leaving any unconventional hydrocarbon activity without a regulatory framework.

432. The government appointed an Expert Commission to evaluate the suspended regulation, the general situation of the oil and gas sector in the country and the possibility for fracking to be developed in Colombia. The commission issued an extensive report with recommendation on the improvement of social license in the industry, a better distribution of benefits with the local community and the need to

198. MME Resolution 18 0742 of 2012.

develop a pilot project to assess the technique as well as the procedures and institutions, before deciding on whether to implement fracking in the country on a commercial level.

433. The government issued Decree 328 of 2020 with the general framework of the pilot projects, as well as Resolution 40185 of 2020 with the technical regulation.

§8. Technical Requirements on Non-conventional Reservoirs

434. Resolution 90341 of March 2014 established the general technical regulation for the development of unconventional hydrocarbons in Colombia. It included issues such as (i) global work programmes; (ii) initial tests, registry and sampling on wells; (iii) casing and cementing work requirements; (iv) specific requirements for hydraulic stimulation operations; (v) situations of suspension of the activities; (vi) injecting well requirements and (vii) inspections by the authorities.

435. Resolution 40185 of 2020 established the rules for the development of the pilot projects for unconventional hydrocarbons. It draws from Resolution 90341; however, its scope is limited only to the pilot projects. This regulation establishes new elements such as the use of minimal impact technology, the creation of a traffic light system for the suspension of activities, the inclusion of a transparency centre that will be fed by technical, social and health information for the public among other measures that respond to a pilot project.

Chapter 3. Transportation

§1. Introduction

436. Colombia's hydrocarbon transport infrastructure has been built by ECOPETROL and private oil producers in accordance with market necessities and new discoveries. In the last years, due to the increase in daily oil production, the pipelines' capacity has proven obsolete for transport. There are certain volumes of daily production that need to be transported by trucks to the ports for exportation. The government has implemented a plan to build pipelines from the main oil production region located at the east of the country, investing important amounts of money in joint ventures between ECOPETROL and private companies.

437. ECOPETROL owns and operates the majority of the pipelines and ports and has the largest capacity to transport oil. There were projects to connect Venezuelan oil production areas to the Colombian Pacific Ocean coast through the national territory in order to facilitate transportation of Venezuelan and Colombian oil production to Asia. Nevertheless, due to political instability, the projects were never build or developed. Other project are under current assessment to connect the Caribbean coast to the Central American countries for gas exports.

§2. Pipeline Construction: Types and Capacity

438. The activity of transporting hydrocarbons through pipelines is considered of public interest. It is a public service that empowers the carrier to request expropriation of land and the imposition of rights of way, whenever the use of private property is deemed necessary.[199]

439. The Petroleum Code establishes two types of pipelines: private-use and public-use pipelines. Private use pipelines are those built by the owners of exploration and production rights or refiners, for their own use. The State has a preference right of up to 20% of the capacity of any type of pipeline to transport state-owned oil, which, in the case of private use pipelines, refers exclusively to oil for royalties. Excess capacity of private use pipelines must be available for third parties. This does not involve making investments to adapt the pipeline for the transportation of said third-party oil.

440. Public-use pipelines are built by private companies considered public transportation companies, which must sign a concession contract with the MME.[200] Public use pipelines concession contracts have a term of fifty years that may be extended in periods of twenty years. The operator must sell the pipelines to the State after thirty years of the contract or at the contract term, if the government provides so. Regarding private-use pipelines, the operator is obliged to sell them when the

199. Article 4, Petroleum Code.
200. Articles 45 and 46, Petroleum Code.

exploration and production contract, to which it is linked, expires. The government must warn the operator about the contract expiration during the first six months of the year prior to the sale and, in case there is no agreement about the price, it shall be determined by experts.[201] Pipelines build after 7 October 1952 are not subject to reversion or restitution of assets to the State without compensation.[202]

441. Pipelines of any type must pay taxes of 6% of the amount resulting from multiplying the volume transported by the applicable fee.[203] For crudes coming from the east or southeast of the eastern mountain chain, the fee is 2%.[204] This tax is charged quarterly to the owner of the crude or gas, as the case may be. Local administrative units must collect this tax and distribute it among non-producing municipalities the pipelines or gas lines pass through, in proportion to the volume and length.

442. The route of the pipelines shall be the most economical and technically convenient and must be approved by the MME, as well as the stations.[205]

443. It is the duty of the Ministry to set transportation fees for the pipeline based on the following criteria: amortization of the capital invested in the construction; expenses of the pipeline running, administration and exploitation; and profit of the operator. This benefit is established by agreement with the State, by taking into account the profits of oil transport companies in other countries. When the agreement is not reached, the fee shall be decided by experts. This fee must be reviewed every four years or when unforeseeable and very serious alterations of the economy arise.[206]

444. The MME has backed the revision of pipeline transport fees in case of terrorist acts.[207] Based on Article 57 of the Petroleum Code, transport fees and economic conditions may be revised in case of force majeure or acts of God that endanger transporter's financial capacity. The Council of State has considered that terrorist acts fit within the force majeure description, provided that such acts are external, irresistible and unforeseeable. In order for the MME to revise the transport fee, and consequently adjust it, a court must qualify such terrorist acts as force majeure.

445. These considerations, though, do not exclude transporter's environmental liability for terrorist acts. Based on a ruling of a district court, the Ministry of Environment and Sustainable Development (MASD)[208] has established that oil transporters are responsible for environmental damage deriving from terrorist acts, such

201. Articles 50 and 51, *ibid.*
202. Article 53, *ibid.*
203. Article 52, *ibid.*
204. Decree-law 2140 of 1955.
205. Article 54, *ibid.*
206. Articles 56 and 57, *ibid.*
207. MME Communication 2014074583 of 2014.
208. MASD Concept 8140-E2-15532 of 2014.

as oil spills, due to the fact that those transporters hold a global environmental license and therefore are obliged to have a contingency plan. These plans shall tackle the impact of oil spills regardless of its cause. Failing to take measures on the occurrence of environmental damage exposes the transport company to the penalties established in Law 1333 of 2009 and further civil liability for damages.

§3. Participating Agencies

I. Hydrocarbons Direction

446. The applicable standards on delivery, transportation and intake of crude through the pipeline were issued through regulations by the MME in 2010.[209] The Hydrocarbons Direction of the Ministry has the following functions: keep a record of carriers, senders and transportation requests by third parties; administrate requests for changes in the carrier handbook; determine the volumes for the preference right in favour of the State; determine the methodology to set the fees for crude oil transportation through pipelines and review the transportation fees; set out the transportation tax; settle disagreement cases between the carrier and third parties about the surplus transportation capacity submitted to the decision of the MME; demand the improvements needed in public-use pipelines for crude oil transportation under the terms foreseen in the law and in the concession contracts; approve, through administrative act, all preliminary studies, the general route, location of the terminals, definitive lay out, construction blueprints and detailed budgets, as well as the corresponding specifications and the pipeline construction notices; make all the procedures for the subscription of the concession contracts of the public use pipelines.

II. Shipper

447. Among others, the following are established as obligations of the shipper: subscribe transportation agreements with the carriers; inform the Hydrocarbons Direction the pipeline and distance to be used; report on the origin (states, municipalities and fields) of the crude oil and the term of the transportation agreement; supply timely to the carrier, pursuant to the time table that he establishes for the purpose, all necessary information to prepare the transportation plan; present, in due time, the nomination to the carrier; to know and put into practice the commercial, operative and administrative procedures from the Carriers Manual; comply with the programme agreed in the month of operations for crude oil deliveries to the pipeline at the entrance node and arrange what is necessary to receive it at the exit node according to procedures defined in the Carrier Manual; deliver and receive from the carrier the crude oil within ranges of quality, volume, opportunity and all other conditions established in the Carrier Manual; respond for all consequences stemming

209. MME Resolution 181258 of 2010.

from the failure to comply with the obligations accorded in the transportation agreement; avoid practising restrictive commercial practices or those considered unfair competition; fulfil all norms established by the corresponding authorities about protection and preservation of the environment; fulfil all norms and procedures established in the Carrier Manual for the connection to the transportation system; pay the established fee for the distance(s) object of the service; supply the information required by the Hydrocarbons Direction of the MME so as to execute adequate control of the activity.

III. Carrier

448. The carrier of crude through the pipeline has, among others, the following obligations: keep the pipeline in adequate operating conditions; allow free access to his pipeline to any sender or third party requesting it, when there is available capacity and all requirements provided in Resolution and the Carrier's Manual; subscribe transportation agreements with the shippers; make, publish and keep updated the Pipeline transportation bulletin (*Boletin de Transporte por Oleoducto* (Bulletin of Transport by Pipeline) – BTO) in a web page in accordance with the Resolution provisions; make the Carrier Manual, send it to the Hydrocarbons Direction, keep it updated and publish it in the BTO; inform to the Hydrocarbons Direction of the MME all transportation agreements within ten days following its signing; give previous notice to the Hydrocarbons Direction about the transport requests made by third parties to use the available capacity; develop its transportation activity independently of other activities executed giving the same treatment to all agents; refrain from doing restrictive commercial practices or those considered as unfair competition; have adequate facilities to handle crude oil and monitor the volumes transported and their quality and carry out the transportation according to the specifications common in the industry; take care of the transportation requests of the agents and put in practice the nomination process; inform the shippers the balance of quality and volume, including the information about the volumes transported, volumes delivered and the inventory of crude oil in the system; establish control and inspection mechanisms needed to maintain the integrity of the transportation system and plan the maintenance and repairs required; calibrate the measuring instruments; and charge fees for the concept of transportation services according to what has been established in the fee methodology set by the Hydrocarbons Direction.

Notably, the MASD has made carriers responsible for terrorist attacks resulting in environmental damage.

449. The Carrier Manual is a document that contains information and operational and administrative procedures of the carrier which are intended to regulate the operation of the system. The Carrier Manual must include, among others, the following: description of the transportation system; rules and procedures to attend connection requests from third parties; rules and procedures for the spare capacity improvement requests, when the effective transportation capacity surplus is not enough cope with oil transportation requests from third parties; rules and procedures for the making of the transportation plan; mechanisms, assignment of responsibilities and rules to carry out the nomination process and coordination of operations; regulation for the sanctions to operating agents for non-compliance with the transportation programme; norms and procedures for measurement of quantities and quality of the crude oil being transported; procedures for the calibration of measuring instruments and applicable standards; minimum quality specifications for the crude oil being transported through the pipeline and the procedure to follow, in order to refuse those non-compliant with these specifications; quality compensation mechanisms for the blend of crudes; procedures for volumetric balance of the pipeline; calculation of losses during transportation; filling of the line in the system and volume transported; mechanisms for the response to claims of the senders and the attention to third-party requests, including terms for presentation and for the response by the carrier; procedures for coordination of operations, communications and attention of emergencies.

§4. Access to Shippers

450. There are some rules in order to grant access to shippers, e.g., petition to the carrier, available capacity and in case of controversies decision by MME; some other rules related to giving permission to build connections, e.g., technical specifications for measurement, quality and safety, the procedure to request this permission and the deadline to answer it, valid reasons to refuse permission; and some other rules describe the way to do enhancements, e.g., allocation of costs, and responsibility; procedure to notify the parties and effects of such modification in the tariff.

451. A transportation plan for, at least, the following five years indicating the yearly and monthly average as well as the available capacity must be put in place. The owner has to present the capacity for the next operational month and the consecutive five months, the shippers have to nominate their needs of volume to be transported, the procedure to offer to third parties the balance of capacity if that is the case and the way to distribute the capacity among the shippers if the capacity is not enough.

452. Lastly, the same regulation indicates the contents of the transportation arrangements and the procedure for filing claims about missing, surplus and quality of the crude oil as well as the intervention of MME to mediate in the relations among different agents.

§5. Fee Setting

453. The MME establishes the obligation to have a fee per distance travelled in the pipeline in US dollars per barrel of crude oil transported, and applicable to shippers and to third parties.[210] The procedure for setting the fee was established, including five sequential stages:

- Summons.
- Agreement among agents.
- Mediation of the Hydrocarbons Direction in case of disagreement.
- Determination of the fee by the Hydrocarbons Direction.
- Setting the fee pursuant to the distance.

454. Each stage has a detail of the procedure to be followed in time frames and actions. In the summons stage, the carrier publishes the base fee to charge for the service according to the distance travelled and summons all interested parties to register in BTO. Then the carrier sends information to the Ministry with the fee and monetary conditions, calculated according to the standard.

455. In the agreement among agents, the carrier and the parties interested in transporting, negotiate the fee and the economic conditions to reach unanimous agreement for each distance in a given period and the annual increase. If there is no agreement, the Hydrocarbons Direction of the Ministry shall gather information and listen to the agents to try to get an agreement. If there is no agreement after two meetings, the Direction sets the applicable fees.

456. In case no agreement about the fee is reached during the mediation stage of the Hydrocarbons Direction, the Resolution establishes a formula to set out the fee by the Ministry, the term and the cases that may cause a review as well as the criteria for the updating and the values to calculate it.

210. MME Resolution 124386 of 2010 and 124547 of 2010.

Chapter 4. Distribution

§1. Introduction

457. Colombia has refineries in Barrancabermeja (central part of the country) and Cartagena (Caribbean coast) of middle conversion, and those in Orito (south) and Apiay (east) of lower capacity and technology. The main refineries capacity are being enhanced in order to satisfy the country needs on fuel consumption and to improve quality and efficiency. The distribution market is shared by private companies in a very regulated and competitive environment. Some products shall be imported and transported to the main consumption locations through the pipelines infrastructure and by trucks.

458. The fuel market is ruled by a set of provisions, grouped in the Petroleum Code, as well as in other laws and decrees establishing the participants of the fuel distribution chain.[211] The agents of the distribution chain of liquid fuels derived from petroleum, with the exception of liquefied gas from petroleum, include: the refiner, the importer, the oil storage operator, the wholesaler, the carrier, the retailer, the industrial marketer and the great consumer.[212]

§2. Refining

459. Refining is a free economic activity and there are no restrictions to private participation. However, at the moment ECOPETROL is the owner of almost 90% of the refining facilities in Colombia. Although there are the necessary conditions to establish a competitive market in oil refining and imports, this market does not have an important development, as there is only one main operator.[213]

460. In order to develop construction and improvement projects for refineries, it is necessary that they be coordinated with the general development plans, for which the MME establishes the requirements and necessary procedures.[214] The ANH must set the oil volumes to be sold for internal refining,[215] with the purpose to meet internal consumption needs.

461. The refiner can only distribute fuels to: other refiners; the wholesaler; and great consumers with fixed facilities and/or using fuel for industrial burners. The special obligations of the refiner refers to maintaining calibration certificates and

211. Law 812 of 2003 and Decrees 4299 of 2005 and 1333 of 2007.
212. Article 2, Law 39 of 1987, modified by Art. 61 of Law 812 of 2003.
213. Mining Energetic Planning Unit (Planning Unit for Mining and Energy Sector (UPME)), *Petroleum Chain 2009* (Bogota, 2009).
214. Article 58, Petroleum Code, and Art. 3, Decree 2657 of 1964.
215. Article 4, Decree 4137 of 2011.

guarantees; providing information to the authorities and authorized agents; keeping records, and meeting environmental and safety standards.[216]

§3. Distribution of Liquid Fuels

462. The transportation and distribution of fuels is regulated by different norms and constitutional provisions. Liquid fuel distribution is considered a public service, therefore the State must endeavour for an efficient and correct service provision.[217] Persons and companies engaged in these activities must carry them according to the regulations issued by the government.[218] The government has the faculty to set out standards about quality, measurement and control of fuels and the sanctions that may be imposed to distributors.

463. The fuel importer must be authorized by the MME. The importer may only supply fuels through contracts to the refiner, the wholesaler, the great consumer with fixed facilities and the great consumer consuming fuels for industrial burners. Its obligations refer to having a conformity certificate, making fuel markings,[219] industrial safety rules and training to its employees and keeping of samples.

464. The oil depot owner or storage operator must be authorized, and must only render the stocking or storage service to: importers, refiners, wholesalers, and retailers earmarked to maritime and aviation stations, great consumer with fixed facilities.

465. The wholesaler must be authorized as such and must fulfil certain requirements, set up guarantees, ensure a minimum dispatch volume and have a plant with storage capacity. Its obligations refer to permits from Municipal and environmental Authorities, the storage in its own or in rented plants, the use of the brand by the retailer, supply only to the great consumer and to the retailer, industrial safety rules, permits and certifications, inspection of the tankers dispatched, addition of additives, payment of surcharges and payment of the global gasoline and diesel oil tax.

§4. Distribution: Fuel Transport

466. Fuel transport may be done through the following means: overland, pipelines, maritime, rivers, train and aerial. It can be done in their own vehicles or by third-party vehicles. The obligations are referred to permitting, guarantees, restrictions in special areas and the use of safety mechanisms. There are no technical regulations for transportation through pipelines.

---

216. MME Resolution 1180 of 2006.
217. Article 365, Political Constitution.
218. Article 212, Petroleum Code.
219. Decree 1503 of 2002 and Decree 3563 of 2003.

467. Retailer is whoever has been authorized to distribute through automotive, aviation, river or maritime service stations. There are regulations requiring the fulfilment of certain requirements according to the type of service station. The retailer's obligations refer to the permits and guarantees, restrictions in the matter of acquisition and sale of the fuels, use of the brand and log of the operations in a system called SICOM.

468. The industrial marketer is an authorized retailer with tanker trucks or with barges for the resell of fuels. Its obligations are referred to restrictions on the type of consumers. Industrial marketers may only distribute liquid fuels derived from petroleum to the final consumer that uses a volume equal to or less than 20,000 (K) gallons per month, to the great consumer without installations and to the property of the military aviation service station.[220]

469. Great Consumers are those facilities using in average more than 20K gallons of fuel per month for its own and exclusive use in its operations. There are different types of great consumers: those with fixed facilities, temporary with and without facilities. They are prohibited from acquiring fuel from several wholesalers, and must sell the fuel and register in the SICOM, among others.

470. There is a sanction regime that allows the MME to impose the following penalties:

- Fines of up to 10 units of the monthly minimum legal salary for infractions concerning permits, licenses, authorizations, information on time, technical requirements, certifications on calibration and quality and quantity of fuel released, and available capacity.
- Service suspension of up to ten days due to lack of timely payment of penalties, failing to meet the authorities' requirements, not delivering the unique transportation guide, receiving or releasing on trucks without minimum requirements, modifications of facilities without authorization, and lack of any authorization from the MME.
- Cancelling the authorization and closing down the establishment due to failures such as behaviours expressly prohibited in the regulation, false information delivered to the authority, marketing of fuels without authorization, acquisition of fuels from non-authorized person, having sanctions of service suspension twice during the last two years, by tenure, illicit trafficking and trade in fuels, and more than ten days of suspension with the same sanctioned behaviour.

220. Decree 4299 of 2005, modified by Decree 1717 of 2008.

§5. Price Regime for Liquid Fuels

471. It is the duty of the MME to set the prices of products derived from petroleum throughout all the production and distribution chain for automotive gasoline, diesel fuel and, additionally the price of biofuels and alcohol with hydrocarbons.[221]

472. The pricing policy for the consumption of fuels within the country aims to its internationalization and liberation. This policy intends to equalize real production cost and the marketing of fuels. It also intends to create competitive conditions starting with the entry of new agents and reducing the weight of ECOPETROL's share. For this, imports have been encouraged and the access to the transportation infrastructure has been eased.[222]

473. Gasoline price has four components: the income received by the refineries for the processing of the crude oil; the value of the fuel alcohol, a biofuel to reduce the pollution levels; the payments for marketing (wholesale distribution, service stations and transportation); and a tax load (including sales tax, global tax and surcharges, which are not applied to biofuels, except the diesel surcharge).[223]

474. The current regime is based on the following measures:[224]

- the income of the refiner or producer is linked to the gasoline and diesel fuel price through a parity with the export price;
- regulated freedom regime for the different capital cities of the country and its metropolitan areas, which consists in setting a maximum selling price for combustibles to the final consumer. These fuels include: standard automotive oxygenated gasoline, standard automotive gasoline and diesel fuel and blends of diesel fuel with biofuels for diesel motors; (this system abolished the regulated freedom in the main capitals, with which there was a liberation of margins for retail distribution); and
- price differential between gasoline and diesel fuel in favour of the later. In summary, the regulation of the sector consists in the existence of de-facto regulated prices for refining and imports, regulated wholesaler margins, regulated retail margins for the main capitals of the Country and for other areas.

§6. Contractual Regime in the Marketing of Petroleum Derivatives

475. As a rule of thumb, there are no restrictions on the type of contract that sign the agents of the marketing chain of hydrocarbons derivatives. It is required that certain contracts be put in place during the process of authorization for its operation by

221. Article 3, s. 1, Decree 4130 of 2011.
222. Resolution 82438 of 1998.
223. UPME, *Petroleum Chain 2009*.
224. MME Resolution 181047 of 2011.

the MME. The importer must prove the existence of a storage and distribution contract; the wholesale distributor must have fuel supply contracts with other wholesale distributors, with retail distributors or with great consumers with certain characteristics, such as the right to use the brand. The retail distributor and the industrial marketer must have a supply contract with the wholesaler and the great consumer must have a supply contract.

Chapter 5. Consumption

476. There is not regulation about this topic.

Part IV. Regulatory Framework Concerning Coal

Chapter 1. Production

477. Coal has historically meant a resource for the energetic basket. Based on that, coal had a special and distinctive set of rules for its promotion and project development for many years.

478. Due to Colombia's scarcity of oil supply, coal was considered an option for the country's energy supply. For years, this condition of strategic resource led to a special legal framework for coal exploration and exploitation. Due to the new policy towards the energetic transition to renewable energies and the decarbonization of the economy, coal is no longer in the energy basket.

§1. History of Coal Regulation

I. Spanish Empire Regulations

479. Our mining legal system has its roots in the Spanish Empire regulations, which ruled the new world and the Viceroyalty of Nueva Granada for many years. The main ruling recognizing sovereign rights to the Crown, and stating the means to obtain mining rights and perform operations were contained in the following laws and decrees:

- Law of Partidas: Rendered by King Alfonso the Wise.
- Ruling of Alcala of 1384: It was issued by King Alfonso XI in 1384, reaffirming the property of the Crown over the mines, and the need of a royal authorization for individuals to exploit mines.
- Birbiesca Ordinance of 1387: It was enacted by the King Juan I in 1387, and implemented a new way as to mine searching, prospection and excavation. The license and mandate procedure was no longer necessary, though the developer had to paid royalties.
- Noverint Universi papal bull of 4 May 1493: Pope Alexander VI, the Borgia, drew a meridian to settle the dispute over the territories administered by Spain and Portugal. Since 1492, the Bull recognized to the Crown of Spain the property on the hills to discover the territories one hundred leagues west of the Azores

Islands or Cape Verde. Both the mountains and the mines of America were subject to special arrangements. The mountains were transferred and the mines in operation were granted through the 'royal favours', paying royalties to the King.
- Royal Decree of 9 December 1526: King 'Carlos I' issued this decree in Granada and it was firstly applied in America. The decree incorporated the mines of America into the Spanish Royal Crown.
- Valladolid Ordinance of 10 January 1559: This Ordinance was issued by King Philip II in Valladolid in 1559 and granted the Crown property rights over the mines of gold, silver and mercury.
- Ordinances of St. Lawrence of 22 August 1584: These ordinances were issued also by King Philip II, revoking all previous laws and ordinances on metal mines. These mines were given to the kingdom of Castile, but were subsequently extended to all realms of the monarchy of Spain. The ordinances were established in America via the 3rd Act, Book II of the Indies Compendium.
- The Compendium of Indies: It was enacted by King Charles II by Royal Decree of 18 May 1680. As its name implies, it contains a compilation of laws and ordinances of the Spanish Crown applicable to its colonies.
- The Mining Ordinances of New Spain of 22 May 1783: these ordinances state the Crown's ownership over the mines, and extend its domain to non-metallic mines, especially coal. The exploration phase is considered implicit in the mining activity, and the reason was that exploration is prior to the discovery of a reservoir.

480. It is worthwhile commenting that these rulings referred mainly to mining rights over metals deposits.

481. The history of coal mining industry in Colombia is almost as old as the beginning of our nation, and starts in 1780 when the Spanish Empire ordered to promote the consumption of coal, in order to prevent forest clearing and wasteful consumption of wood. For the same purpose, by Law 2 of 1789, coal trading and trafficking by land and sea was declared free, for it was not a metal or other substance declared as state-owned resources.

482. It was a principle then, as for other mineral substances, that coal did not belong to His Majesty the King but was part of the property of the landowners, provided that they burned it permanently.

II. Independence Years

483. Having gained independence from Spain, the Liberator Simon Bolivar issued the first national mining statute on 24 October 1829.

484. Later on, in the Grenadine Confederation and upon the issuance of the Constitution of 1858, the Nation reserved the rights on emeralds, rock salt and salt sheds, which left Sovereign States the domain over other minerals, including coal. At this stage, the Confederation did not recognize any importance to this mineral.

485. The approach gradually changed with Law 69 of 1867. This act, issued by the United States of Colombia, established that the demarcation of public and private lands included those lands called *Cerrejón* in the Department of Padilla, sovereign State of Magdalena, which contained coal. The purpose was to request information about the location and characteristics of a coal deposit, as well as quality and quantity, and to establish how exploitation could be carried out. Due to the scarce technical capacity of the State, Law 69 of 1867 authorized the government to incorporate a company abroad with public and foreign capital for the development of mining projects. The terms had to be advantageous to the national interest and subject to congressional approval.

486. In order to keep this idea, the State 'reserved' the ownership of mining coal deposits.[225] These deposits could not be sold or granted with the land where they lay. The State had to enter into contracts administered by the Federal government in order to access those deposits. The same power was conferred to the State to benefit from privately owned reserves, under the condition that they were previously offered to their owners through contracts.

487. In those days, the mining industry represented public and national interest, which encouraged the State to promote this activity. Law 13 of 1868 empowered the Executive to 'build railways or roads, canals to connect the operating points, and sea ports and river valleys, where appropriate, to give way to coal, and the docks, piers and other works necessary in such ports'. This was applicable to all mines and coal deposits located on vacant land in the entire country, not just in the State of Magdalena. For the time being, coal gained prominence in the local economy.

488. Subsequently, and improving the regulatory framework for the development of the coal industry, through Law 90 of 1873 the Executive was authorized to enter into contracts of up to sixty years with individuals, for the design and implementation of mining projects. The project included the construction of a railway from the port of Riohacha to coal mines within this district and, if feasible, in Salguero port on the Cesar river, going through the municipalities of Barranca, Fonseca, San Juan del Cesar and Valledupar. This project was free of taxes and import tariffs. The government also foresaw the free reversion of all property and free deposits to the State, at the end of the contract.

489. Later, after the promulgation of the Constitution of 1886 on the new Unitary Republic, mines of non-precious metals and non-metals existing in public lands by 28 October 1873, became property of the nation. The nation, hence, took over property over coal mines.

490. As for the vacant lots that had been transferred to private holders, it was decided that those mines would be respected as constituted in favour of third parties by the Sovereign States, and were excluded from the assignment to the Unitary

225. Law 13 of 1868.

Republic. This meant that those rights granted by States on mines and mineral rights of private property during the federal period, would be respected in the future.

III. Republican Legal Framework

491. The Mining Code of the former Sovereign State of Antioquia was adopted at national level, by Law 38 of 1887. This code kept the reserve on coal deposits and excluded such deposits from the granting process, when located in vacant lots. However, in relation to the reservoirs located on private land, the situation was different.

492. Concerning precious metals, owners had one year to look, search and report any mines on their land. It was silent in relation to mines other than metals, including those of coal. Many legal discussions arose about the possibility to claim private ownership of underground coal in this period. That is why Law 20 of 1969 is considered a milestone in the history of mining in Colombia. Thanks to this law it was clear that in the future, regardless of the underground type of mining ore, they all belonged to the Nation.

493. Therefore, the rights of individuals on mines allotted, redeemed or purchased by perpetual accession to subsurface soil and other similar titles, would be respected only if they acquired, maintained and exercised mining over 'discovered deposits'.

494. It should be recalled that Law 20 of 1969 determined that the mines owned by the Nation declared as special reserve could only be exploited by concession or '*aporte*' given to industrial and commercial or mixed owned State companies, and it had special implications for reservoir coal, which were declared as a special reserve. Another important idea is the acknowledgment of coal as an energy resource of national importance. That is why by Decrees 1704 and 2533 of 1973 almost all coal deposits are declared special reserves.

495. By Law 61 of 1979, better known as the 'Coal Law', was then determined that the exploration and exploitation of coal could only be done by the 'aporte' system, through the industrial and commercial companies of State ownership. The 'aporte' system was adopted to perform a public policy. According to this policy, the Colombian State was in charge of performing mining activities as any other entrepreneur and a mining title called 'aporte' was granted to its companies incorporated with this special purpose. It thus sought to give special status to the development of projects related to this resource, again considered as strategic for the Nation. To this purpose, these state-owned companies were not subject to limited areas, or the terms of exploration, construction and operations, or any other permitting systems.

496. The Coal Law also created the National Fund for Coal as an account management system, aimed at financing projects and programmes of exploration, exploitation, benefit, transportation, shipping and marketing of coal, with resources from the newly created coal tax. The duty on coal was equal to 5% of the mine ore production at mine mouth, and was due as of 1 January 1980. Non-coking coal used in thermal power plants for public service, production of synthetic fuels and other products that replaced the use of hydrocarbons, was exempted from the tax.

497. In order to complement the regulatory framework, Decree 1155 was issued in 1980 authorizing state-owned companies receiving 'aporte' to carry out the work of prospecting, exploration and construction, transportation infrastructure construction and shipping coal, ore processing and marketing, directly or through partnership with private company or persons. The contracts used for this purpose included operation, services, administration or any other class of agreements.

498. Mining association contracts, widely used in the coal industry, were often seen as exotic, given its special features.

499. Another stage of the coal industry occurred with the enactment of Decree 2655 of 1988 or the Mining Code, adopted by the National Government, when it was still possible to issue codes by decree. With this code, funds were created to promote mining, such as the account management systems (*sistema especial de cuentas*) designed to provide earmarked financial resources to the mining industry in all its activities, technical and financial assistance, and improvement of social and economic conditions for small and medium mining operations. In line with this idea, Decree 2655 of 1988 created the Coal Development Fund for the same purposes, but geared exclusively to the coal industry. The new Mining Code also established categories for mining activities: small, medium and large scale mining, with some differences, such as technical and environmental obligations.

500. Concerning coal contracts concluded under the 'aporte' system, which was a mining title held by the industrial and commercial companies of the State, Resolution 24 of 1994[226] established criteria for the development of large mining projects. Due to these regulatory provisions, the Nation launched large coal projects based on contracts such as Cerrejón and La Loma from the early eighties. As a result, Decree 2056 of 1996 was issued defining the system of allotment for five large coal mining areas known as: Cerrejón South, Cesarito, Guaimaral, El Descanso and El Hatillo, where some big mining projects are being developed today.

501. After several years, there was widespread criticism on the 'aporte' mining regime in Colombia, based on the State performance as entrepreneur, which eventually led to its demise. However, it is pertinent to mention that this system gave way to major initiatives, such as the mining and rescue programme of technical assistance and training to small miners. These initiatives improved the operational conditions in productive region's coal mines.

226. Replaced by Resolution 81468 of 1994.

502. The most important regulatory statutes aforementioned were the result of the exercise of extraordinary powers.[227] They were also adopted as part of the emergency powers given to the government, such as the Mining Code of 1954. Other regulations were issued on the basis of the government's regulatory powers with limited scope.[228] Since the issuance of the 1991 National Constitution, it was no longer possible to issue codes by the government, for this authority was embedded in the Congress. Pursuant to a constitutional clause, the Congress is the only authority empowered to issue or amend codes in all branches of law, as provided in section 10 of Article 150.

IV. 2001 Mining Code: Current Legislation

503. Law 685 of 2001 approves the Mining Code of 2001, which is the first Mining Code that Congress issued since 1887, when it adopted for the whole nation the Mining Code of the extinct Sovereign State of Antioquia (Law 38 of 1887). The 2001 Mining Code is the current applicable legislation as modified by emerging legislation including the laws of the national development plan.[229]

504. The Mining Code redefines the role of the government as non-entrepreneur, and facilitator of the development of mining activities by private persons. The emphasis of this role focuses on overseeing developers' compliance with mining obligations, and dictating the mining policy, plans and projects to support mining.

505. Concerning mining operations, the Code sought to ensure that projects where economically, technically and environmentally feasible, regardless of their extension. For the exploration and exploitation of coal, the provisions of the Mining Code did not differentiate between coal deposits and other minerals and metals. The granting system is the same for every type of mining project. This orientation was recently modified through Law 1753 of 2015 and Decree 1666 of 2016 by bringing back a differentiation between large-, medium- and small-scale projects, with the sole purpose of implementing a policy by which the small miners' obligations are less rigid and demanding.

506. Due to criticism of the permitting system, the modifications of the Mining Code through Law 1735 of 2015 included the possibility of having reserved areas to be granted through special contracts with additional requisites and obligations, regarding the so-called 'strategic minerals'. Therefore, the applicable law for these types of contracts will be partly the Mining Code and the contract's own provisions, previously negotiated. Obtaining additional considerations and other benefits for the State are the goals of these new contracts. A bid shall be implemented, so the best proposal is selected to obtain the concession.

---

227. For example, Decrees 223 of 1932, and 2514, 1952, 2665 of 1988.
228. For example, Decrees 805 of 1947, 2419*bis*, 1958, 1163, 1967, 292, 1968 and 1275 of 1970.
229. Law 1450 of 2011, Law 1753 of 2015 and Law 1955 of 2019.

§2. PRINCIPLES

507. The basic principles of mining law in Colombia include.

– State Ownership of Mineral Deposits

508. Article 4 of the Mining Code states that the minerals of any kind and location, lying on the ground or underground in any natural physical state, are the exclusive property of the State. This principle applies regardless of the ownership or tenure of the land. Where individual, subjective and concrete rights over private property titles are based on earlier laws, the principle will not apply.

509. However, if those with property rights over ground and underground mines fail to explore and/or exploit them for more than twelve continuous months, without good cause that constitutes a fortuitous event or force majeure, their rights will be considered expired.

510. No activity of prospecting, exploration or exploitation or physical possession of such resources, whatever their age, duration or characteristics, confer any right or priority to acquire mining title or oppose against title applications from third parties.

– Mining Activities and Investigation Is of Public Interest

511. Article 13 of the Mining Code provides that the mining industry is of public interest and social benefit in all its branches and phases. The status of public interest and social benefit translates into the promotion of technical exploration and exploitation of mineral resources of public property as well as the privately owned.

512. According to the mining law, regional research and global subsurface is considered of public interest, for it seeks to obtain, complete and deepen the knowledge of the country's potential in mineral resources and subsurface soil. The results of these studies should be part of the National System of Mining and Geo-Scientific Information Service. Research and studies will in any event be coordinated by the State or by the Geologic Service at the national level.

– Mining Is a Regulated Activity

513. Access to mining subsoil resources is only possible through a mining title granted by the Mining Authority, prior compliance with the legal requirements and conditions.

514. The concessionaire, title holder, is considered an independent contractor for purposes of all civil, commercial and labour contracts. In carrying out the work, studies and exploration work, assembly, construction, operation, trading and transformation, the concessionaire has complete technical, industrial, economic and commercial autonomy.

515. The concessionaire can choose the nature, form and order of execution of the systems and processes and to freely determine the location, movement and timing of use and dedication of staff, equipment, facilities and works, within the legal framework.

516. The public agency that grants concession titles and the environmental authority carry out control activities to ensure proper conservation of resources purpose, and compliance with health and safety standards and environmental sustainable mining.

– Sustainable Mining

517. Article 1 of Law 685 of 2001 provides that the use of mineral resources must be done in harmony with the principles and norms of rational exploitation of non-renewable natural resources and the environment. The concession agreement involves environmental obligations included in the respective environmental license, which must be guaranteed by the concessionaire.

– Legal Certainty of Mining Rights

518. Perhaps, the most valued principle is the legal certainty of the mining concession. This principle involves different aspects.

519. The regulation provides exhaustive knowledge and consistent application of the rules by compiling and promulgating it in an orderly and logical way. It creates harmony among its numerous and diverse components so that all constitute a conceptual and policy system, properly integrated.

520. There is a limited listing of requirements and formalities, which develop Article 84[230] of the Constitution and makes mining operation more reliable. No authority may establish or require permits, licenses or additional requirements for the submission of applications or for granting of, execution or exercise of the mining title.

521. The principle of preferred application is granted in favour of mining developers, for it prevents general law to be applied to mining activities.

522. Transparency requirements on the pre-contract phase refer to the objective selection of the contractor. This selection is made by the simple criterion to implement the principle of first come first served (*prior tempore, prior jure*), known and accepted in traditional mining laws in Colombia, specially in Articles 270, 274 and 299 of the Mining Code. This principle would no longer be applicable to the so called strategic resources.

230. Article 84. When a right or an activity has been regulated in a general way, the public authorities may not establish or demand permits, licenses, or impose additional conditions for its exercise.

523. Unlike previous regulations (Decree 1275 of 1970 and the Mining Code of 1988), which established separate and distinct mining rights for all the stages of the mining project, the Code of 2001 establishes a unique title to all these stages or phases. The mining title must fulfil the same procedures and requirements to be valid.

524. The administrative protection and the expropriation of goods for the development of mining activities are considered protective measures in favour of the mining title holder. Administrative protection refers to the right of the concessionaire against incursions or trespassing from third parties. It is a measure of police that seeks to prevent or halt visible disorders that disturb public order or harmony among citizens, instead of final ruling on rights or preferences. These disorders occur when works from individuals invade the concessionaire's activities or simply disrupt or impede operations.

525. In exceptional situations, the Code opened the possibility of ordering the expropriation of goods or land for the benefit of miners. This expropriation is possible whenever reasons of public interest or social benefit arise, as previously defined in the law.

– Permanent Work in Mines

526. Given the importance of the mining industry, the regulatory framework provides for the preservation of workers' rights. The unjustified suspension of operations without prior permission exposes the concessionaire to losing its mining rights.

Chapter 2. Exploitation

§1. Licensing Regime

527. The first application or proposal of concession does not confer in itself the right to enter into a concession agreement with the State. Regarding third parties, the first application only confers the right of preference to obtain such concession, if it complies with all legal requirements.

528. The licensing process concludes with the issuance of the Concession Agreement. This agreement involves three main stages: exploration, construction and assembling, and exploitation. Prospection activities are not part of the mining concession granting procedure.

I. Prospection

529. Prospection is legally defined as a process to investigate the existence of minerals and delimiting promising areas. Prospection methods consist, among others, in the identification of rock exposure, geological cartography, geophysical and geochemistry studies, and superficial investigation in areas that are not subject to exclusive rights.

530. Prospection of mines is free and no mining concession is required, except in territories defined as mining areas for ethnic minorities, where an authorization of the community is required.[231]

531. When prospection has to be done in areas of private ownership, a previous notice has to be given to the owner, holder or tenure, directly or through the Mayor of the municipality. When it has to be done in areas of public service under jurisdiction of the General Marine Agency (DIMAR), its favourable technical concept will be required, pursuant to Article 2 of Decree-Law 2324 of 1984.

II. Mining Concession: Application Procedure

A. Applicant

532. According to the Mining Code, the following can be applicants for a mining concession:

- National and foreign legally capable individuals.
- National corporations whose by-laws include the exploration and exploitation of mines, as part of its main businesses.

231. Article 39, Mining Code. Prospection is understood as the previous activities to a technical exploration.

- Foreign corporations with a branch in Colombia. This is needed when applicants are to sign the Concession agreement.
- Joint ventures. In case of setting a joint venture, a branch must be established in Colombia.
- Partnerships. Under this structure, the participants of the partnership are jointly liable for the obligations from the concession agreement.

B. Application Requirements

533. The application is called 'proposal for a concession agreement' and it can be submitted electronically. The electronic application form requires the following information:

About the Area

- Identification of the municipality, department and the environmental authority of the area or route location.
- Description of the area covered by the application and its extension.
- Indication of the mineral or minerals in the application.
- Mention of ethnic groups permanently settled in the requested area. If applicable, the applicant must indicate whether part or the whole area is inhabited by Indigenous people, Afro-Colombian or mixed communities. If so, the applicant must include a concept according to Article 35. This article refers to urban perimeter of cities and municipalities, areas occupied by rural constructions, areas of special archaeological, historical or cultural interest, beaches and fluvial paths served by public transportation companies, areas occupied by public works or attached to a public service and indigenous mining areas and afro-Colombian mining areas. In these cases an authorization of the beneficiary or responsible of the area is required.
- Indication of the terms of reference and guidelines to be applied in mining exploration work and the estimation of the investment amount, after applying such terms and guidelines.
- A map that meets the specifications laid down in Articles 66 and 67 of the Code.

Project Information

- A technical appendix describing exploration works has to be included, which must be at or above a minimum standard fixed by the MME, according to the area and the characteristics of the mining project.
- The requirement for information in the technical appendix has been increased with labour and environmental sufficiency data. Due to a Constitutional Court ruling,[232] the terms of reference of the technical appendix were modified. Labour aspects according to Article 251 of the Mining Code and Environmental aspects

232. Constitutional Court, Ruling C-389 of 2016.

in compliance with Articles 198 and 272 were adjusted in order to require specific personnel and activities to perform a minimum and necessary works for exploration. The developer must indicate what kind of professional will be in charge of the specific activity and equipment required. These new information requirements tend to assure the sustainability of mining works.

Applicant's Information

- Name and identification number of the applicant.
- In case of projects over 150 ha, the applicant has to demonstrate economic capacity. This capacity must meet the criteria set by the MME, which is proportional to the requested area. If the applicant lacks the necessary financial capacity, it may require a third party to provide the funds and to guarantee the investment. That third party is required to prove the legal and financial capacity. If the documentation required to prove the legal and financial capacity comes from abroad, it must be translated into Spanish and meet the requirements of Colombian law.
- Proof of payment of the surface fee for the first year of exploration.
- Information about other miners: indication of the existence of some kind of mining activities, with its location and the methodology used to determine the existence of such mine.
- A special regime has been adopted for the small-scale projects, that voluntarily can be accessed. The maximum area is 100 ha, and it is only applicable to a single contract. These special conditions apply to areas of traditional miners who apply for legalization of their irregular conditions, primarily, but can also be used by new applicants with small projects willing to be subjects of this new legal framework.

Mining Grid System

As of 2018, mining titles and proposals in process were migrated to a mining grid system. New mining proposals must be submitted based on this system to establish the geographical coordinates of the areas of interest.

Additionally, the administration of mining titles is carried out through a platform called 'ANNA MINERIA' that eliminates paper handling and systematizes all processes and procedures. All information and obligations compliance must be filled in the platform. Access codes must be obtained by users (titleholders, lawyers, geologists, engineers, accountants) according to the role they play in the administration of a mining title.

III. Project Viability

534. Based on the legal stipulations and regulations in force, the structure of an extractive mining project in Colombia requires demonstrating the feasibility of four basic aspects:

(1) Technical: The technical feasibility of the exploitation is taken from positive results of exploration activities, according to the report of exploration regarding resources and reserves. These results allow designing a Program of Mining Works for exploitation, based on the terms of reference adopted by the MME.[233]
(2) Financial: It is presumed that the exploitation will be economically profitable due to the quantity and quality of the mineral found during exploration, and, likewise, it is also part of the Program of Mining Works as financial commitment of investment.[234]
(3) Environmental: Environmental feasibility means that the exploitation must be environmentally sustainable. This aspect is proved by obtaining the environmental license, which is subject to compliance with legal requirements and the submission of an Environmental Impact Study (*Estudio de Impacto Ambiental* – EIS). There is one exception to this rule, in the case of activities initiated prior to the issuance of Law 99 of 1993. These activities are subject to a transitory regime and require an Environmental Management Plan instead of an environmental license.[235]

    Mining activities are prohibited in designated and defined zones according to regulations the protection and development of renewable natural resources or the environment.[236] Exceptionally, if the area is located in areas with environmental restrictions, the interested party must carry out the appropriate procedure in order to process the corresponding environmental license.[237]
(4) Social: There are two obligations related to the attention and management of social impacts in mining: (i) one derived from the concession contract and the other (ii) derived from the environmental license:

According to mining legislation there is a contractual obligation to provide a Social Management Plan which consists of a management instrument that includes programmes, projects and activities to prevent, mitigate and address the social risks generated by the mining project, as well as to increase the opportunities and benefits that it can generate.

From the environmental perspective, the social aspect is part of the environmental license and corresponds to the chapter on social impacts, which must be positive. Should the social impact be negative, it has to be properly mitigated and compensated. The Mining Social Management Plan produced for the National Mining Agency (NMA) can improve and add to any measures suggested and included in the environmental license.

535. Finally, since 2018 Colombia is a member of CRIRSCO (Committee for Mineral Reserves International Reporting Standards) and the international standard

233. Articles 80, 82, 84, 89.
234. Articles 271, 80.
235. Decree 1753 of 1994 and Decree 2041 of 2014.
236. Decree 2372 of 2010.
237. Law 1450 of 2010 and Resolution 1526 of 2012.

was adopted through the 'Colombian Standard for the Public Reporting of Exploration Results, Mineral Resources and Reserves –ECRR'. Therefore, the exploration works and its results have to prove sufficient reserves to justify the exploitation project, applying the modifying factors (technical, economical, social etc.) that may have an impact on the project's development.

§2. Mining Concession

I. Characteristics

536. The mining concession is an administrative agreement involving the State as part of the contract. For that reason, public law and its principles apply to this kind of agreement. The law itself gives it a distinctive name to the concession agreement.[238] This nomination limits the possibility to use analogue criteria to assimilate the concession agreement to other existing contracts in administrative, civil or commercial law.[239]

537. In order to execute the agreement, it must be embedded in a written document and meet certain formalities, apart from the covenants. In the absence of such formalities the agreement becomes unenforceable or no legal effect is produced. The requirement of formalities has, besides conservation purposes and material durability, binding and advertising effects of undeniable importance and usefulness to the contractors and to third parties.

538. The mining concession is also a standard form contract, also known as a standard contract. The contractor has no possibility to negotiate the terms and conditions of the agreement.[240] In consequence, the agreement's terms, conditions and procedures are all contained in the Code regardless of the quality of the contractor and the nature and size of its works and operations, besides what has been adopted as a special regime for small-scale miners. As an exception to the general rule of the administrative law and public contracts, the mining concession agreement cannot be modified, finished or interpreted unilaterally by the authority.[241]

539. The NMA has adopted the standard form of the mining concession agreement, which provides the contractual terms and conditions for the exploration, construction and exploitation of the mineral resource.[242] This contract form has been modified by the government with the purpose to strengthen the mining industry while ensuring that activities are developed in a sustainable fashion.

238. Article 14, Mining Code.
239. Article 45, *ibid.*
240. Article 49, *ibid.*
241. Article 51, *ibid.*
242. National Mining Agency, Resolution 420 of 2013, modified by Resolution 409 of 2015.

540. The State ownership over non-renewable natural resources is inalienable and not subject to limitations in time.[243] The right to explore and exploit can only be acquired through a mining concession,[244] which does not confer ownership rights to the ore in-situ but a temporary right to appropriate the ore.

541. The State is not obliged to guarantee the existence of the minerals or the viability of its technical and economic exploitation.[245] Accordingly, the concessionaire shall not claim payment, reimbursement or compensation for not finding minerals in quantity or quality that makes them marketable. The State may be responsible in the event that third parties, based on mining rights registered in the Mining Register before the conclusion of the contract, deprive the State from all or part of the contracted area.

II. Contractual Stages

542. The mining concession covers different project phases. All stages and phases of the project are included in the contract. The agreement's purpose is to perform exploration, installation, construction and assembly of mining infrastructure, the commercial exploitation of the extracted minerals, the trading of production and the closure or abandonment of mining pits and the environmental restoration works.

543. The periods for each state include:

- Exploration: Within the three years following the date of the contract registration, the concessionaire should make the technical exploration of the contracted area. Upon request of the applicant, an inferior period of exploration can be indicated in the concession agreement, as long as it does not imply liberating him from the minimum obligations required during this phase of the agreement.
- Construction and assembling: Once the period of exploration has ended, the period of three years will start for the construction and erection of equipment for the exploitation works and operations.
- Exploitation: The maximum period of exploitation will be the time of the concession minus the periods of exploration, construction and assembling, with its deferrals.

544. Extension of contractual milestones. The Mining Code provides different rules for each phase of the contract. For the exploration phase, the concessionaire can only request the extension for periods of two consecutive years until completing eleven years, provided that each extension is justified and has carried out the basic works called phase Iso that the necessary studies are completed to determine

243. Article 5, *ibid.*
244. Article 14, *ibid.*
245. Article 56, *ibid.*

the existence of minerals and the economic feasibility of its extraction. For the construction and assembling phase, the extension may only be requested for an additional year, which, if granted, automatically extends the exploitation period of the concession. In order to request the extension of contractual phases, concessionaires must demonstrate they have complied with all contractual obligations and have paid any penalties imposed by the authority.[246]

545. In an attempt to further regulate the requirements for the extension of contractual phases, the MME issued Decree 943 of 2013. Some of the conditions included in this piece of legislation for contract extension included submission of technical reasons and economic perspectives, fulfilment of Mining and Environmental Guidelines, description of works to be executed, specification of the duration of the works, investments to be made, and payments of the exploration surface fee. The Council of State has considered that the national government, through the MME, exceeded its regulatory power when issuing Decree 943 of 2013. In the Council's view, this decree creates additional requirements of those established in the Mining Code and does not, as it was intended, provide further detail on the existing conditions. At the moment, some of the provisions of Decree 943 of 2013 have been eliminated by the Council of State.[247]

546. In addition, the NMA has adopted a *Unique protocol for evaluating mining contract extensions*. It is applicable to the mining contracts of all existing legal regimes.

547. According to the protocol, extending the term of these contracts is feasible to the extent that it is demonstrated that the extension will benefit the State by increasing or maintaining the value of the mining project. The extension is no longer an acquired right, which is why the mining concessionaire must prove it will be able to offer more and better conditions to the State, if additional years are granted to the project. The Colombian Standard for the Public Reporting of Exploration Results, Mineral Resources and Reserves – ECRR is an important tool to prove feasibility of the extension.

548. The concessionaire may also request a deferral of the period of construction and assembling for a term of up to one year.

246. Articles 74 and 76, *ibid.*
247. Council of State, Third Section, Sentence of 30 Apr. 2014, Magistrate: Carlos Alberto Zambrano Barrera.

§3. SPECIAL REQUIREMENTS

I. Open Pit and Underground Mining

549. Mining can be performed in open pit or underground exploitation. There are specific mining and environmental requirements depending on the selected system. The requirements are fixed in the terms of reference issued by the authorities according to Article 278 of the Mining Code. The terms of reference for mining studies were issued through Resolution 18-0859 of 2002.

550. There are also technical restrictions on health and safety for open pit and underground mining, which are included in Decrees 133 of 1987 and 222 of 1993. Breaching the technical rules is cause for termination of the concession.

II. Environmental Restrictions

551. Through recent national development plan laws, changes were included in the mining legislation to harmonize it with environmental legislation with regards to excluded and restricted areas for mining.

552. The zones excluded from mining activities are those that have been established as areas that integrate the national natural parks system. They also include regional natural parks, protected forest reserve areas, protective and other areas of forest reserves, as well as *páramo* ecosystems and wetlands designated in the list of the international Ramsar Convention.

553. These zones, in order to be mining excluded areas, must be geographically defined by the environmental authority based on technical, social and environmental studies. Law 1450 of 2011 adopted the Von Humboldt's cartographic information as the official limits of the 'páramo lands', and Law 1753 of 2015 gave more clarity over the issue. Several resolutions from the MASD have declared and delimited the different 'Paramos' as the law required. Some are still pending declaration due to the socio-environmental conflicts derived from the mining and agricultural activities of the population.

554. In addition, Law 1930 of 2018 or Paramos Law, in its Article 10, provided that the MME and their attached or linked entities and territorial entities, in coordination with the Regional Autonomous Corporations, and under the guidelines of the MASD, must design, train and implement substitution and reconversion programmes for the activities of small traditional miners.

§4. Royalties and Compensation

555. The concessionaire must pay the Colombian State royalties and compensations during exploration, construction and exploitation of state-owned minerals as follows:

I. Surface Fee

556. The surface fee is paid during exploration and construction. The payment shall be equivalent to an SMDLV for each hectare per year, from the first to the fifth year; and from then, the payment shall increase every two additional years as follows:

- sixth and seventh year: the payment shall be equal to 1.25 minimum legal wage per legal valid day for each hectare per year; and
- eighth year: the payment shall be equal to 1.50 minimum legal wage per legal valid day for each hectare per year.

557. The surface fee must be paid in advance every year. The first year should be paid ten days after the concession is registered in the National Mining Registry. For any additional construction, assembly and exploration activities, the same payment than for the exploration shall be made. The concessionaire must pay the surface fee, regardless of the project land owners.

II. Royalties

558. Royalties must be paid during the exploitation stage. Every exploitation project generates royalties as a compulsory counter-benefit. This consists of a percentage, fixed or progressive, of the exploited gross product and its sub-products, calculated or measured at the mine mouth, payable in currency or in kind. It the reception of minerals coming from natural sources that are technically considered mines triggers the payment of royalties.

559. In the case of private owners of the subsoil, they have to pay no less than 0.4% of the value of the production, calculated or measured in the same way as state-owned minerals.

560. The amount of royalties and the system to liquidate and readjust them is the one applicable at the entry into force of the concession agreement, which remains applicable during the concession term. According to the Mining Code, any amendments on royalties or compensations only affect the contracts celebrated and completed after the entry into force of such modifications.

III. Other Compensations

561. In addition to royalties, the concession agreement can establish other compensations for the exploitation of the subsoil's natural resources. For example, additional payments to the State, increase in publicly owned shares, or participation in higher prices.

§5. Special Concessions and CBM

I. Reserved Areas and Special Concessions

562. As a result of the new mining policy and the issuance of Law 1450 of 2011 there is a possibility of creating new reserved areas to explore and exploit strategic minerals. According to Resolution 180241 of 2012, these areas are reserved where ordinary concessions cannot be granted.

563. The State also reserved some specific minerals and metals to be granted through special concession agreements.[248] Some of these minerals are gold, silver, platinum, iron ore, copper, uranium and thermal and metallurgic coal. Those concession agreements will be granted through open bids in which the participants are compelled to offer the best technical, financial, environmental and social conditions to explore and exploit the deposits, in order to be a beneficiary of a concession agreement.

II. Coal Bed Methane

564. The legal nature of coal bed methane was uncertain in Colombia until legal issues arose and decisions on the matter were taken. The Mining Code establishes that, in addition to minerals included in the concession agreement, the concessionaire has the right to exploit those minerals that are linked or associated with them or that are obtained as sub-products of the exploitation.

565. The legal definition of this concept involves:

- Intimately linked: it refers to those minerals that make part of the material extracted and which separation can be only obtained by means of subsequent physical and chemical processes of beneficiation.
- Sub-product: It is considered that one mineral is a sub-product of the concessionaire's exploitation, when it is necessarily extracted together with that mineral established in the contract, and that due to its quality and amount it would not be economically exploitable in a separate form.
- Associated minerals: it refers to those minerals that make integral part of the mineralized body object of the concession contract.

---

248. Resolution 180201 of 2012.

566. Concerning the coal bed methane, it has been asked whether or not it can be considered one of these kinds of products to which the concessionaire has the right to exploit. The answer was given by the CONPES, responsible at the highest level for coordinating the economic policy in Colombia. During a CONPES of 12 May 2008 a document was produced setting out recommendations on this matter to both the MME and the ANH. The document expresses the matter as follows:

> 'The methane gas in coal deposits (GMDC) is a naturally occurring gas in unconventional reservoirs, which is part of the energy supply of fossil fuels. The behaviour of the supply and demand for oil is associated with the growing need for energy from different sources … ' '(…) Countries like USA, Canada, Australia, South Africa and India have legislation that classifies the GMDC as a hydrocarbon, and not as part or component of coal subject to the rules of it.
>
> Gases in unconventional reservoirs are those which are different from those in reservoirs where the natural gas occurs. These gases are typically included: (…) and iii) the methane gas in coal deposits'.[249]

567. The CONPES concept perfectly coincides with the universally accepted standard under which methane gas from coal beds is an unconventional source of natural gas. This view is based on the fact that, with respect to methane gas from coal seams, the recovery process in the ground is very different from that applied in conventional fields.

568. As a result of the analysis of the technical definitions in the CONPES and the recommendations to the ANH, under the new interpretation the Mining Code cannot be applied to bed methane deposits. Due to the fact that the coal bed methane was defined as a hydrocarbon, then Article 2 of the Mining Code applies and expressly states that the exploration and exploitation of liquid and gaseous hydrocarbons, must be governed by special provisions on the matter, and excluded from the mining regulations.

569. At the moment, there is no harmony between the regulation of this hydrocarbon and regulations on mine safety. Actually, what is a resource of national interest for one sector, for the other is a factor to be regulated as hazard in mining operations.

570. The MME has regulated non-conventional hydrocarbons and its technical aspects for exploitation, through Resolution 180742 of 2012. During the Open Round 2012 of the ANH, there were no areas included for coal bed methane.

---

249. www.upme.gov.co.

§6. ENFORCEMENT

571. As illustrated throughout this chapter, holders of mining titles are subject to a number of requirements established in the title itself, the law or the mining concession. Infringement of those requirements not only triggers contractual consequences, but also exposes the miner to certain penalties established by the MME. Resolution 91544 of 2014 sets out different penalties, the criteria to determine their gravity and the contractual stage where they can be imposed. The NMA graduates the pertinent sanction and administers the proceeds of the enforcement activity.

572. Penalties are established in terms of minimum monthly legal wages (mmlw), and are imposed according to the type of requirement infringed. Penalties have been classified by the MME according to the obligation infringed: legal, technical or environmental. For example, if the title holder carries out mining activities in indigenous territories and fails to engage or train the surrounding indigenous community members, then the title holder would be considered in violation of a legal requirement established in the Mining Code. This infraction, for example, is considered of low gravity, pursuant to the tables adopted by the MME.

573. It is worth mentioning that penalties vary according to the contract phase. During exploration or construction works, the amount of the sanction is fixed according to the gravity of the infringement. For example, low gravity violations expose the title holder to penalties of 13.5 mmlw. During production phase, the penalties are applied according to the mineral under exploitation. For coal mining, the NMA looks at the annual production, normally ranging from 24,000 to 800,000 tonnes per year, and then determines whether the infraction was moderate, serious or very serious. As a matter of example, if a title holder extracts more than 800,000 tonnes per year and commits a serious infraction, the penalty would range between 30.1 and 400 mmlw.

Chapter 3. Transport

574. Transport is part of the activities involved in the mining cycle. There are easements of legal source for this kind of activity when required by the mining project.

§1. Transport Means

575. In Colombia there are two main means of transport for coal: railways, in the big scale mines; and trucks, for the medium and small scales projects. In some cases there are used barges in the Magdalena River.

576. From the total coal produced in the country 80% is transported by truck and costs vary according to the region where it is produced and the distance to the ports or consuming centres.

577. The main railway system operates for the Large Scale mines in the north of the country.

§2. Regulation

578. The regulations for transport by road for mining are specially referred to their weight capacity. The administrative authorities responsible for the national, regional and local roads, establish the technical specifications of the roads and determine what kind of vehicles are allowed for transit. In some local roads, big trucks are not allowed.

579. Regarding ports, there are public and private ports. The management of ports in Colombia is granted through concession contracts. There are private coal ports, which have their own coal handling facilities. The Superintendence of Ports oversees their operation.[250]

580. Due to environmental concerns and according to Law 1450 of 2011, as of 1 January 2012, loading of coal in the sea and river ports must be done through a direct loading system without any cargo transference (Article 113).

---

250. Decree 2741 of 2001, Decree 3083 of 2007, Decree 4286 of 2009, Decree 700 of 2010.

Chapter 4. Distribution

581. There are no specific regulations regarding trading or distribution of coal in national or international markets.

Chapter 5. Consumption

§1. Fixed Prices

582. Regarding consumption, it is important to mention that for the purpose of determining the compulsory counter-benefit in concession agreements the governmental planning UPME, fixes a trading price for domestic and foreign consumption, according to the international and national markets prices.

583. This trading price is fixed at least twice per year. Royalties and additional compensations must be paid according to this fixed price.

§2. Main Consumers

584. Several industries in the country require coal as an energetic resource, such as cement, steel, bricks and clay derivatives, glass and others.

585. The coke coal produced in Colombia was only intended for national consumption in the steel industry. However, in the past few years a new industry has arisen involving coking coal plants to produce coke for exportation.

Part V. Interaction Between Energy and Environmental Law

Chapter 1. Regulatory Framework

586. Environmental regulation is set by international conventions, the national constitution and domestic laws and decrees. Environmental topics are mostly regulated by ordinary laws and further developed by decrees and regulations, such as the creation of the Ministry of Environment (Law 99 of 1993), the enforcement procedure for environmental infractions (Law 1333 of 2009), or Law 1159 of 2007 approving the Rotterdam Convention for application of the Prior Informed Consent (PIC) Procedure on the export and import of pesticides and hazardous chemicals. Laws adopted by the President under special legislative powers granted by the Congress are known as Decree-Laws. For example, Law 23 of 1973 empowered the President to adopt the regulation on natural resources and environmental protection, which was finally adopted through Decree-Law 2811 of 1974 establishing the National Code of Renewable Natural Resources and Environmental Protection.

§1. Constitutional Provisions

587. The enactment of the 1991 Constitution served as catalyser to provide environmental issues with a higher degree of protection. The 1991 Constitution is said to be an ecologic constitution due to the number of provisions containing environmental aspects, including the right to a healthy environment; the duty to protect the environment, conserve special areas, promote education on environmental issues, prevent and control polluting factors, provide the means to ensure community's participation, and control the entry and exit of genetic resources. This document integrates the environmental dimension into national planning, gives environmental policy the same hierarchy as other matters of national policy, introduces the concept of sustainable development, grants environmental competences to administrative units known as territorial entities, and establishes that the property has an inner ecological purpose. On top of that, the 1991 Constitution provides citizens and groups with expedite and accessible mechanisms to protect environmental rights.

588. The making process of the 1991 Constitution was surrounded by an international desire to turn ecological good intentions into effective environmental protection, which was reflected in the various provisions on natural resource conservation and protection, the establishment of the right to a healthy environment and the inclusion of environmental considerations as a matter of public policy.[251] According to the Constitutional Court, the 1991 Constitution has a three-fold environmental dimension: the protection of the environment; the right of every person to enjoy a healthy environment; and the range of obligations imposed to public authorities and citizens. The number of environmental provisions established in the Constitution, the fundamental connotation that the right to a healthy environment bears, and the close relationship between the right to a healthy environment and the rights to public health, decent life and personal integrity, attribute the Constitution an ecologic nature that has been acknowledged by the Constitutional Court.

589. Concerning constitutional provisions related with the environment, the following could be listed: Article 8 on the obligation to protect nation's cultural and natural wealth; Article 49, on health care and environmental sanitation; Article 58, establishing the ecologic purpose of the property; Article 66, on agricultural credits for environmental calamities; Article 67, on education for environmental protection; Article 79, establishing the right to a healthy environment and participation in environmental decision-making; Article 80, on the management and exploitation planning of natural resources; Article 81, on the prohibition of chemical, biological and nuclear weapons; Article 82, establishing the duty to protect cultural and natural resources; Article 215, establishing situations of emergency for the perturbation or threat to ecological order; Article 226, on the internationalization of ecological affairs; Article 268 No. 7, on the surveillance of natural resources and the environment; Article 277 No. 4, establishing environmental protection as one of the functions of the Public Attorney; Article 282 No. 5, establishing the People Ombudsman and Popular Actions as mechanisms for environmental protection; Article 289, on cooperation and integration programmes for environmental preservation in bordering areas; Article 300 No. 2, on Departmental Assemblies and the environment; Article 301, on fiscal and administrative management according to the department's natural resources and ecological circumstances; Article 310, on the population density control in San Andres and Providencia to preserve the environment and natural resources; Article 313 No. 9, on Municipal Councils and ecological heritage; Articles 317 and 294 on land appreciation tax for environmental and natural resources conservation; Article 330 No. 5, on Councils of Indigenous Territories and preservation of the environment; Article 332, on the State ownership over the subsoil and non-renewable resources; Article 333, on limitations to economic activities for environmental reasons; Article 334, on State intervention to preserve natural resources and a healthy environment; Article 339, on environmental policy in the National Plan of Development; Article 340, on the representation of ecological sectors in the National Council of Planning; and Article 344 on the provision of environmental sanitation and potable water as part of the aims of the State.

590. These provisions and the right to a healthy environment are regarded as the legal basis for environmental legislation in Colombia. The Constitutional Court

251. Constitutional Court. Sentence No. T-092 of 19 Feb. 1993. Magistrate: Simón Rodríguez Rodríguez.

allocates special value to the ecologic character of the 1991 Constitution by using an environmental-protective interpretation criterion when testing the hierarchy of constitutional rights and values.

§2. AUTHORITIES

591. Law 99 of 1993 establishes two main environmental authorities: the MASD, and the Autonomous Regional Corporations (CARs), which include environmental authorities in highly populated areas. It also grants specific competences on environmental matters to administrative units known as territorial entities (departments, municipalities and districts). Law 99 of 1993 creates sixteen additional CARs for a total of thirty-three CARs and empowers them to be the highest authority within their jurisdiction. The Ministry of Environment is the highest authority nationwide for environmental matters.

592. Environmental competences and authorities created by Law 99 of 1993 do not follow the territorial or administrative decentralization of Colombia. Colombia is administratively divided into the national state, departments, and municipalities and/or districts, in which departments and municipalities are subject to national regulations and have exclusive powers within their jurisdictions on the specific matters established in the law expressly provides so. This territorial division differs from the approach of the CARs to environmental matters, for the CARs are regional authorities that follow geographical and environmental criteria, such as river basins, strategic ecosystems or nature parks. The jurisdiction of one CAR can comprise more than one department, and can also lead to situations where two municipalities of the same department are subject to the environmental competence of two different CARs. Environmental authorities must coordinate harmonically their competences between the national State, the CARs, departments, municipalities and/or districts.

I. Ministry of Environment and Sustainable Development

593. The MASD, created by Law 99 of 1993 is the main environmental governmental institution at national level. The MASD has the duty to protect Colombia's national natural resources and the environment. The structure, functions and aims of the MASD have been amended in different occasions, due to the planning and administrative policies of each government.

594. The MASD is responsible for establishing the national environmental policy and coordinating environmental management, through the definition of policies and regulations on renewable natural resource recovery, conservation, protection, zoning, management, use and exploitation. The policies and regulations of the MASD apply to all economic activities regardless of their specific sector, and must be regarded and complied with in all regions, departments, municipalities and/or districts. The roles of the MASD include the protection of renewable natural resources, including air, soil, forests and water; issuance of environmental licenses according to the system of Environmental Impact Assessment (EIA), through the National Authority of Environmental Licenses (ANLA); regulation of contamination from economic activities; assessment of environmental aspects of development programmes; protection of biodiversity and nature park conservation; control of biotechnology activities; and the negotiation of international treaties relating to the protection of the environment.

595. The MASD used to be responsible for the authorization of major polluting projects, namely big scale mining and hydrocarbon projects, hydroelectric facilities, infrastructure projects, airports and harbours. Concerning energy matters, the MASD used to issue licenses for activities such as mineral carbon exploration in quantities equal to or in excess of 800,000 tons a year, or the operation and construction of hydropower and power plants with a capacity equal to or above 100 MW. This competence was delegated to the ANLA, established with the aim of centralizing all the procedures on environmental licenses, permits and authorizations.[252] The ANLA is administratively and financially autonomous and reports to the MASD, who holds its legal representation.

596. The MASD also coordinates the national system of environmental information (SINA), which is a set of guidelines, standards, activities, resources, programmes and institutions that allow the execution of the environmental principles contained in the law. For example, the MASD adopts the terms of reference that activities requiring an environmental license must fulfil, in order to obtain the environmental license. The MASD issues a series of guidelines for the sound environmental management of certain activities in specific sectors, which allow the authority and the developer to follow the same rules. For the hydrocarbon sector, the MASD has issued guideline guides on the drilling of oil and gas wells, seismic terrestrial exploration, development of fields, transport by pipeline, service stations and distribution of natural gas.

597. In addition, the MASD has at its disposal the National Environmental Council, which stands as a public advisory body responsible for the coordination of environmental and renewable natural resource conservation policies with the economic sectors involved. The National Environmental Council acts as an advisory body to the MASD by issuing the necessary recommendations for the development of national environmental regulations, action plans and programmes on land planning and zoning procedures, and procedures for environmental pollution prevention and control of risk factors.

598. Regarding energy matters, the National Environmental Council plays a significant role in the environmental policymaking. The Council helps coordinate the insertion of environmental policies and regulations in the mining, electric and hydrocarbon sector. The MME, the president of ECOPETROL and representatives

252. Decree 3575 of 2011.

from the mining industry are included as members of the Council. Some of the policies and regulations discussed in this forum include water management, zoning, hazardous waste management and public participation.

II. Regional and Local Level Authorities

599. According to Law 99 of 1993, the CARs are the entities in charge of creating regional policies of environmental protection within their jurisdiction. The CARs are defined as regional institutions integrated by territorial entities that due to their features constitute a geopolitical, bio-geographical or hydro-geographical unit. The entities in charge of the Colombian Amazon, San Andres, Uraba, the Mojana and the Macarena have been named as Corporations of Sustainable Development due to the eco-systemic importance they have. The CARs and the Corporations of Sustainable Development cover thirty-three specific regions of the national territory, which are different from the existing departments, municipalities and districts, and which respond to strategic ecosystems criteria. The legal competences of the CARs exclusively concern environmental matters.

600. The actual role of the CARs consists of being the maximum environmental authority in the region, responsible for the administration of natural resources and the execution of environmental policies, plans and programmes from the MASD. The CARs' inspection and surveillance powers are executed through follow-up and control activities aimed to ensure environmental protection. Follow-up and control activities focus on the use of water, soil, air and other renewable natural resources, as well as the movement and trade of such resources. The CARs have enforcement powers to ensure the sound disposal of waste, and the appropriate performance of activities involving exploration, exploitation, transport or deposit of non-renewable natural resources.

601. CARs are the entities in charge of approving or rejecting projects entailing significant negative impacts within their jurisdiction, as established in Article 9 of Decree 2041 of 2014 (compiled in Decree 1076 of 2015, under Article 2.2.2.3.2.3). This important role allows the CARs to authorize the development of activities and projects, and the consequent use or affection to natural resources through concessions, permits, authorizations or environmental licenses. The CARs also develop biodiversity conservation and protection plans and provide technical advice to territorial entities in disaster planning and prevention.

602. Law 99 of 1993 refers to Great Urban Centres as municipalities or metropolitan areas with a population higher than 1,000,000 inhabitants. In these areas, local environmental authorities take over the environmental powers that the CARs have in the regions. Law 768 of 2002 creates other municipal environmental authorities provided with the same environmental powers of the CARs, which include the Districts of Cartagena, Barranquilla and Santa Marta. The environmental powers given to Great Urban Centres and the aforementioned districts concern the issuance of licenses, concessions, permits and authorizations for the works and projects taking place within their jurisdiction; the follow-up and control of wastewater discharges, disposal of solid, toxic and hazardous waste; and the adoption of the necessary mitigation, decontamination, sanitation and correction measures to tackle environmental degradation.

603. At local level, environmental authorities play an important role in the authorization of economic activities, enforcement of environmental law, participation mechanisms and environmental awareness of citizens. This role is comparable to the one played by the CARs at regional level, with the difference that authorities of Great Urban Centres are often subject to political wilfulness of local administrations. A good example of these authorities is the District Secretariat of Environment (SDA) in Bogota, which decides on requests for ground water exploitation, concessions, surface water, occupation of water flows, wastewater discharges, and atmospheric permits. The SDA also imposes sanctions for environmental infringements.

Chapter 2. Environmental Legislation and Energy

§1. POLLUTION CONTROL

I. Permitting: Environmental License

604. In Colombia, projects with significant negative environmental impact are required to obtain a permit before starting construction and operation. This permit is known as the environmental license (*licencia ambiental*), which has been in force since 1993. Energy-related projects including hydrocarbon, coal mining and electricity are included in the list of activities requiring an environmental license. This license works as integrated pollution prevention and control, for it contains all the necessary authorizations to use natural resources, and release pollutants into the air, water and soil.

A. *Historical Background*

605. The National Code of Renewable Natural Resources and Protection to the Environment (NCRNR) required natural and legal persons to declare the likely hazards of their economic activities. The purpose of this declaration, known as the declaration of environmental effect, was to warn authorities on the possible or harmful effects that activities, projects or works could cause to the environment. The evolution on international environmental law drove lawmakers towards requiring operators to carry out impact assessments and obtain an environmental license before starting the desired activities. As a result, Law 99 of 1993 created the Environmental License system in Colombia and Decree 2041 of 2014 provided for its detailed regulation.

B. *Concept*

606. Law 99 of 1993 conceives the environmental license as a policy instrument of environmental management, economic intervention and administrative planning. The procedure to obtain an environmental license allows for assessing the environmental performance of proposed activities at their planning, execution and follow-up stages. Permitting of new activities and projects is based on the precautionary principle; with the information available, the project developer assesses the risks a project may pose and the measures to mitigate, minimize or compensate negative impacts.

607. The environmental license is the authorization issued for the construction and execution of a work or activity that is likely to cause significant negative impact to natural resources, the environment or the landscape. This license covers the whole life cycle of the project, work or activity, including construction, operation, maintenance, dismantling and site closure. The environmental license comprises all the authorizations or concessions for the use or exploitation of renewable natural resources, which are needed to carry out the proposed activity, work or project. Environmental license holders are subject to compliance with the terms, conditions and obligations established therein.

608. The environmental license must be obtained prior to the start of the project. No project or activity is required to have more than one license.[253] Any other authorization, concession, permit or license required to construct or operate the proposed project, will generate effects as soon as the environmental license is obtained. The license is granted for the entire life of the project.

C. Activities Required to Obtain the Environmental License

609. Decree 2041 of 2014 establishes a list of activities requiring environmental license. The list is divided into two groups: the ones authorized by the ANLA, and the ones authorized by regional environmental authorities (CARs and environmental authorities in big urban centres). The ANLA issues environmental licenses to activities that represent a major risk to the national territory. In other countries, these activities are known as federal jurisdiction projects. The second group is composed of those activities with minor impacts and/or effects that remain within a single jurisdiction, authorized by regional agencies. There are cases where national and regional permitting competences conflict, such as the construction of a highway involving two different jurisdictions. In this case, the ANLA establishes the competent authority.

610. Activities not listed in Decree 2041 of 2014 do not require an environmental license or environmental management plan. They must obtain, however, the necessary environmental authorizations for operation, such as wastewater discharge or atmospheric emissions permit. For example, although open-pit and underground mining must be authorized by an environmental license, the accumulation, loading and unloading of coal outside the works site are exempted from this license. The MASD has clarified that this rule applies when the ports where these activities are executed are authorized to do so by the environmental agency, or when the activities are covered by specific pollution-prevention permits.[254]

611. The following are activities and projects relevant to the energy sector requiring environmental license, granted exclusively by the ANLA (Article 9 of Decree 2041 of 2014):

612. Hydrocarbon sector:

- Seismic exploration requiring the construction of roads for vehicle transit; and seismic exploration activities in maritime areas, when they are carried out at less than 200 m deep.

253. Article 3, Decree 2041 of 2014.
254. MASD, Communication E2-23685, 22 Jul. 2014.

- Drilling of wells out of existing hydrocarbon production fields, according to the area declared by the applicant.
- Exploitation of hydrocarbons. This includes drilling any type of wells, construction of installations, complementary works for internal transport of oil by ducts, onsite oil storage, internal roads and other oil infrastructure. In case the area for hydrocarbon exploitation corresponds to an exploration area already covered by the license, the applicant will only need to request the modification of the existing environmental license.
- Transport and carriage of liquid and gaseous hydrocarbons involving the construction of pipelines of more than 6 inches (15.24 cm), including oil pumping and pressure reduction stations, infrastructure for storage and flow control. Activities related to the distribution of household, industrial and commercial use are excluded.
- Terminals and transfer stations, understood as storage infrastructure related with the transport of hydrocarbons, by-products and derivates through pipelines.
- Construction and operation of refineries, and petrochemical developments belonging to a refinery facility.

613. Mining sector:
Coal mining when the projected exploitation is more than or equal to 800,000 tonnes per year.

614. Electric sector:

- Construction of power stations with installed capacity of more than or equal to 100 MW.
- Exploration and use of alternative energy sources with an installed capacity greater than 3 MW.
- Construction of dams or reservoirs with a capacity of more than 200 million m^3 water.
- Laying of overhead electrical power lines with a voltage of 220 kW, including connection sub-stations, etc.
- Nuclear energy projects.

615. Some other projects under the exclusive competence of the ANLA include the construction and operation of deep water ports, and deep dredging in navigable canals, and projects, works or activities affecting the areas of the System of National Natural Parks, among others.

616. The projects falling under the exclusive competence of the Regional Autonomous Corporations (CARs), Great Urban Centres (*Grandes Centros Urbanos*) and the environmental authorities created by Law 768 of 2002, include:

617. Mining sector:

- Coal mining when the projected exploitation is less than 600 tonnes per year.

618. Electric sector:

- Construction of power stations with installed capacity of more than or equal to 10 MW and less than 100 MW.
- Construction of dams or reservoirs with a capacity of less than 200 million water cubic metres.
- Laying of overhead electrical power lines with a voltage of 220 kW, including connection sub-stations, etc.
- Construction and operation of hydropower stations with a capacity of less than 100 MW; except those small hydropower facilities operating in non-connected zones, with a capacity equal to or less than 10 MW.

Other projects include the construction and operation of landfills, wastewater treatment facilities, and storage of hazardous substances, excluding hydrocarbons, among others.

D. Global Environmental License

619. The global environmental license is a permitting instrument designed for hydrocarbon and mining projects. It was thought as an authorization for works that integrated an environmental unity, with the aim to simplify the licensing of activities taking place in the same area. Decree 2041 of 2014 establishes that for the development of works and activities related to hydrocarbon or mine exploitation, the competent authority will issue a global environmental license.[255] This license covers the whole exploitation area requested by the developer.

620. In order to obtain the global license, the operator must prepare and submit an Environmental Management Plan (Plan de Manejo Ambiental). This plan is not subject to approval, but it must be followed during the construction and execution of the project. The Environmental Management Plan, the contingency plan and in some cases, the restoration plan, establish obligations for the operator on top of the conditions set out in the license. The authority, hence, evaluates compliance against the license and the environmental management plan.

621. Concerning mining activities, the global environmental license includes construction, assembling, exploitation, production and internal transport of materials.

622. One example that better illustrates the use of the global environmental license is the case of Petrominerales.[256] Petrominerales Colombia Ltd, Colombian

255. Article 4, Decree 2041 of 2014.
256. Resolution 2401 of 2008 of the Ministry of Environment, Housing and Land Development granting a global environmental license and establishing other provisions.

Branch, requested authorization to exploit the production field 'Campo de Producción Corcel'. This project involved the operation of seven platforms for the exploitation of oil wells and construction of several facilities, including pools, camps, access ways, injection lines, etc. Instead of a license for each well, the global environmental license allowed the exploitation of the whole Corcel production field. Petrominerales had to submit an Environmental Management Plan and a follow-up programme, which was to be reported by using an Environmental Compliance Report (Informe de cumplimiento ambiental – ICA).

623. Some environmental experts affirm that the global environmental license is often replaced by modifying a regular environmental license.[257] For example, an oil exploration project covered by a regular environmental license can request the authority to modify the license, in order to include the exploitation phase. In this case, the application for a global environmental license is no longer necessary.

E. Environmental Studies

624. In Colombia, the EIA is a process whereby a project developer, environmental authorities and sector-specific agencies evaluate the effects of the proposed activity. All projects required to hold an environmental license must carry out the EIA by preparing and submitting environmental studies. There are two types of environmental studies: Declaration of Environmental Alternatives (*Declaración de Alternativas Ambientales* – DDA) and EIS. Decree 2041 of 2014 establishes the list of activities requiring a DDA or an EIS. Depending on the type of environmental study the environmental license application procedure will be different.

625. Environmental studies must observe the terms of reference established by the MASD, and fulfil the requirements of the General Methodology for the Presentation of Environmental Studies, adopted by Resolution 1503 of 2010. The General Methodology establishes the requirements for preparing and submitting the DDA, EIS and Environmental Management Plans. Likewise, the methodology provides guidelines to carry out environmental zoning, identification and assessment of environmental impacts, design of environmental management measures, configuration of follow-up and monitoring plans, and contingency plans. The general methodology is a mandatory instrument of consultation and orientation.

1. Declaration of Environmental Alternatives

626. The DDA seeks to provide information on the different alternatives under which a proposed project or activity may be carried out. Every alternative must take

257. Legal Analysis, Macías Gómez & Asociados, 11 Mar. 2011. Available at: http://www.maciasabogados.com/NewsDetail/272/1/BrevesComentariosenTornoalDecreto2820de2010SobreLicenciasAmbientales.

into account geographical conditions, biotic and abiotic factors, social and economic circumstances, as well as possible solutions and control measures for each alternative.[258]

627. The DDA is mandatory for the following projects/activities:

- Seismic exploration for hydrocarbons requiring the construction of roads for vehicular transit.
- Transport and carriage of liquid and gaseous hydrocarbons involving the construction of pipelines of more than 6 inches (15.24 cm).
- Hydrocarbon infrastructure for the storage of hydrocarbons that are transported through pipelines.
- Refineries and petrochemical facilities.
- Construction and operation of power stations.
- Projects for the exploration and use of alternative energy sources with an installed capacity greater than 3 MW.

628. Developers of these types of projects must ask the authority whether or not they must prepare and submit a DDA. This petition must be accompanied by the project's description, object and scope, as well as its coordinates and blueprints. If the authority deems the project must have a DDA, it will issue the terms of reference to draft this environmental study. For hydropower projects, the applicant must attach evidence of the project's registration with the UPME. The environmental authority has a thirty-day period to assess the DDA and select the alternative under which the project must be carried out. The authority also orders the developer to draft and submit an EIS for the selected alternative.

629. In order to accurately select the best alternative for rationalizing the use of natural resources and for risk prevention, the DAA must include at least the following information:

- Project location and information of its geographical, environmental and social surroundings.
- A comparative analysis of the project inherent effects.
- A comparative analysis of possible solutions and control measures for each one of the proposed alternatives.
- Identification of neighbouring communities and the mechanisms to inform them about the project.
- Information of the project's compatibility with land uses, according to the local zoning plan, and
- Selection of the best alternative.

258. Article 17, Decree 2041 of 2014.

2. Environmental Impact Study

630. Projects that are not required to present DDA must prepare and submit an EIS. In other words, the EIS is the general rule for projects requiring environmental license. The EIS must contain information such as the location of the planned development/project, a description of the environmental abiotic, biotic and socio-economic factors which may be impacted by the proposed project and other data that the environmental licence petitioner must submit to the environmental authority. The EIS must also address environmental impact prevention, correction and compensation measures, as well as a proposed Environmental Management Plan.

631. Activities that have a negative environmental impact which cannot be tackled through mitigation or prevention measures must compensate biodiversity loss. Compensation measures for biodiversity loss must be conducted in accordance with Resolution 1517 of 2012 adopting the Manual for biodiversity loss compensation. Resolution 1517 of 2012 provides the list of projects where biodiversity loss is required, including mining, hydrocarbon, infrastructure, and energy sectors; port and marine infrastructure; power generation; construction and operation of international airports and new landing strips; and public works, etc.

632. The EIS is submitted along with the license application form to the corresponding environmental authority. Once the authority has acknowledged receipt of the application, it gathers information from other governmental agencies on the feasibility of the project. The petitioner may be requested to submit additional information, and it can always submit further documents before the authority declares having gathered all the necessary information. The authority has twenty-five business days to decide on the issuance of rejection of the environmental from the date it acknowledged receipt of all documents.

633. Project developers applying for an environmental license must pay the applicable fees according to Resolution 260 of 2011. Environmental fees represent the costs of the assessment and follow-up services provided by the authority,[259] including value of professional service fees, cost of travel expenses necessary for the study, issue and/or monitoring of the environmental license, permit, concession or authorization; and cost of analysis and studies. The environmental fee is calculated by applying the administrative fee to the sum of the costs (travel expenses, professional fees, etc.). The administrative fee is fixed at 25% of the total cost of the project.[260]

259. Law 633 of 2000.
260. Resolution 2613 of 2010.

F. Content of the Environmental Licence

634. The environmental license is issued through a resolution (administrative decision) from the MASD or the competent environmental authority and contains the following elements:

- Identification of the individual or company, public or private, authorized to develop the project, work or activity, indicating the company name, number of identification and address.
- The general purpose and location of the project, work or activity.
- A detailed account of the environmental motivations that have been taken into account for granting the license.
- A list of the different activities and works authorized by the environmental license.
- Natural resources authorized for use, exploitation, as well as the conditions, prohibition and requisites of use.
- Requirements, conditions and obligations in addition to the Environmental Management Plan that must be complied with during the construction, operation, maintenance, dismantling, abandonment or finalization of the project, work or activity.
- Publication of the administrative authorization notice required under Article 71 of Law 99 of 1993.
- Any other information that the authority deems relevant.

635. The requirements and obligations laid down in the license can be quite strict. The global license granted to Drumond Ltd. for the exploitation of the coal mine El Descanso in the Cesar Department, with an output of 50 million tonnes per year, is one example that reflects this situation.[261] The maximum limits and management conditions set in the license on atmospheric emissions, wastewater discharges and hazardous waste generation were fixed by following the highest standards. Drumond challenged the terms of the licence arguing that other mining companies operating in the area did not have as many requirements and conditions. Some of these conditions included relocating neighbouring communities which were impacted by other projects, as well as the prohibition to abstract surface water in certain areas.

G. Prior Consultation Procedure

636. One of the topics triggering considerable debate and being the subject matter of a current bill in the Congress concerns public consultation (*consulta previa*). The prior consultation procedure is a mechanism, and fundamental right,[262] whereby any project, work, activity or administrative measure which has an impact

261. Resolution 414 of 2008 of the Ministry of Environment, Housing and Land Development granting a global environmental license and establishing other provisions.
262. Constitutional Court. Sentence SU-039 of 1997.

on ethnic communities is required to be consulted to such communities. Project developers and government agencies must carry out this procedure through the Ministry of Internal Affairs' designated office. Bearing in mind that 14% of the territory is inhabited by ethnic communities and they are settled in rich natural and mineral resource areas, the prior consultation procedure has brought up a considerable number of issues for energy-related activities.

637. Prior consultation must be carried out when a project affects indigenous settlements (*zonas de resguardo o reservas indígenas*) or zones granted to afro-descendant communities. The Ministry of Internal Affairs certifies the presence of those communities in the areas affected by the proposed activity. Projects requiring environmental license, meaning all major energy developments, must include ethnic communities in the preparation and drafting of environmental studies.[263] The steps, documents and certifications of this procedure are established in Decree 1320 of 1998.

H. Public Participation

638. Any projects requiring environmental license or permit can be subject to public hearings. Public hearings are mechanisms aimed at involving affected communities, social organizations, the society and project stakeholders to participate in the environmental decision-making process. According to Article 72 of Law 99 of 1993, entities with legal standing to request a public hearing include the General Attorney of the Nation, the Ombudsman of the People, the MASD, environmental authorities, governors and majors, at least one hundred people, and three non-profit organizations. The authority responsible for assessing the environmental viability of the project can also call for public hearings when it deems it convenient, due to the importance of the project or the impact it can have on the community and the environment.

639. The public hearing can be requested before the project license is granted, modified or revoked, in which case it will be named prior hearing. Public hearings can also take place once the project has been authorized and they will aim at raising concerns on the project's non-compliance of the conditions established in the license. In this case, the authority verifies the evidence supporting non-compliance and establishes the applicable sanctions accordingly. The procedure for carrying out public hearings includes a formal request, submitted by those with legal standing to request public hearings; a public convocation called up by the competent authority, which involves the posting up of a public edict for ten days at the authority's offices, and the publication in a local newspaper. The public edict contains the time and place of the public hearing, so that interested parties can prepare their queries and arguments. The public hearing is recorded in an act containing: the project identification, place and time of the hearing, the main discussed issues, the documents

263. Decree 1320 of 1998 of the Ministry of Internal Affairs regulating prior consultation to indigenous and afro-descendant communities.

presented during the hearing and the interventions of the hearing participants. The hearing act is later considered in the administrative act that grants or rejects the environmental license.

640. Public hearings can play a decisive role in the way activities are conducted. The hydroelectric project 'El Quimbo' involving the construction of a 2,601 hm^3 dam and a flooded area of 8,250 ha for an installed capacity of 400 MW exemplifies the case. The public hearing was requested by the regional environmental authority – CAM – and one of the municipalities where the project was to take place. As a result of the hearing, the President of Colombia had to intervene to establish coordination table rounds in order to find a compromise between the developer, administrative units, environmental authorities and the community. As a result of the hearings and negotiation tables, the developer had to modify its initial Environmental Management Plan to satisfy the demands of certain economic sectors affected with the project.[264]

II. Atmospheric Pollution

641. Atmospheric pollution is identified in the 1974 NCRNR as one of the factors amounting to contamination in Colombia. Articles 73–76 of the NCRNR lay down the main provisions on outer space and the atmosphere, requiring the government to keep the atmosphere in good conditions, and to avoid harming or interfering with the normal development of human, animal or nature life or the natural renewable resources. Decree 948 of 1995 regulates atmospheric pollution and repeals former Decree 2/1982. Decree 948 of 1995 sets out the legal framework for air quality standards, polluting emissions, mobile sources, noise and odour emissions, public authorities and their powers, atmospheric emission permit for fixed sources, certification mechanisms for mobile sources, contingency plans for contamination incidents, air contamination control and enforcement, and mechanisms for public participation in air-related matters.

642. In general, operators of facilities releasing pollutants into the air must obtain an environmental permit, keep the emissions below the maximum permissible limits and report to the authority. The activities subject to the Atmospheric Emission Permit are established in Article 73 of Decree 948 of 1995 and include:

- Release of smoke, gas, vapour, dust and particulate matter from industrial chimneys or ducts.
- Dispersed emissions from open-pit mining activities.
- Solid, liquid or gas waste incineration.
- Storage, transport, loading and unloading operations causing air emissions.
- Industrial or commercial operation of boilers or incinerators.
- Fuel burning operations in oil and gas facilities.

264. Resolution 899 of 2009 of the Ministry of Environment, Housing and Land Development granting the environmental license to 'El Quimbo' Project.

- Processes causing toxic air emissions.
- Manufacture of lubricants and fuels.
- Oil refineries.
- Operation of thermoelectric plants.
- Nuclear reactor operations.
- Activities generating offensive odours.
- Any other activity established by the MASD.

643. When writing the permit, the environmental authority looks at the existing air quality standards, zoning of polluted areas and the maximum permissible limits applicable to the facility. Resolution 909 of 2008 establishes the maximum permissible limits for fixed sources and the measurement methods. Fixed sources include punctual, dispersed sources, and area-source. The maximum limits apply to:

- Industrial activities: Resolution 909 of 2008 establishes threshold values for atmospheric pollutants associated with each type of industry, as well as for dioxins and furans.
- External combustion equipment.
- Thermal power stations, establishing different limits for those generating more than, equal to or less than 20 MW, as well as for those working with gas turbines.
- Refinery of oil products.
- Incinerators of hazardous and non-hazardous waste, among others.

644. Operators of fixed sources must report their emissions to the authority by using the IE-1 Report on Emissions *(Informe de Estado de Emisiones).*

645. Restrictions, obligations and necessary authorizations on atmospheric emissions for fixed and mobile sources applicable to energy projects are established in their corresponding environmental license. One of the cases where the environmental authority has clarified the applicability of atmospheric permit in energy-related activities is in the use of liquefied or natural gas when used in boilers and kilns. Pursuant to the Council of State, only boilers and kilns using mineral coal, ACPM or cane bagasse are required to obtain an atmospheric emissions permits, whereas the use of natural or liquefied gas falls within the exemptions of Decree 948 of 2015 and are thus only subject to non-binding technical standards.[265]

III. Water Use and Wastewater Discharges

A. Water Use Rights

646. The use of public domain water for activities different than satisfaction of the own needs is subject to authorization from the government. This authorization is issued by environmental authorities and is known as concession. According to

265. Council of State, Internal No. 000213 of 16 Apr. 2015.

Decree 1541 of 1978, concessions are needed to carry out activities such as the supply of household water, irrigation activities, nuclear or power generation, mining, oil exploration, geothermal generation, hydroelectric power generation, transport of toxic materials and minerals, transport of wood logs, fishing and aquiculture, sport and recreation, medicinal use activities, and certain mining applications. Decree 1541 of 1978 establishes special permits for abstraction or use of sands, stones and gravels from waterbeds, streams or deposits. The authority gives priority to certain water uses, including water for human consumption, individual domestic needs, community agricultural uses, hydropower, industrial or manufacture uses, mining activities, and recreational uses.

647. Concession holders must not change or alter the uses for which the concession has been granted. In addition, hydraulic works required to abstract water must be approved by the authority and control devices must be installed so the amount of abstracted water can be measured. Pursuant to the NCRNR, water users are obliged to use water in an efficient way according to the concession terms, and pay the applicable fees. In order to ensure the efficient use of water, users must construct and maintain installations and hydraulic works in good conditions, avoid any water deviation, leaks or spills, or exceeding water usage limits.

648. For energy projects, the concession for water use is granted through the environmental license. The authority sets out a specific chapter in the license establishing the maximum water amount, the sources, applicable fees and obligations. The license also contains the permits necessary to carry out the project, such as the authorization for occupying a river flow or carrying out hydraulic works.

B. Wastewater Discharges

649. Wastewater discharges into water bodies, soil and the sewerage system are regulated in Decree 3930 of 2010. Any natural or legal person discharging wastewater into surface or marine water, or soil, has to obtain a wastewater discharge permit. The authority grants the permit on the basis of the existing water resource classification, assessment of the information submitted by the applicant, facts and considerations from the technical visit and the corresponding report. Permit holders must comply with the maximum allowable limits, necessary treatment works and implement a risk management plan, as part of the conditions set out in the permit. This authorization is valid for a maximum of ten years.[266]

650. Wastewater discharges into the sewerage system must comply with the maximum allowable limits, including greases and oils, temperature, heavy metals, etc. The public sanitation company that renders the sewage service must ensure that

266. Article 47, Decree 3930 of 2010 of the Ministry of Environment, Housing and Territorial Development, partially regulating Title I of Law 9 of 1979, as well as Ch. II of Title VI – Part III – Book II of Decree-Law 2811 of 1974 concerning water use and liquid waste.

users do not exceed those limits. For such purpose, operators have to submit a characterization of discharges according to the protocol approved by the MASD.

651. Concerning energy projects, the wastewater discharge permit is contained and granted through the environmental license. For instance, the MASD authorized the discharge of industrial wastewater for the development of Block Buenaventura involving the operation of two oil wells. The MASD required the developer to use overhead irrigation within a specific zone with six sprinklers, and limited the discharge to 0.9 l per second. The developer had also to carry out a soil study in the area every six months to monitor pH, arsenic, cadmium, electric conductivity and other parameters. Decree 3930 of 2010 only allows the re-injection of liquid effluents from hydrocarbon exploration and exploitation activities, as long as it does not harm the aquifer.[267]

IV. Waste Management

652. There are two main classes of waste regulated in Colombia: solid and hazardous waste. Solid waste is regulated by Decree 1713 of 2002 and requires municipalities to ensure that all citizens are provided with sanitation services, including solid waste collection, transport, treatment, cleaning of public spaces and final disposal. Hazardous waste is regulated by Decree 4741 of 2005, and engages generators in managing waste in an integrated way, from cradle to cradle. Companies responsible for hazardous waste management must be authorized.

653. Waste management and related obligations are established in the environmental license, for energy projects. The permit sets out specific conditions such as developing a dumping site for debris or handing recyclable waste on to authorized companies. It can also require the developer to fulfil statutory duties, such as managing hazardous waste pursuant Decree 4741 of 2005 on the integrated management of this kind of waste. This was the case for El Descanso coal mine[268] in which the operator was not allowed to landfill plastic bags containing residues from explosives, but ensure and report they were managed by authorized companies.

§2. Nature Conservation

654. The relationship between nature conservation and energy projects is a matter of heated debate in a country where most of the extractive activities take place in biodiversity-wealthy areas. Electricity is not the exception, for it is largely based on hydro power.

655. Decree 2372 of 2010 establishes the National System of Protected Areas (SINAP) integrated by six public areas: the ones of the System of National Nature

267. Resolution 2401 of 2008.
268. Resolution 2401 of 2008.

Parks (SPNNN); reserve forests; regional nature parks; districts of integrated management; districts of soil conservation; and recreational areas. The SINAP also includes private zones designated by the civil society.[269] Since protected areas have been officially designated for conservation purposes, developers of economic activities need to obtain permission. Each area has management rules allowing the development of certain activities to a greater or lesser degree, such as investigation, recreation, recovery, conservation, education, etc.

656. Any project affecting the SINAP requires an environmental license from the ANLA or the regional authority, depending on the area category. The license application is considered so long the proposed activities match the management category of the affected area. If not, the developer will have to ask the designating authority, normally the SPNNN administrative unit, to remove the area from the SINAP (*sustracción de area*). When deciding on this request, the authority will have to take into account conservation and environmental criteria provided in the regulation.

657. Not seldom the authority rejects a license application for taking place in protected areas, such as a construction material mine that was to be developed near the reserve forest of Bogota, or a gold extraction project involving the installation of an open-pit mine on a high plateau. In other cases, the authority has endorsed the development of activities in designated areas by using the legal instrument of *sustracción de area.* It is the case of El Quimbo hydroelectric project, where the authority approved the exclusion of 7.482 ha from the Amazonian reserve forest.

269. Decree 2372 of 2010 of the Ministry of Environment, Housing and Land Development, regulating Decree-Law 2811 of 1974, Law 99 of 1993, Law 165 of 1994 and Decree-Law 216 of 2003, in relation to the national system of protected areas and its management categories.

Part VI. Interaction Between Energy and Tax Law

658. Pursuant to the up growing energy industry in Colombia of the last decades, the Colombian tax regulation has introduced different rules providing energy companies special features for a more suitable tax regime. However, this work is of the opinion that a greater effort must be done to provide more special tax features to the energy industry, so as to reach international energy taxation standards.

659. This part describes the general tax regime regarding the main taxes applicable to any industry and company developing business in Colombia. Later on, it focuses on the tax regulations applicable to the energy industry.

Chapter 1. General Tax Regime

§1. Income Tax

I. General Rules

A. *Colombian Source Income*

660. As a general rule, income derived from services rendered in Colombia; from the transfer of any kind of assets located in the country at the time of the transfer, or income derived from the exploitation of assets in Colombia, is deemed to be income of a national source. Interest paid on loans granted by foreign entities are also treated as national source income.

661. On the contrary, income derived from services rendered abroad; from the transfer of any kind of assets located outside the country; or from the exploitation of assets located overseas, constitutes income of a foreign source.

662. Foreign investors are taxed depending on whether the investor has established a permanent establishment, including branch offices (*permanent establishment definition is provided below*) or an affiliate (*subsidiarias*) in Colombia (Tax Code, Article 12). Affiliates (i.e., corporations, limited liability companies, and similar entities) are subject to income tax on their worldwide income, because they are treated as domestic companies for tax purposes.

663. Foreign non-domiciled entities (such as branches or permanent establishments of foreign companies) are subject to income tax on their Colombian source income and on their worldwide income attributable to them.

664. Per Law 1607 of 2012 the concept of permanent establishment was introduced into Colombian legislation. In this regard, it is defined as a fixed place of business, through which the businesses of a foreign enterprise, either a company, entity or a non-resident individual, are wholly or partly carried on.

665. This concept includes branches of foreign entities, agencies, offices, factories, workshops, mines, oil or gas wells, quarries or any other places relating to the exploration or the exploitation of natural resources.

666. It is also understood as permanent establishment when a person (different from an agent with independent status) is acting on behalf of an enterprise and has, and habitually exercises, in Colombian territory an authority to conclude contracts on behalf of the enterprise. That enterprise shall be considered to have a permanent establishment in Colombia in respect of any activities which that person undertakes for the enterprise, unless the activities of such person are preparatory or auxiliary.

667. An enterprise shall not be considered to have a permanent establishment in Colombia merely because it carries on business through a broker or any other agent of an independent status, provided that such persons are acting in the ordinary course of their business. However, the agent shall not be considered as an agent with independent status when it carries on all or nearly all the activities on behalf the enterprise and the conditions set forth between the enterprise and the agent are those which would not have been established between independent enterprises or parties.

B. Taxable Income

668. Corporate entities are required to pay income taxes on their net income ('taxable income'). It is defined as the sum of all operating income plus non-operating income, minus: (i) the cost of goods sold or services, and (ii) the general business expenses incurred during the year (Tax Code, Article 26).

669. However, a corporate taxpayer may be required to pay income tax based on the so-called presumptive income. This is an alternative minimum taxable income, whenever it exceeds regular net income in any given year. Presumptive income is equal to 1.5% of net worth as of 31 December of the preceding tax year (the tax year is the same calendar year in Colombia) (Tax Code, Article 188). 'Net worth' is defined as assets minus liabilities as reported on the income tax return. As of 2021 presumptive income rate should be 0%.

670. Taxpayers are required to report assets and liabilities on their returns for several purposes, three of which are to: (i) calculate presumptive income; (ii) provide means for the Tax Office to check the level of taxable income as it relates to increases in equity (Tax Code, Article 236); and (iii) be the tax base of equity tax as explained further.

C. Income Tax Rates

671. The general corporate income tax rate applicable to foreign companies obtaining profits through a permanent establishment is 32%. Foreign companies and entities whose income is not attributable to a branch or permanent establishment are taxed at a rate of 32%. The applicable corporate income tax is set at 31% for 2021 and 30% as of 2022.

672. Pursuant to the above, foreign shareholders of a Colombian subsidiary are required to pay, through tax withholding, a 32% tax on dividends from earnings not taxed at the subsidiary level.

673. Dividends distributed out of profits taxed at the corporate level are subject to a 10% dividends tax when distributed to foreign shareholders. This withholding can be potentially reduced per the application of a tax treaty.

674. Dividends distributed to Colombian shareholders are subject to a 7.5% withholding. This dividend tax will not apply when a control situation between the subsidiary and its shareholder is duly registered with the Chamber of Commerce, and when the company receiving the dividends is classified as a Colombian Holding Company (CHC).

D. Transfer Pricing

675. The Colombian transfer pricing regime is aimed at avoiding manipulation of prices, against commercial/market practices, in transactions with foreign-related parties. Transfer pricing provisions became enforceable on 1 January 2004. To this end, income taxpayers must adjust their income, costs, deductions, assets and liabilities derived from transactions with foreign-related parties. The adjustment is made by taking into consideration a profit margin comparable to the one obtained in transactions with unrelated parties; this is, in accordance with the arm's length principle.

676. Additionally, taxpayers must comply with formal obligations, such as filing information returns annually, and preparing and preserving contemporaneous documentation. Only taxpayers with equity above 100,000 Tax Value Units (UVT's) (1 UVT is equivalent to approximately USD 9) or revenues in excess of 61,000 UVT's have to file the annual information returns.

677. The methods set forth to determine the arm's length profit margins are: (i) the Comparable Uncontrolled Price Method; (ii) the Resale Price Method; (iii) the Cost Plus Method; (iv) the Profit Split Method and (v)the Operational profit margins in comparable transactions. The best method rule applies.

678. When operations take place with entities or individuals located in jurisdictions classified as tax havens it will be presumed that such transaction takes place between related parties. As a result, this transaction will be subject to transfer pricing regulations and restrictions. For this purpose the Colombian Government has issued a list with the jurisdictions considered as tax havens.[270]

679. Cost Sharing Arrangements (CSA) are allowable but not specifically ruled by the law. Thus, payments will be allowable in accordance to general tax rules and principles.

E. Tax Havens

680. Colombian legislation states that payments made to entities or individuals located in tax havens are subject to the maximum income tax withholding rate

270. Hong Kong, Antigua y Barbuda, Cook Islands, are examples of Tax Heavens under Colombian legislation.

(32%).[271] Payments that have been subject to tax withholdings will be deductible. Income tax payers that fail to comply with this obligation will not have the possibility to deduct such expenses.

681. The list of Tax Havens is set forth in section 1.2.2.5.1 of Decree 1625 of 2016, and is reviewed and updated, if necessary, on an annual basis.

F. Permanent Establishments and Subsidiaries

682. Permanent establishments and subsidiaries are subject to the general rules explained above and to the specific rules that follow.

683. In the case of a subsidiary, the foreign shareholder(s) is (are) required to pay, through tax withholding, a 32% tax on dividends from earnings not taxed at the corporate level. Remittances of non-taxed profits at the corporate level obtained through branches or permanent establishments are taxed at the rate applicable to dividends (Tax Code, Articles 48, 49, 245).

G. CHC Regime

684. Colombia adopted a holding regime, initially through Law 1943 of 2018,[272] by which Colombian companies which hold participation in two or more companies (Colombian or foreign) for at least twelve months are subject to a special tax rule for dividends distributions and capital gains resulting from the sale of shares.

685. Specifically, dividends received by a CHC from foreign entities are exempted from corporate income tax, and dividends distributed by the CHC to a foreign tax resident are qualified as foreign-source income. Dividends distributed from a Colombian entity to a CHC will not be subject to the 7.% dividends tax.

Capital gains received by a CHC resulting from a sale of shares in foreign entities are exempted from Colombian tax. The sale of CHC shares by its shareholders will be exempt from Colombian tax except for the part attributable to profits from activities carried out in Colombia.

---

271. When these payments have been subject to tax withholdings, then they may be deductible for the local party making the payment. On the other hand, if said payments do not constitute Colombian taxable income, then they would not be subject to the referred withholdings, and they would not be deductible for the party making the payment. (Tax Code, Art. 124-2).

272. Law 1943 of 2018 was held unconstitutional and repealed entirely by Law 2010 of 2020.

II. Specific Rules

A. Technical Assistance and Technical Services Rendered Abroad

686. Fees paid for technical assistance, technical services or consulting rendered abroad are subject to a flat 20% withholding tax and are fully deductible for the payer.[273]Technical assistance or technical services always involve labour or work from the service provider (actual training, design work or hands-on service), as opposed to the fact of applying for patents, know-how, formulae, etc., which are available to a third party under a license (Tax Code, Article 408).[274] This withholding can be reduced if a tax treaty is applicable.

B. Overhead and Royalties

687. Management overhead expenses, royalties, and other amounts charged for the acquisition or exploitation of intangible assets that are paid to (or credited to the account of) the parent company or a related 'foreign office' may be deducted for income tax purposes, as long as the (corresponding) withholding taxes are paid.

C. 15% Ceiling

688. The deduction of direct operating costs and general business expenses incurred abroad cannot exceed 15% of taxable income, as computed before deducting said costs and expenses. The following items are not subject to the 15% ceiling (Tax Code, Article 122):

- those subject to statutory withholding tax;
- commissions paid to foreign agents on the procurement and/or sale of merchandise, raw materials and other assets;
- interest paid on foreign import/export credits;
- repairs and maintenance of equipment;
- training of personnel of state-owned companies;
- the cost of any tangible assets;

273. This type of agreement must be previously registered with the Tax Administration (DIAN in Colombia).

274. For example, the difference between *know-how* and *technical assistance* is the following: *Know-how* is defined as a type of intangible asset, basically a *secret experience* about the way of doing something, which has been formed in an art or technique and which can be transferred for efficient application in the same field. *Technical assistance* is defined as the *advice* supplied under a service contract for the use of technological knowledge that is applied by means of an art or technique; this advice being one that also involves the training of people for the application of said knowledge. Thus, one thing is to license the practical knowledge called know-how for the use of a third party, and another thing is to *communicate* that knowledge to the licensee. The process of communicating said knowledge is called *technical assistance.*

- those which are capitalized for future amortization under generally accepted accounting principles; and
- those incurred pursuant to a specific legal requirement (as opposed to a contract requirement).

D. Deductible and Creditable Taxes

689. Real state tax is fully deductible for income tax purposes. They must have a direct relation with the taxpayer's income. Also, income taxpayers are allowed to deduct 50% of the financial transactions tax (GMF) and of their turnover tax (as of 2022 they should be able to deduct 100% of the turnover tax, which is a local tax) (Tax Code, Article 115).

E. Foreign Borrowing and Cross-Border Leasing

690. Interest payments on foreign borrowing and cross-border transactions are subject to withholding tax in Colombia. The rate applicable to the withholding tax varies according to the term of repayment of each disbursement as follows:

- For disbursements to be repaid in less than one year, as well as lease agreements for the same term, the applicable withholding tax rate is 20%.
- For disbursements to be repaid in a longer term, so as for lease agreements, the applicable withholding tax rate will be 15%.

691. Interests are fully deductible when the taxpayer withholds and pays the income tax applicable to interests payments, complies with the foreign exchange regulations and fulfils the other conditions set forth in section 107 of the Colombian Tax Code.[275]

III. Withholding Taxes for Non-resident Companies

692. Non-resident foreign companies are only taxed on Colombian source income, by means of withholding taxes. The most common withholdings include:

- Royalties paid or accrued to foreign non-resident licensors (other than 'royalties' paid under software and film licenses) are subject to 20% withholding tax (Tax Code, Article 408).
- Technical assistance, technical services and consulting services rendered either inside the country or abroad by non-resident companies are subject to a flat withholding tax of 20% (Tax Code, Article 408).

275. Tax payers may deduct from its income the costs and expenses accrued during the taxable year, provided that the relevant cost or expense is: (a) related to revenue producing activities; (b) necessary to obtain the revenue and; (c) proportioned to the revenue.

- Compensation paid to foreign non-resident licensors for software licenses or for film licenses (or film distribution) is subject to withholding taxes in Colombia at a rate of 20% (Tax Code, Article 408).

IV. Income Tax Incentives

693. Colombian tax legislation establishes different income tax incentives in the form of special deductions and exemptions. Most of the benefits are established for a specific period of time.

A. *Exemptions*

694. The following activities have been exempted from corporate income tax for fixed periods of time. However, it must be taken into account that the benefits obtained by a company as a result of an income tax exemption cannot be transferred to its partners or shareholders:

- Income resulting from activities qualified as creative industries[276] per the definitions set forth in the law is exempt for a seven year period.
- Income received from investments in the Colombian agriculture sector could be exempt for ten years.
- The sale of electrical energy generated with wind resources, biomass or agricultural waste for a fifteen-year term as of 2017.
- Income related to the sale of social interest or priority housing, provided certain requirements are met.
- Income received from the investment of forestry activities, sawmills and processing plants.
- Fluvial transportation services with shallow draft boats and barges for a fifteen-year period as of 2019.

B. *Special Corporate Income Tax Rates*

695. Free Trade Zones are areas within Colombian territory but considered out of the customs territory in which different logistics and manufacturing activities can be developed. Free Trade Zone users (operator, goods and service industrial users) are subject to a 20% corporate income tax rate (Tax Code, Article 240-1). Commercial sers, which are those developing activities of marketing, merchandising and storage of goods, are subject to the ordinary 32% corporate income tax rate.

276. Some examples are book editing, music recording, software editing, movie and video production etc.

696. Another special corporate income tax rate refers to 'mega-investments'. In this case, the rate is 27% for projects qualified as mega investments. Investments need to be over USD 280 million and create 400 direct employments.

V. International Aspects

A. Double Taxation Treaties

697. Colombia has entered into a few agreements aimed at preventing double taxation. The first one was entered into by the members of the Andean Community of Nations (Bolivia, Colombia, Ecuador and Peru) and it was modified by Decision 578 of 2004. This agreement establishes that, except for specific rules, income is taxed by the source country. Furthermore, it states that corporate benefits for technical assistance, consulting and technical services are taxed in the member country in which the benefit is produced.[277] In addition, labour income is only taxed in the country in which the employee renders his personal services.[278]

698. As of 2005 Colombia has signed Double Taxation Treaties (DTT) with the following countries: Spain, Chile, Switzerland, Canada, Mexico, Korea, India, Portugal, Czech Republic, and the United Kingdom. The following treaties have been signed but have not yet entered into force: Italy, France, Japan, United Arab Emirates.

B. Foreign Tax Credit

699. Colombian taxpayers can credit against their corporate income tax, income taxes paid on foreign source income. Colombian tax law contemplates both a direct tax credit and an indirect tax credit. The tax credit cannot exceed the tax levied in Colombia for the same income (Tax Code, Article 254).

VI. Losses

700. Colombian taxpayers are allowed to carry forward their Net Operating Losses (NOLs) for the following twelve years. The use of losses to reduce taxable income is without prejudice of the assessment of the alternate minimum presumptive income tax. NOLs may not be transferred from the companies to its partners or shareholders. NOLs may not be carried back.

---

277. Revenue Ruling 44126 of 2 May 2008.
278. Revenue Ruling 52813 of 20 May 2008.

§2. Value Added Tax

701. VAT (or IVA in Spanish) is levied on the importation and sale of goods, and the rendering of services. The export of goods is subject to zero rate (exempt). Certain goods (raw food, vegetable products, some medicines, oil, gas, electricity, and others) and services (health care, transportation, and others) are excluded from VAT.

702. The applicable tax rates are 0%, 5%, and 19%. As the tax is designed to cover the value added of goods and services in circulation, it is the end user who normally pays the cost of the tax. While those who sell goods and render services are legally accountable for VAT, they act as true tax collectors: they set off the VAT they pay on raw materials, supplies and merchandise with the VAT they collect from customers, and pay the excess of the latter over the former to the government.

703. VAT taxpayers are required to register as VAT vendors with the Tax Office; disclose the VAT they charge on their invoices; carry a General Ledger account for entries related to the tax called 'Impuesto a las Ventas por Pagar' (VAT payable); and file bimonthly returns reporting the VAT charged to customers and the VAT paid to suppliers or paid on imports (Input VAT).

704. All services consumed in the country and provided by non-resident companies are subject to VAT. For B2B services reverse-charge mechanism will apply, and thus the Colombian consumer will need to account and pay 19% tax to the tax authorities. For B2C services, the foreign provider needs to register before the tax authority and comply with all VAT formal and substantial requirements (Tax Code, Articles 420 et seq).

§3. Carbon Tax

705. In 2016, the Colombian Government enacted the Carbon Tax[279] which taxes the carbon component of fossil fuels, including all fossil gas types used with energetic purposes, as long as they are used for combustion.

706. The tax is levied on the amount of carbon dioxide emissions produced by the fossil fuel. Taxpayers can offset this tax with carbon credits duly certified.

§4. National Gasoline Tax

707. This tax, created by Law 1607 of 2012, levies the sale, import or consumption of gasoline and other liquid motor fuels. Producers and importers are responsible for charging and collecting this tax. The tax is determined based on a fixed rate established yearly by the government per gallon.

---

279. Law 1819 of 2016.

708. State and local authorities apply a Gasoline Surcharge to the consumption of gasoline and other liquid motor fuels, and the wholesalers are responsible for charging and collecting the tax.

§5. Industry and Commerce Tax (District/Local Taxes)

709. This municipal tax applies to industrial and commercial activity, as well as to services rendered within a municipality. However, it does not apply to exports. Municipal treasurers and finance secretaries are the authorities responsible for collecting and managing the tax. The rate is set by each municipality according to the limits established by law: (i) The Industrial Activity is taxed at rates between 0.2% and 1.1% each month on income from the sale of goods other than exports, and from the sale of fixed assets, refunds, subsidies and withholdings; and (ii) commercial and services activity is taxed at rates between 0.2% and 1.4% each month on average monthly income in the preceding year, excluding the items mentioned above.

§6. Financial Transactions Tax

710. The financial operations tax was established by means of Decree 2331 of 1998 and was in force until 31 December 1999. Its initial purpose was to gather funds for the reconstruction of the so-called *Eje Cafetero*, a geographical area affected by an earthquake in early 1999. Although the transaction tax was meant to be transitory, throughout different tax reforms has become a permanent tax.

I. Taxable Events

711. The taxable event is the performance of financial operations by which individuals or legal entities use funds that are deposited in checking or savings accounts, as well as the issuance of certified checks, except for certain transactions performed between accounts of the same holder, among others.

712. Also debits made to accounting balances, different from checking, saving or deposit accounts, for purposes of payments or transfers to a third party.

II. Taxable Base

713. The taxable base is the total value of each financial operation.

III. Rate

714. The tax is levied at a rate of 0.4%, and accrues at the moment in which the financial operation takes place.

IV. Accrual

715. The financial operations tax accrues at the moment the corresponding financial operation is performed. The financial operations tax must be withheld by the financial entities through which the operations are performed. The financial entities must file the relevant returns and pay the collected amounts to the tax authorities. Additionally, they are responsible for compliance with these obligations, and shall be subject to the applicable fines and interests.

V. Deductibility of the Financial Operations Tax

716. Income taxpayers are allowed to deduct 50% of the GMF (Tax Code, Article 115).

Chapter 2. Specific Tax Regime: Energy

717. This chapter elaborates on the special tax features the Colombian tax regime provides for Oil, Gas, Mining and Non-conventional energy sources companies.

§1. Income Tax

I. E&P Investments Amortization

718. One of the most relevant and significant features of the Colombian tax regulation for oil industry companies is the special E&P investment amortization conditions, which are contemplated in Article 143-1 of the Tax Code.

719. Regarding amortization of E&P investments in oil and gas fields, the law establishes two scenarios for amortization:

(1) *First scenario – unsuccessful field*: the asset may be amortized in the following year in which the unsuccessful condition is determined, and in any case, at the latest within two years.
(2) *Second scenario – successful field*: the value to be amortized is determined by an equation which is the following:

$$CA_t = \frac{UP_t}{R_{t-1}} \times SA_{t-1}$$

Where:

- CA_t is the amortization cost in the taxable year or period.
- UP_t equals the units produced in the taxable year or period.
- R_{t-1} equals the remaining proven developed reserves or remaining recoverable reserves, duly audited by the expert in the field, at the end of the immediately preceding year. In the first year of production, R corresponds to the value of proven reserves and consigned in the respective contract, work programmes and PTO-projects and/or the technical reserve study.
- SA_{t-1} equals the balance to be amortized at the end of the immediately preceding year or taxable period.

  In case the production of the oil field runs out before the term established in the contract, the outstanding balance may be amortized the year in which the situation is verified and, in any case, in the following two years at the latest.

720. E&P-related assets described in section 4 from Article 74-1 from the Tax Code, include (i) acquisition of exploration rights; (ii) seismic, topographic, geological, geochemical and geophysical studies linked to a discovery of the non-renewable natural resource; (iii) exploratory drilling; (iv) sampling; (v) activities related to the evaluation of the commercial viability can be capitalized and amortized in accordance to the rules described before. However, if those investments are made between 1 January 2017 and 31 December 2027 the amortization straight-line method for a five-year period should be used (unless the oil field is unsuccessful in which case, the special rule would apply).

721. In summary, items that can be capitalized in E&P investments for being used in the development of this activity will have the following treatment: (i) if said investment is successful it will be amortized in accordance with the successful field rule and if applicable, the five-year term straight-line method; (ii) if the investment is unsuccessful, it will be amortized in accordance with the unsuccessful field rule.

II. VAT as Tax Credit in Income Tax

722. Article 258-1 of the Tax Code establishes that VAT paid in acquisition, construction or formation, and import of real productive fixed assets, including services necessary for the assets to perform the required functions, can be used as a tax credit to offset Corporate Income Tax.

723. Real productive fixed assets are those which comply with the following criteria:

- Are classified as fixed assets (not sold in the ordinary course of business).
- Are tangible goods.
- Are acquired, build or formed, or imported to be part of the gross worth of the taxpayer.
- Participate permanently and directly in the main economic activity of the taxpayer to produce goods and/or services.
- Are subject to fiscal depreciation or amortization.

III. Withholding Tax on Exports

724. Oil, gas and mining exporters will be subject to withholding tax on the gross income received in currency from the export of said products.

- 3% on hydrocarbons.
- 1% on mining products.

725. For that purpose, the beneficiary of the income acts as self-withholding agent and shall determine the value of the tax according to the exchange rate of the day of payment or accrual. Finally, the beneficiary shall pay the tax within the time-frame stated by the National Government.

§2. VALUE ADDED TAX

I. VAT Exclusion on Temporary Imports

726. The temporary import of heavy machinery, which is not manufactured in Colombia and is to be used in basic industries, is not charged with VAT. Mining, Oil & Gas, electric energy production and transmission, and attainment, purification and transportation of hydrogen oxide.

727. Notably, heavy machinery can be imported on a temporary basis for a maximum five year period or for the time agreed on the lease agreement. After said period, the machinery must be re-exported abroad or definitely imported by paying the relevant VAT and customs duties.

II. VAT Excluded

728. Transportation of oil & gas, sale of gas and coal, and sale of electric energy are VAT excluded (exempted without credit).

III. Imports out of VAT Scope

729. Equipment and machinery imports, which are not produced in the country, destined for investment in environmental control, will not be subject to import VAT. Environmental control projects include those aimed at obtaining measurable results in the reduction of atmospheric gases emissions and demand for non-renewable natural resources.

IV. Creditable VAT for Offshore E&P Projects

730. Taxpayers whose main economic activity is the exploration of oil & gas can credit the input VAT incurred in the acquisition or import of goods and services used in the exploration and development stage. The amount resulting from said creditable input VAT can be subject to a refund request within the next year. Acquired goods and services need to be capitalized so that this benefit applies, making this benefit different from the tax credit of VAT paid in acquisition, construction or formation, and import of real productive fixed assets.

§3. Mining Industry Special Tax Features

731. Colombian tax regime provides for a special tax feature regarding Presumptive income tax, which is granted to companies who belong to the Mining Industry. Mining companies which exclusively develop mining activities, for purposes of assessing its presumptive income, can exclude from its net worth the assets directly linked to the mining activity.

§4. Alternative Energy

732. As of 2014, Colombia enacted tax incentives for the production of electric energy with non-conventional energy sources and the efficient energy management. Non-conventional energy sources are defined as environmental sustainable energy resources that are not used or broadly commercialized in Colombia.

733. Efficient Energy Management is defined as all actions aimed at securing the energy supply by implementing energy-efficient methods such as good practices of fuel substitution.

734. Tax incentives include the following:

- Special deduction in the Corporate Income Tax assessment equivalent to 50% of the investment in production of electric energy with non-conventional energy sources and efficient energy management projects.
- No import taxes (VAT and tariff) on equipment, machinery and supplies for production of electric energy with non-conventional energy sources projects.
- Accelerated depreciation for assets acquired or built for the electric energy generation with non-conventional energy sources.

735. The sale of electrical energy generated with wind resources, biomass or agricultural waste is exempt from income tax for a fifteen-year term. For such purpose, companies must obtain and sell CO_2 certificates in accordance with the Kyoto Protocol. Finally, at least 50% of the revenues perceived from such sale must be invested in social projects in the region where the company is established.

736. Companies performing investments on control and protection of environment may credit 25% of the value of such investments from their corporate income tax.

737. The Tax Authority has clarified that the purchase of goods and machinery intended for projects or programmes for energy consumption reduction or energy efficiency are not eligible for tax incentives, when such acquisitions are carried out in compliance with an environmental obligation or when they fall out of the targets on clean energy established by the MASD and the MME.[280]

738. For obtaining the benefits set forth above, taxpayers are required to qualify their project before the competent environmental authority.

280. Tax Authority, Official Letter No. 000953; 11 Sep. 2014.

Part VII. Interaction Between Energy Law and Competition Law

Chapter 1. Introduction

739. In Colombia, Competition Law in the energy sector has evolved dynamically since the 1991 Constitution, which laid a new foundation and principles for the national economic regime. It also modified the structure of public utilities' supply, including electricity and gas.

740. In fact, competition regulation in Colombia affects mainly the electricity and gas industry, as there is a special competition regime for these services, which has been recently modified by Law 1955 of 2019 regarding limits to integrated electricity companies. Regarding mining and oil, the rules that apply to these sectors are mainly related to the general competition regime, which is why this part will make a much more extensive reference to the relationship between electricity and gas regulation with competition law.

§1. Constitutional Principles

741. In the 'Economic and public finances regime' governed by title XII of the Colombian Constitution, Article 333 enshrines a social market economic model based on principles such as freedom of economic activity, private initiative, free competition and freedom of enterprise.[281]

742. As for the principles of free economic activity and free private initiative, they refer to the right of any individual to participate in the market, performing whichever activity they wish as long as it is carried out within the limits of the common good.

743. Meanwhile, free competition is a right that involves responsibilities and is complemented by the principle of free enterprise, which is seen as the foundation for progress.

---

281. Political Constitution of Colombia, Art. 333.

744. However, concerning the exercise of free enterprise and free competition, the Colombian constitutional system also enshrined limits. Article 333 establishes the duty for the State to prevent the obstruction or restriction of economic freedom and prevent or control any abuse that any person or company makes of their dominant position in the domestic market.

745. It is necessary to emphasize that although individuals are allowed complete freedom when developing economic activities, the State remains with the power to direct and intervene in the economy, when authorized by the law, in order to improve the quality of life for its residents. This intervention, according to Article 334 of the Constitution, includes the exploitation of natural resources, land use, production, distribution, use and consumption of goods, as well as public and private services.[282]

746. Thus, the Colombian state with its power to address the economy may intervene, when authorized by the law, in the regulation of several sectors, such as the exploration and exploitation of hydrocarbons, mining and electricity, including public services and the exploitation of natural resources.

747. From this approach, we present a brief description about the constitutional regime of public services – such as electricity and gas – and its link with the concept of competition.

§2. Constitution, Public Services and Competition

748. The Colombian constitutional regime has a chapter exclusively dedicated to the regulation of public services and its importance for social development.[283] This chapter defines who can provide these services, the purpose of its provision, the state's responsibilities, and the functions of organizations such as the SSP, among other aspects.

749. The State has the obligation to provide all public services efficiently to all inhabitants of the country. This service may be provided by the same State or by individuals or organized communities without stating they should be exercising a public role.[284]

750. Therefore, the principle of economic freedom and free enterprise also has application in the field of public services by allowing private persons or communities to become providers of these services. Regardless of who is in charge of providing a public service, the State keeps regulatory, monitoring and control functions.

282. Article 334, Constitution.
283. Chapter V, Title XII, *ibid.*
284. Article 365, Constitution.

751. This means, according to the legal framework, that the State is no longer a stakeholder, nor does it reserves the sole and direct provision of public services, such as electricity or gas. This new standard of service exists along with a business model in which the State maintains three main functions: regulating the service, and monitoring and controlling all participating companies.[285]

752. Similarly, the right of individuals to provide public services is not absolute. The Constitution, in the same Article 333, allows the State to keep the provision of some strategic activities or public services for itself, and it compensates beforehand all individuals who may be affected by this decision. By having a social market economy model, it is clear that the provision of public services shall be guided by principles for the improvement of the citizens' quality of life. It should be noted that the Constitution makes specific reference to those public services that affect households, that is, a special category of services delivered through networks in order to meet basic needs, such as the electric or gas service.[286]

753. The Constitutional Court has defined the characteristics of the electric service as a public domiciliary service and has concluded that it is:

> an essential public service for the normal development of social and economic activities in the country. Electricity, as the subject of the provision stated in the resulting service, meets a general need that is substantially linked to the population's welfare and the vital requirements of many processes and social activities. Electricity in Colombia, taking into account its current technological and economic conditions and the high dependence on this resource, is therefore an essential public good as its deficiency compromises the fate of the community.[287]

754. According to constitutional provisions on the public service system, the law must define the users' rights, requirements on quality in the provision of these services, the level of coverage, funding and also the tariff system of public services, which is not structured in a free manner. For the establishment of tariffs, the regulator must take into account cost criteria, solidarity and income redistribution. This explains why in some public services, users, including the electric service, pay subsidies on their utility bill to finance the cost of servicing those low-income users.[288]

---

285. Article 370, Constitution. This task of monitoring and control has been entrusted to the Superintendence of Public Utilities.
286. The Constitutional Court has defined the concept of domiciliary public service as follows: 'those that are provided through natural or human networks, with end points in users' homes or workplaces, which serve the specific purpose of meeting people's essential needs'. Known also as public utilities. *See* Constitutional Court, Judgment T-578 of 3 Nov. 1992. Available at: http://www.corteconstitucional.gov.co/relatoria/1992/T-578-92.htm.
287. Constitutional Court, Sentence C-447of 1992, Magistrate: Eduardo Cifuentes Muñoz.
288. Articles 367, 368 and 369, Constitution.

755. In conclusion, electricity and gas are subject to principles defined by the Constitution for public services. Among the principles to be considered in the energy sector are the State's role as regulator and responsible for monitoring and supervision of providers, free economy, free private initiative, free competition, free enterprise, efficiency in service delivery, quality, coverage and implementation of cost criteria, solidarity and income redistribution in issuing rates. All these principles are the starting point and have a direct impact on the accrual basis, general and specific, applicable to the energy sector in Colombia.

Chapter 2. Competition Law and Energy: General Regime

756. As we mentioned previously, competition law in the energy sector is regulated by two different legal regimes: first, the general competition regime and, second, the special rules for the public service sector and the energy sector, which specifically governs competition in these markets.

757. Before referring to the general competition, it is necessary to note that as from the issuance of Law 1340 of 2009, the Superintendence of Industry and Commerce (SIC) is, with few exceptions,[289] the only competition authority in the country, responsible for hearing solely the procedures, administrative investigations, fines and other decisions related to unfair competition, restrictive business practices (agreements, actions, abuse of dominant position and mergers) competition advocacy, consumer statute application, among others. In this sense, it is clear that any case involving the application of the general or special competition regime in the energy sector is administered by this authority.[290]

758. However, regarding the general competition rules applicable to the energy sector, Law 256 of 1996 defines an extensive list of forbidden conducts considered as actions of unfair competition, as it covers all economic activities. Pursuant to the Constitution, Law 256 of 1996 must be interpreted in accordance with the principles of free economy and free enterprise, within the limits of the common good and also according to the principle of economic competition freedom required, which must be exercised with responsibility and loyalty.[291]

§1. Unfair Competition

759. Law 256 of1996 applies to all sectors of the economy. The effects of inequitable conduct must take place in the Colombian market and are mandatory for any market participant. Naturally, the standard must be met by traders, regardless of their activity, profession or trade.[292] In consequence, all energy companies must compete in the market following the principles of responsibility, loyalty and, of course, avoiding any unfair competition behaviour.

760. Also for the conducts referred to in Law 256 of1996 to be considered actions of unfair competition, they must be made for the purpose of maintaining or

---

289. For example, the Civil Aeronautic retains jurisdiction for the approval of all commercial transactions between aircraft operators. Also, the Financial Superintendence retains jurisdiction for the approval of mergers or corporate reorganization involving only the entities supervised by it. Law 1340 issued 24 Jul. 2009, Arts 9 and 8.
290. Law 1340 issued 24 Jul. 2009, Art. 2 y 6.
291. Article 6, Law 256 of 1996.
292. Articles 1, 3 and 4, *ibid.*

increasing market share of the one who exhibits this behaviour, or to maintain or increase market share of a third party.[293] This behaviour is called competing purpose.

761. In the unfair competition regime, in addition to actions expressly stated in the law as such, there is a general clause prohibiting unfair conduct, which is not in itself an act of individual competition but has the general characteristics of this type of behaviour. In this sense, it is considered unfair competition any act or event which takes place in the market for competing purposes, when it is contrary to sound business practices, the principle of commercial good faith and honest practices in industrial or commercial matters. Any act or event which affects or seeks to affect the purchaser or consumer's decision freedom, or the competitive operation of the market,[294] shall also be considered unfair competition.

762. The actions of unfair competition are defined in the following specific conducts:[295]

- Customer diversion conducted in an opposite manner to honest commercial practices.
- Actions aimed at generating internal disorganization in businesses.
- Actions that seek to create confusion or deception regarding the commercial activities and services of other establishments, incorrect indications or false statements, omission of the true facts and any other practice which has the purpose or effect of discrediting the activity, services, or business relations of a third party.
- Actions of public comparison using incorrect indications or allegations, true or false comparisons taken to extremes that are not similar, nor verifiable.
- Actions of imitation when they generate confusion about the business source involved in the provision, or taking unfair advantage of another's reputation. In this sense, it is considered unfair the unauthorized use of trademarks or appellations of origin that are false or misleading.

763. It is also considered inequitable the disclosure or exploitation without the owner's authorization, of trade secrets or any other kind of secret to which the individual has legitimately had access with the duty to keep in strict confidence, or has accessed illegally by espionage or similar procedures. It is also considered unfair to induce workers, suppliers, customers and others to violate the basic contractual obligations they have undertaken with competitors. However, this last conduct only qualifies as unfair when it are meant for the expansion of an industry or business or accompanied by circumstances such as deception or intent to eliminate a competitor from the market.

764. Finally, it is considered unfair to acquire a significant competitive advantage through the violation of one or more legal rules. In addition, agreeing to unfair

293. Article 2, *ibid.*
294. Article 7, *ibid.*
295. Articles 8–17, *ibid.*

exclusivity clauses when their object or effect is the restriction of access of competitors to the market, or monopolize the distribution of products or services, is considered unfair competition.

765. In practice, the SIC and the local courts[296] have seen multiple cases of unfair competition in which the companies involved belong to the energy sector: between electricity distributors, retail fuel distributors,[297] natural compressed gas vehicle companies, etc. These trials have involved several actions defined in Law 256 of 1996 as unfair competition.

766. For example, the complaint filed by Energía Confiable S.A. ESP (electricity trader) arguing that a procedure to restrict the supply front by Electricaribe S. A. ESP (distributor and marketer of electricity) should be considered an act of unfair competition,[298] or Gas Natural Comprimido S.A. (GNC S.A.) and Gas Natural Comprimido de Colombia S.A. (GASCOL S.A.), dedicated to marketing, distribution and operation of compressed natural gas service stations, in which GNC SA denounced its competitor for engaging in some of the general prohibitions included in the Competition Act, such as diversion of customers and exploitation of the competitor's reputation.[299]

§2. Restrictive Practices

767. In addition to conducts considered unfair competition, we must refer to practices that restrict competition, the second major branch of competition law in Colombia. Competition restrictive practices cover: anticompetitive actions or agreements; prohibition of the abuse of dominant position; and control over mergers. This entire legal regime, together with the rules of unfair competition, is applicable to companies active in the energy sector, although it should be made clear that it only applies as long as there is no rule from the special utility or energy sector to deal with the matter.[300]

296. 'In terms of unfair competition there are two kinds of jurisdictions. On the one hand the administrative jurisdiction and civil jurisdiction on the other', *see* Mauricio Velandia. *Competition Law and Consumption*. 2nd ed. 407 (Universidad Externado de Colombia 2011).
297. Supreme Court of Justice, Civil Cassation Chamber, Case 6869 of 9 Apr. 2002, MP Ardila Manuel Velazquez.
298. Superintendence of Industry and Commerce, Case No. 01425 of 2004.
299. Superintendence of Industry and Commerce, 015 Judgment 17 Mar. 2011.
300. As stated in Art. 4 of Law 1340 of 2009: 'Law 155 of 1959, Decree 2153 of 1992, this Act and other provisions which amend it or supplement it, constitute the general system of competition protection, applicable to all sectors and all economic activities. If there are special rules for certain sectors or activities, these will prevail only for the specific topic.' For example, as discussed below, the special legislation of the public services sector in Colombia, Law 142 of 1994, regulates the abuse of dominant position in this area.

768. Decree 2153 of 1992 defines the kind of agreements or actions considered as restrictive of competition.[301] The effects of agreements considered against free competition do not necessarily occur in the market, meaning that an agreement may be anticompetitive due to its purpose or its effect. As stated by the competition authority, anticompetitive agreements by purpose are those that, regardless of whether they have effects on the market or not, their purpose is anticompetitive by nature. On the contrary, an agreement has an anticompetitive effect when its outcome, independently from the parties' purpose, has anticompetitive effects in the market.[302]

769. Therefore, agreements are considered anticompetitive whenever they have as their purpose or affect the following:

- Direct or indirect fixing of prices.
- Determining conditions for sale or marketing in a discriminatory manner against third parties.
- The allotment of markets between producers, or between producers and distributors.
- The allocation of production or supply quotas.
- The allocation, distribution or limitation to input production and supply sources.
- The limitation on technical developments.
- Conditioning the supply of a product to the acceptance of additional obligations, which, by their nature, were not intrinsic to the business.
- Refraining from producing a good or service or affecting its production levels.
- Preventing others from accessing markets or marketing channels.
- The bid-rigging or collusion in selection processes or similar ones that have the purpose of awarding contracts, and distribution of tenders as well as setting terms for proposals.[303]

770. It is important to distinguish anticompetitive actions from the abuse of dominant position. In this regard, there is a clear explanation by Mauricio Velandia for this distinction. According to this author, 'restrictive actions are unilateral behaviors aimed at all traders. They differ from the dominant position in the fact that these restrictive actions do not require a specific qualified subject, for they are aimed at the entire universe of merchants'.[304]

301. The rationale behind this rule is found in Law 155 of 1959 (as amended by Art. 1 of Decree 3307 of 1963) which states in Art. 1: 'agreements that are directly or indirectly by to limit the production, supply, distribution or consumption of raw materials, products, goods or services or foreign, and in general all kinds of practices, procedures or systems designed to limit competition and maintain or fix unfair prices are prohibited'. *See* Art. 1, Law 155 of 1959.

302. Superintendence of Industry and Commerce, *What is an Anticompetitive Agreement?.* http://www.sic.gov.co/es/web/guest/practicas-restrictivas, May 2012.

303. Article 47, Decree 2153 of 1992.

304. *See* Velandia, *supra,* p. 195.

771. Consequently, the breach of the advertising rules contained in the consumer protection statute is considered an anticompetitive action, as well as influencing a company to raise the prices of its products, services, or to desist from their intention to cut prices; to refuse selling or providing services to a company or practice discriminatory behaviour against a company, when it can be inferred that this behaviour is a retaliation to their pricing.[305]

§3. ABUSE OF DOMINANT POSITION

772. The abuse of dominant position implies that the company or individual holds a dominant position in a determined relevant market. Furthermore, the mere fact of being the dominant competitor in a market is not sanctioned by the norms of competition, as this position can be achieved by legitimate means, such as economic and administrative efficiency, innovation technology, research, etc. What the Colombian law punishes is the abuse of this position, which results in an assault to fair competition and a distortion of the natural conditions of competition in a given market. The Constitution makes the State responsible for preventing any abuse of dominant position in the domestic market.

773. According to this constitutional mandate, competition law has defined what a dominant position means and has identified a number of behaviours that constitute an abuse of that position. Accordingly, an entrepreneur will be in a dominant position when he has the possibility to determine, directly or indirectly, the market conditions. The behaviours that represent an abuse of this position are the following:[306]

- The decline in prices below the cost level, when it intends to remove one or more competitors or prevent their entry or expansion.
- The use of discriminatory conditions to equivalent transactions, thereby placing a consumer or supplier in disadvantage compared to other consumer or provider under similar conditions.
- Those conducts that have as their purpose or effect to subject the supply of a product to acceptance of additional obligations, which by their nature were not intrinsic to the main business.
- The sale to a buyer under different conditions from those offered to another buyer, when this is intended to reduce or eliminate competition in the market.
- Selling or providing services in any part of the country at a different price from that which is offered elsewhere in the Colombian territory, if the intent or effect is to reduce or eliminate competition in that area and the price does not correspond to the structure cost of the transaction.
- Obstructing or preventing third parties from accessing markets or marketing channels.

---

305. Article 48, Decree 2153 of 1992.
306. Articles 45 and 50, Decree 2153 of 1992.

– In the energy sector, is common to find cases of restrictive practices or abuse of dominant position. The SIC has investigated and sanctioned fuel retailers due to tacit pricing agreements. For example, in Resolution 71794 of 2011, the authority fined several petrol stations in the municipality of Duitama for agreeing to set fuel sale prices; and Resolution 14540 of 2002 the authority sanctioned gas stations for price fixing as a result of consciously parallel practices.[307]

774. Regarding abuse of dominant position in the energy sector, the competition authority began in 2009 an investigation against Gas Natural SA E.S.P. due to the abuse of its dominant position, which became an obstruction to access this market. According to the Superintendence, Gas Natural SA E.S.P exploited the dominant position it held in Bogota in the distribution and marketing of gas (which gave it direct access to information of all service users, the ability to create and maintain a register of providers recognized by the market, as well as the legal authority to certify facilities). The company seemed to have implemented a penetration market strategy that would secure itself the complementary services of gas supply by limiting the ability of competitors to independently participate in the market.[308]

775. Also, in 2012, the Superintendence began an investigation against Empresa de Energía de Boyaca E.S.P (EBSA).The Superintendence found that EBSA abused its dominant position in the distribution and retailer market by creating a competitive advantage in the electricity metre calibration market. This market deals with verifying the metre's correct operation to know precisely the amount of energy consumed by the end user. The metre calibration market tends to be a competitive market in which multiple companies participate, including EBSA. However, EBSA acting as a retailer and distribution company began charging a fee for the homologation of metres calibrated by other companies, making it more expensive for other retailers and distribution companies to contract their services. Although EBSA incurred administrative and operative costs by the homologation and registration of metres calibrated in different laboratories, such expense was ultimately paid by the consumer through the electricity bill, so there was no actual need for charging companies an extra fee.[309]

776. Similarly, in the field of vehicular natural gas distribution, it can be cited the case in which the Superintendence accepted the guarantees provided by two companies under investigation, due to the alleged abuse of their dominant position

307. Superintendence of Industry and Commerce, Resolution 71794 of 2011, Distribuidora de Combustibles El Sol S.A., Estación de servicio LA ISLA LTDA., Estación de servicio VILLA DEL RÍO LTDA and others; Resolution 14540 of 15 May 2002, Servicentro La Sultana; Estación de Servicio Texaco 10 Start Mart; Estación de servicio Belalcázar and others; Resolution 7951 de 15 Mar. 2002, Servisur Ltda, Estación de Servicio Andina and others. http://avancejuridico.sic.gov.co/sic/docs/arbol/1778.htm, May 2012.

308. Superintendence of Industry and Commerce, Resolution 43270 of 2009, Gas Natural S.A. E.S.P, Meltronic LTDA. http://www.sic.gov.co/siyc/memoria/resolucion/superindustria/2009/resolucion_superindustria_43270_2009.html, May 2012.

309. Superintendence of Industry and Commerce, Resolution 3694 of 2013, Empresa de Energia de Boyaca E.S.P. https://www.sic.gov.co/sites/default/files/estados/RESOLUCION_3694_DE_05_DE_FEBRERO_DE_2013_SANCION_EBSA_ESP.pdf.

(Gases del Caribe ESP SA and Gas Natural Comprimido SA). According to the investigation, the two companies conditioned the gas supply to service stations to the acceptance of additional obligations, such as the collection of portfolio obligations, which were not intrinsic to their business.[310]

777. It is important to mention that control over mergers and acquisitions is primarily governed by Law 155 of 1959 and Law 1340 of 2009.[311] It is a general scheme applicable to all economic sectors in Colombia, except the mergers of entities supervised by the Superintendence of Finance, and those between the aircraft operators.

778. Due to the importance of the mining and energy sectors for the national economy, there was a remarkable increase in completed mergers between mining and oil companies.[312] Indeed, according to Gabriela Mancero, between 2000 and 2011, the SIC was notified of twenty mergers in the mining sector and seventy-four

310. Superintendence of Industry and Commerce, Resolution 28463 of 5 Aug. 2008, Mundogas S.A., Gases del Caribe S.A. E.S.P., Gas Natural Comprimido S.A. http://www.sic.gov.co/siyc/memoria/resolucion/superindustria/2008/resolucion_superindustria_28463_2008.html, May 2012.

311. Other relevant norms regarding merger control are Decree 3523 of 2009, Decree 1687 of 2010, Resolution 35006 of 2010, and Resolution 52778 of 2011. In addition, the Superintendence of Industry and Commerce has recently published a guide to analyse mergers: horizontal, vertical and conglomerate types. This information is available at: www.sic.gov.co.

312. Certainly, the recent intense activity on mergers covers the mining and oil sector with unique intensity, but it is also common to find mergers in electricity and gas sector. In order to assess this dynamic, below is a list of some concentrations carried out in mining, oil, fuel, electricity and gas in the last years: twenty years: Year 2016, ISAGEN, an public company involved in electricity generation, sold 57.61% to the Canadian Company Brookfield Renewable Energy Partners L.P Year 2013, the Advent International investor group acquired the 22% of Ocensa Central S.A, Colombia's largest crude oil transportation system. Later in 2020, Advent International sell its 22% stake to Cenit S.A, which is a wholly-owned subsidiary of ECOPETROL S.A. Year 2012: Emerald Energy PLC-Tepma B.V. (Rad. 12-061102); ExxonMobil de Colombia S.A.-Grupo EDS AutoGas S.A.S (Rad. 12-053350); 2011: Gran Tierra Energy Inc-Petrolifera Petroleum Limited (Rad. 11032044), Promigas-Organización Terpel S.A-Corporación Financiera Colombiana en Transoriente (Rad. 10146981); 2010: Gas Natural del Oriente-Gas Natural del Cesar (Rad. 9099373), Petrobras Colombia Combustibles S.A-Petrobras Colombia Downstream S.A. (Rad. 10035792), Termocandelaria Power-Termocandelaria S.C.A –Termoencali (Rad. 10049266); 2009: Empresa de Energía de Bogotá S.A. E.S.P. – Electrificadora del Meta S.A. ESP. – Empresa de Energía de Cundinamarca S.A. E.S.P. – Empresa de Energía de Boyacá S.A. E.S.P., – Electrificadora de Santander S.A. E.S.P. – Centrales Eléctricas de Norte de Santander S.A. E.S.P. (Rad. 8138117), ECOPETROL S.A. – Hocol S.A. – Homcol Cayman Inc.(Rad. 9033696), Amcor Ltd. – Rio Tinto International Holdings Limited (Rad. 9106659); 2008: Meta Petroleum Ltd – Tethys Petroleum Company Ltda-Quifa Petroleum Ltda-Major International Oil S.A-Petrorubiales Corporation Corp – Pacific Stratus Energy Colombia Ltd Sucursdal Colombia – Oleoductio De Los Llanos Orientales S.A – Kappa Resources Colombia Ltda-Great North Energyu Colombia Inc. (Rad. 08/75138); Compañía Minera de Caldas S.A. – Mineros S.A. (Rad. 08/57525); 2007: Promigas S.A. ESP – Sociedad de Inversiones en Energía S.A. (Rad. 7026372), Compañía Energética del Tolima S.A. ESP – Servicios Generales Empresa de Servicios Públicos de Carácter Privado S.A. ESP – E.L.E.C. S.A – Servicios Integrales del Valle S.A. ESP – Empresa de Energía de Pereira S.A. ESP (Rad. 7118869); 2006: Fenoco S.A. – Carbones del Caribe S.A., – Consorcio Minero Unido S.A., – Carbones de los Andes S.A., – Compañía Carbones del Cesar S.A., – Drummmond Coal Mining LLC., C.I.-Prodeco S.A. – Carbones de la Jagua S.A. (Rad. 6027462); Glencore International AG – Consorcio Minero Unido S.A. (Rad. 6057587); 2005: Proyecto de Energía S.A. – Promotora de Energía

in the oil sector.[313] Of these operations, most of them have not been objected by the authority, only a small percentage have been challenged or approved under certain conditions, such as the merger between Indac Colombia Ltda. and Acerías Paz del Río S.A. No significant mergers and acquisitions have been observed in recent years.[314]

---

y Gas S.A. (Rad. 5073693); Sociedades Gases del Norte del Valle S.A. E.S.P. – Gases de Occidente A.E.S. (Rad. 50110623); 2004: Colombiana de Servicios Energéticos S.A. – Soluciones Equipos y Proyectos Sep Ltda – Colombiana de servicios Petroleros y Energéticos S.A. (Rad. 4111201); 2003: Meta Petroleum – Turnsector – Coplex – Rubiales (Rad. 3104187), Sociedad invercolsa S.A – Metrogas de Colombia E.S.P – Inversiones Extrogas S.A – Gases del Oriente S.A E.S.P (Rad. 3017105); 2002: Chevron Texaco: Industrias Texaco S.A., Texas Petroleum Company, Chevron Petroleum Company, Chevron Oil Colombia Limited, Chevron Oronite Latin America S.A, Guajira Gas Services Inc. y Chevron San Jorge S.A (Rad. 2089513), Empresas Publicas de Medellin E.S.P (EEPPM) – Central Hidroelectrica de Caldas S.A. E.S.P (CHEC) – Empresa de Energia del Quindio (EDEQ) (Rad. 2034032), Flores holding Ltda – Flores II S.A – Flores III S.A – Flores II S.A y Cía SCA ESP – Flores III S.A y Cía SCA ESP (Rad. 2091078); 2001: Proyectos de Energía S.A. – Betania Gen Inc (Rad. 1046064), Empresa Antioquena de Energía S.A E.S.P – Empresas Publicas de Caucasia (Rad. 1027174), The AES Corporation – Chivor S.A E.S.P (Rad. 1076520); 2000: Empresas Públicas de Medellín – Empresas Antioqueña de Energía (Rad. 14686), Empresa de Energia del Pacífico – Cidral S.A. E.P.S. (Rad. 00048921), Empresas Públicas de Medellín S.A. ESP – Isagen S.A. ESP (Rad. 00030604), Triton Colombia I.N.C. – Preussag Energy (Rad. 00079638), Occidental de Colombia I.N.C. – Occidental Andina I.N.C. (Rad. 00078148), Terpel Norte – Terpel Bucaramanga – Terpel Occidente – Terpel Centro – Terpel Sur (Rad. 00083664); 1999: Carbones Del Cerrejón S.A. – Oreganal S.A. (Rad. 99011005), Esso Colombiana Limited – Mobil De Colombia S.A. (Rad. 99038315), Bogotana de Gas S.A. E.S.P. – Supergas S.A. E.S.P. (Rad. 9904482); 1998: Gas Natural E.S.P. – Gas Natural del Oriente S.A. E.S.P. (Rad. 9800799), Alcanos del Huila S.A. E.S.P. – Gran Colombiana de Gas S.A. (Rad. 98051155). Available at: www.sic.gov.co.

313. Gabriela Mancero Bucheli, *Adquisición de Empresas en el Sector Minero y Petrolero Colombiano*, in *Colección de Estudios en Derecho Minero y Energético 4* (Universidad Externado de Colombia 2012).

314. This merger was objected to by SIC Resolution 35379 of 21 Dec. 2006 but subsequently authorized by Resolution 2489 of 20 Feb. 2007.

Chapter 3. Energy Regulation and Competition: Special Regime

779. Concerning electricity and gas, there are special rules on anticompetitive practices and unfair competition for these industries. The starting point of all special regulations on competition in the energy sector is Law 142 of 1994, which establishes the general legal framework for public services, including electrical service and gas distribution.

780. This law defines that the State should intervene in public services according to the competition rules established therein, which develop the constitutional economic regime aforementioned. One of the purposes of State intervention in these services is to ensure that companies do not abuse their dominant position and that a system of free competition operates.[315]

781. In order to enable the State to achieve this, and all the objectives set by the Constitution and the law on public services, Law 142 of 1994 creates a mechanism known as the regulatory commissions. These are independent authorities from the sector and include the CREG.[316] In general, the role of these commissions is to regulate monopolies in the areas of public services where competition is not possible and, where possible, to promote competition so that operations are economically efficient, companies are not involved in an abuse of dominant position and quality services are provided.[317] To meet this general function, the Commissions are empowered to:[318]

- Identify general criteria on the abuse of dominant position in public service contracts.
- Establish mechanisms to avoid concentration of stock ownership in companies with complementary activities in the same sector or related sectors for each public service.
- Order a utility company to spin-off into new companies with the same purpose or a purpose that is limited to a side-line activity. A spin-off order may occur in the following cases: when the firm uses its dominant position to prevent the development of competition in a market where this is possible; when the company subsidizes one of its intensely competitive services with resources from another service that does not have as much competition; or, in general, when performing anticompetitive practices.
- Order the merger of companies where there are studies showing to the need to extend coverage and lower costs for users.

315. Article 2, Law 142 of 1994.
316. Through Law 142 of 1994, the Water and Sanitation Commission (CRA, after its wording in Spanish) and the Communications Regulation Commission (CRC) were also created.
317. Article 73, Law 142 of 1994.
318. Articles 73.13, 73.14, 73.21, 73.25 and 74.1, *ibid.*

782. Law 142 of 1994 provides that the CREG should regulate in order to promote competition in the mining and energy sector, propose the necessary measures to prevent the abuse of dominant position and seek the gradual release of markets into full competition.

783. Free enterprise on public services is defined in Law 142 of 1994 as the right that everyone has to organize and operate businesses for the provision of these services. It requires that when there is no possibility of competition, companies must refrain from monopolistic or restrictive practices.[319] This purpose is consistent with the interpretation criteria according to which these should be interpreted in accordance with the principles contained in the preliminary title of the Law and in the manner that best ensures fair competition and prevents dominant position abuses.[320]

§1. Dominant Position

784. Law 142 of 1994 defines the abuse of dominant position in the public service sector. Consequently, the companies that have a dominant position in regards to their users, market and replacement market, are the ones that serve 25% or more of the users that make up their market.[321] In addition to this general definition, the standard public service contract defines twenty-six clauses whose presence presumes the existence of an abuse of dominant position by the company. Among these clauses we emphasize the following ones:[322]

- Exclusion or limitation of the company's liability according to general Law or those that assign the user the duty of obtaining evidence, for instance, in a claim procedure.
- Those that give the company the right to terminate the contract, change the conditions or suspend its validity, revoke or limit any of the user's rights, for reasons other than breach of contract or force majeure.
- Conditioning any contractual or statutory right of the user to the approval of the utility company.
- Requiring users to purchase goods or services from the utility company or another person, which are not directly related to the contract. Also, clauses that limit the users' freedom to choose the service provider, evidence an abuse of dominant position.
- Imposing the user a waiver of any right awarded in the contract.
- Subjecting the use of any resource or activities to which the user is entitled to terms or conditions not covered by the law.

319. Articles 10 and 11.2, Law 142 of 1994.
320. Articles 1, 2.6 and 30, *ibid.*
321. Article 14.13, *ibid.* In regards to utility companies that have a dominant position in the market, and whose principal activity is the distribution of goods or services provided by third parties, the law requires that they must acquire the good or service through procedures that ensure the possibility of competition for potential contractors and on equal terms for them.
322. Article 133, Law 142 of 1994.

- Empowering the company to choose the place where the arbitration or conciliation has to take place, in case of disputes.
- Entitling the company to modify its obligations based on the company's interests.
- Limiting the users' right to request the termination of the contract or damages in the event of the company's total or partial non-compliance.

§2. Anticompetitive Practices

785. Regarding anticompetitive practices, it is clearly stated that public service companies must avoid unjustified discrimination in all their actions and contracts. Public service companies must also refrain from any practice that has the capacity, purpose or effect of creating unfair competition or that unjustifiably restricts competition. Hence, the law defines the conducts identified as anticompetitive practices, such as:

- Charging fees that cover service operation costs.
- Offering additional services for free or for a price that is below cost rates.
- Entering into agreements with other companies to share fees or certain types of services, or establishing rates that create supply constraints or raising rates above of what would occur under competitive conditions.
- Any agreement with any competitor during the processing of any act or contract, which should have citations to the public or potential competitors and that may seek a change in the result that would have been obtained in full competition.
- All acts of unfair competition under the general regime defined in Law 256 of 1996 and the abuse of dominant position under the terms of Article 133 of Law 142 of1994, regardless of the counterpart or type of contract.[323]

786. Similarly, the law provides for specific behaviour types that are considered anticompetitive in the utility fees area. These practices are:

- Establishing fees that are below operational costs, especially when the same company provides services in other markets where it is dominant or where the fees are subject to regulation. This behaviour takes place when fees are established in a competitive market, or such rates are not subject to regulation.
- Setting lower rates than average operating costs with the intention to displace competitors, prevent the entry of new suppliers, obtain a dominant position in the market or reach potential clients.
- Discriminating customers with the same commercial features as others, by charging these costumers with higher rates. This behaviour is anticompetitive even if this discrimination occurs in a competitive market or a market with non-regulated fees.

---

323. Article 32, *ibid.*

Chapter 4. Electricity

787. Based on the general legal framework on public utilities, Law 143 of 1994 was enacted for the electricity sector. This law regulates the electricity service under a market scheme that introduces competition in generation and marketing activities, establishes the principle of open access to networks, develops the functions of the CREG, regulates the sector's institutional structure and the tariff structure and, naturally, sets important competition rules.[324]

788. The State's role in the electric sector, is, among others, to promote free competition in the sector's activities, i.e., production, transmission, distribution and marketing; prevent practices which constitute unfair competition or abuse of dominant position; and regulate situations where, due to the existence of a natural monopoly, competition cannot ensure an economically efficient service.[325]

789. Additionally, taking into account the principle of free enterprise, all operators (public, private or mixed capital entities) are allowed to participate in the activities of the power sector and are free to carry out activities in a context of free competition.[326]

790. Regarding the concept of dominant position in the electricity sector, any practice that prevents an unregulated user or company to freely negotiate their supply contracts, or any attempt to fix prices by previous agreements between sellers, buyers or both, is considered a violation of the competition norms and an abuse of dominant position.[327]

791. Power companies established after Law 143 of 1994 cannot develop more than one activity (generation, transmission, distribution) together (unbundling), except electricity retailing, which can be performed in combination with generation or distribution activities.[328]

---

324. In the gas sector, the regulation has also defined specific rules on competition, such as the definition of restrictive practices, separation of activities and limits to business growth. For example, among companies providing gas service contracts, actions or conditions which differ from those that are customary in the market are considered anticompetitive practices, including those made among gas service providers and their parent companies, the subordinates or related branches, or their owners. Also, to break the principle of neutrality and tariff treatment to customers or users, to keep accounting records that do not reflect fairly the separation that must exist between the services provided by the same company, or the one that must exist with other companies that have owners in common or complementary purposes; to exploit the confidential information of a parent company or subsidiary, where there is common ownership, in order to obtain unfair advantage or to unfairly trade actions or contracts, allowing information that must be kept secret by law, to be disclosed to those not entitled to it, and especially the parent companies, subsidiaries, or others with owners in common. CREG Resolution 057 of 1996, Art. 9.
325. Article 3, Law 142 of 1994.
326. Article 7, *ibid.*
327. Article 43, *ibid.*
328. Article 74, *ibid.*

792. Law 143 of 1994 provides the legal basis for the CREG to set maximum investment thresholds in the electricity sector. These limits, horizontal and vertical, must be respected when a merger is completed, as they have been set to preserve the desired competition conditions in this segment.[329]

793. Prior to a merger, companies should check their participation rates[330] in the market or business, so that the new company does not exceed the limits set by the authority.

794. In this sense, we highlight some of the most important thresholds for horizontal mergers in the electricity sector.

Production

795. As a general rule, any natural or legal person may not, directly or indirectly, own more than 25% of electricity generation capacity rate in the national network system. The CREG states that no person or company may increase its market share of generation by any kind of merger, if the share resulting from it exceeds 25%.[331]

---

329. Case law has supported the functions of the Colombian CREG aimed at preventing abuses of dominant position and achieving free competition in the sector through market investment thresholds. Indeed, according to the Council of State's criteria, 'to promote competition between those who provide utilities is a counteraction against monopolistic practices, while this helps to obtain quality services. The more competition there is, the better the delivery of services will be, since every company aims to offer better conditions in order to attract more demand. The norm of requiring a limit on investment in generation, distribution and marketing provides a mechanism to avoid concentration of stock ownership. This power is enshrined in Article 73, paragraph 73.25 of the said Law 142'. Then in the same ruling, the Council of State added: 'the mechanism to set limits to participation in a generation company, marketer or distributor of energy, as noted, leads to develop the purpose provided for in Article 73, number 73.25 of Act 142 of 1994, to avoid the concentration of stock ownership, which indirectly helps to prevent the abuse of dominant position … . since when there is a greater concentration of share ownership in a company this can contribute to the fact that at any given time it may start adopting actions that result in an abuse of that position … '. *See* Judgment of the Council of State, Division of Administrative Litigation, First Section, File 4443, 12 Feb. 1998.
330. Based on Law 142 of 1994, the electricity industry regulation defines the concept of enterprise as follows: 'Enterprise: A natural or legal person, as provided by Article 15 and Paragraph 1 of Article 17 of Act 142 of 1994, that develops the activity of generating, transmitting, distributing or selling electricity, either developing one of these activities in isolation or in combination with other activities in the electricity sector, any of them being the main activity'. It also includes persons or companies with whom they have a controlling relationship, either as a parent, affiliate, subsidiary or subordinate person or company. When the provider of this activity is a public entity, the subordinate status should be determined towards the nation, the province, district, or municipality, whichever the territorial order to which it belongs is, and its respective decentralized territorial entity. *See* CREG Resolution 001 of 10 Jan. 2006, Art. 1.
331. Article 2, CREG Resolution 042 of 1999 and Art. 6, CREG Resolution 060 of 2007.

796. Similarly, no individual or company may increase their share, directly or indirectly, in the generation market through any kind of merger, when the total power output, measured in MW of effective net capacity is greater than the power strip calculated by CREG.[332]

797. The method to calculate the market share of each operator is not left to the discretion of each company, but is expressly stated in CREG resolutions, so there is clarity in the process and amounts to be used.[333] The participation in the generation activity is calculated based on the concept of 'Firm Energy for Reliability Charge (ENFICC, for its initials in Spanish)', which is the maximum power a generation plant can produce continuously, in low hydrology, over the period of one year. Based on this concept and by an arithmetic calculation, any operator can estimate their contribution in the generation market.[334]

798. If a generator's participation in production is greater than or equal to 25% and less than 30%, and the HHI is greater than or equal to 1800, the CREG must report this situation to the SSPD in order to initiate the appropriate investigation.[335]

799. Also, if the CREG states that the participation of a generator is greater than or equal to 30% and the HHI is greater than or equal to 1800, the generator must make available the necessary energy to other companies in order to reduce its share to the permitted extent.[336]

Transmission

800. In order to prevent the abuse of dominant position and to avoid concentration of companies' stock ownership, the CREG, establishes the following rules for participation in the activity of national transmission. The main operator of the transmission sector, Interconexión Eléctrica S.A. E.S.P. (ISA), and the companies with

---

332. The power strip is the result of subtracting the average annual peak demand of energy from the annual average availability. Article 1, CREG Resolution 042 of 1999. and Luis E. Arbeláez & Milton Montoya, *Límites a la participación horizontal en la actividad de energía eléctrica en Colombia*, in *Colección de Regulación Minera y Energética No 1, Regulación de Energía Eléctrica y Gas: Estudio Jurídico y Económico* (Luis F. Moreno ed., Universidad Externado de Colombia, Bogota, 2010).
333. Articles 3 and 4, CREG Resolution 060 of 2007.
334. To calculate the ENFICC, CREG defines what a controlled and an uncontrolled company is, based on the concepts set on corporate law and competition law. In this sense, a controlled company is the one that is 'found in a subordinate position of a natural or legal person whatever their nature, in accordance with business and tax law definitions and Numeral 4th, Article 45 of Decree 2153 of 1992.' On the other hand, a non-controlled company is one that 'has in its assets or property, the involvement of a person or company, whatever their nature, without the existence of a relationship of subordination between them, according to what is defined by commercial and tax law and the paragraph 4, Article 45 of Decree 2153, 1992'. *See* paras 1 and 2 of Art. 7 of CREG Resolution 042 of 1999 and Art. 3 CREG Resolution 060 of 2007.
335. The method of calculating the HHI index is also indicated by CREG. CREG Resolution 060 of 28 Jun. 2007, Art. 4. Available at: www.creg.gov.co.
336. Article 4, CREG Resolution 060 of 2007.

whom it has a control relationship, can only increase their participation in the transmission activity when they are chosen as beneficiaries in the expansion plans' selection processes of the national transmission system. ISA cannot acquire equity interest or shares in other national transmission companies, or increase its participation in other transmission companies, present or future ones, except in those in which it has a control relationship.[337] Similarly, ISA cannot acquire transmission assets of other companies that are chosen in the national network expansion programmes' of the transmission system, except the transmission assets of businesses over which it has a control relationship.[338]

801. Applicants participating in the same selecting process of the national transmission system's expansion cannot have a control relationship, either as a parent, affiliate, subsidiary or subordinate company.[339]

Distribution

802. CREG Resolution 128 of 1996 provided that no company could own more than 25% in distribution activities. However, this limitation was annulled by CREG Resolution 001 of 2006.[340]

Marketing

803. No company can own, directly or indirectly, more than 25% in an electricity trading company. In order to calculate this percentage in a merger, the sum of the companies' shares must be taken into account from the time the control relationship between them started. If a company exceeds the limit, it will have a maximum of one year, as soon as it exceeds the limit, to take the necessary steps to adjust its market share.[341]

804. With the adoption of Law 1955 of 2019, no limits are longer imposed to vertical mergers in the electricity sector.

Production

337. Letter (b) of Art. 10 of CREG Resolution 001 of 10 Jan. 2006. Available at: www.creg.gov.co.
338. The limitations set forth in subparagraph (b) of Art. 10 of Resolution CREG 001 of 2006, only apply to ISA in its capacity as the dominant operator of the electricity transmission network in Colombia, it is not applicable to other transmission companies. These differential measurements over ISA are justified as the company operates on more than 70% of the country's transmission network.
339. Letter (d) of Art. 10 of CREG Resolution 001 of 10 Jan. 2006.
340. Article 4 of CREG Resolution 001 of 10 Jan. 2006 and Art. 5 of CREG Resolution 128 of 17 Dec. 1996.
341. To calculate the market share, the percentage of direct involvement that the company has in marketing, is added to the percentage of direct participation held by other companies having a control relationship with the first one, either as a parent, subsidiary, or subordinate company. Article 1 of CREG Resolution 024 of 16 Mar. 2009. Available at: www.creg.gov.co.

805. A generator can freely develop a marketing activity,[342] but no generation company may hold shares or capital stock representing over 25% of the capital of a distribution company.[343] Meanwhile, generators (or vertically merged companies, i.e., those that jointly develop generation, distribution and marketing)[344] may not hold shares or capital stock representing over 15% of a national transmission company's capital stock. Power generators must not have a control position and/or be a controller of that transmission company.

Transmission

806. No company incorporated after 1994 can simultaneously develop activities of electricity generation, distribution and marketing.[345] Meanwhile, ISA, as the company responsible for domestic interconnection at the entry into force of Law 143 of 1994, cannot participate in the activities of generation, distribution and marketing.[346] All companies established as utility companies (ESP, for its initials in Spanish) wishing to participate in the selection process of the national transmission system expansion plans must have the sole purpose of national transmission activity in the electricity sector.[347]

Distribution

807. The distribution activity can be performed freely alongside with the marketing activity.[348] However, no distribution company may hold shares, quotas or capital stock representing more than 25% of the generation company's capital.[349] Distributors may also hold shares, quotas or capital stock, representing over 15% of the capital of a national transmission company.

Marketing

808. As mentioned above, marketing can be developed simultaneously with generation or distribution. However, marketers cannot have shares, quotas or capital stock, representing over 15% of the capital of a national transmission company.

342. Article 74, Law 143 of 1994.
343. Article 6, CREG Resolution 128 of 1996.
344. Vertically merged companies are those which, before the entry into force of Law 143 of 1994, were simultaneously performing the activities of generation, distribution and marketing. These companies may continue with this business structure due to the authorization provided in Art. 80 of Law 143 of 1994. However, CREG Resolution 095 of 2007 limited their participation in other companies, as follows: 'utility companies established before the effective date of Act 143 of 1994, aimed at the provision of electricity in the national network, cannot absorb utility companies aimed at developing any activities of transmission, generation and distribution of electricity, created after the effective date of the Law'. *See* Art. 1, CREG Resolution 095 of 2007 and Art. 80 of Law 143 of 1994.
345. Article 3, CREG 001 of 1994.
346. Paragraph 3, Art. 32, Law 143 of 1994.
347. Article 8, CREG Resolution 001 of 2006.
348. Article 74, Law 143 of 1994.
349. Article 6, CREG Resolution 128 of 1996.

Marketing companies must not control or be controlled by transmission companies. However, they may hold shares, capital stock or quotas, representing over 15% of stocks in a transmission company, as long as the profits do not cover more than 2% of the total revenues from the STN transmission.[350]

809. It should be noted that this sector's regulation follows the general competition law procedure for mergers. The SIC must be notified previously of all mergers, spin-offs, acquisitions or control acquisitions, by submitting all the relevant information and taking into account the counter arguments against the transaction.[351]

810. In investigations on restrictive practices or merger control, the SIC must report these procedures to the CREG and the SSPD, so these agencies can send a technical report on the matter to the competition authority. These concepts are not binding for the SIC, but if it does not agree with any such, it must state specifically the legal or economic reasons for its decision.[352]

811. Finally, Law 1340 of 2009 gives the SIC the possibility of submitting a previous concept on draft regulations that may have an effect on competition in the markets. Regulatory authorities, including the CREG, should inform the SIC on the administrative acts that they intend to issue. The SIC releases an opinion, which is not binding; however, if the regulatory authority departs from the opinion, it has to state the reasons. This function, known as competition advocacy,[353] is critical for the regulatory process in the energy sector and has already been implemented in the most recent reform of the electricity trading regime: CREG Resolution 156 of 2011.[354]

812. However, Law 1955 of 2019 allows electricity companies to integrate all the activities (bundled of activities). For this, the law establishes that the electricity authority, CREG, is in charge of regulating the terms of it.[355] So far, such regulation has not been enacted yet. This law breaks the paradigm of the expected unbundling of activities in a liberalized electricity industry. The law restricts bundling by establishing that when an integrated electricity company (generation and/or retailer and or distribution) controls more than 25% of the demand of the grid-connected system, the company cannot supply with its own energy more than 40% of the regulated users' demand.[356] The government or CREG may establish a percentage lower

350. Letter (c) of Art. 10, CREG Resolution 001 of 2006 and Art. 2, CREG Resolution 095 of 2007.
351. Article 4, CREG Resolution 042 of 1999.
352. Article 8, Law 1340 of 2009.
353. Article 7, *ibid.*
354. Indeed, at the request of the CREG, the SIC presented a concept of regulatory projects that changed the electricity trading regime. This concept, dated 3 Nov. 2011, is in CREG document No. 123 of 17 Nov. 2011, entitled 'Análisis de los Comentarios a la Resolución CREG 143 de 2010'. Available at: http://www.creg.gov.co/html/i_portals/index.php?p_origin=internal&p_name=content&p_id=MI-75&p_options= (14 Jun. 2012).
355. Article 298, Law 1955 of 2019.
356. Article 298, Law 1955 of 2019.

than 40%. The provision is controversial because it may increase the dominant position of already dominant players while allowing them control or set prices and quantities unilaterally, on top of the market restrictions that can be imposed on new players.

813. The primary purpose of allowing vertical integration was as a special and urgent measure taken by the government to ensure electricity supply to the Caribbean Region. Therefore, eliminating legal restrictions that deter strong energy companies from being involved in the energy supply in that area. For the last decade, the Caribbean region was poorly supplied by Electricaribe, an energy company controlled and owned by the Spanish Company Gas Natural Fenosa. Since 2016, the Colombian Government intervened to guarantee the security of supply of the region, and since 2018, it has been looking for a new operator for the area. This is the reason why in the Law 1955 of 2019, the development plan of the current government (2018–2022), allows vertical integration, so current and robust companies that were operating in nearby areas, such as EPM, could generate, distribute, and trade energy in the Caribbean region and finally guarantee the investment that the area required to ensure the security of supply. Therefore, although the decision to allow vertical integration serves a particular and valid interest as is to guarantee the security of supply of the Caribbean region, it is also controversial because it may increase the dominant position of already dominant players, while allowing them to control or set prices and quantities unilaterally, and imposing more restrictions to new players.

Selected Bibliography

Books

Arbelaez Orozco, L. & M. Pardo. *Límites a la participación horizontal en la actividad de energía eléctrica en Colombia.* In Moreno Castillo, L, *Colección de Regulación Minera y Energética No 1, Regulación de Energía Eléctrica y Gas: Estudio Jurídico y Económico.* Universidad Externado de Colombia, Bogotá, 2010.

Barreiro, R. *Derecho de la energía eléctrica.* Buenos Aires: Ábaco de Rodolfo Depalma, 2002.

Colombian Comisión De Regulación De Energía Y Gas (CREG). *Upstream Issues in Colombian Gas Supply.* A report commissioned by the Colombian Comisión de Regulación de Energía y Gas (CREG), Bogota, April 2010.

Comision de regulacion de energia electrica y gas. *Análisis de los Comentarios a la Resolución CREG 143 de 2010.* CREG Document 123 of 17 November 2011.

Cortázar Mora, J. *Curso de Derecho de la Competencia (Antimonopolios) Course of Competition Law (Antitrust).* Bogotá: Editorial Temis S.A. Pontificia Universidad Javeriana, 2011.

Cramton, P. *Auctioning Long-term Gas Contracts in Colombia.* A paper commissioned by the Colombian Comisión de Regulación de Energía y Gas (CREG), Bogota. 2008.

Fedesarrollo. *Obstáculos para el desarrollo del Gas Natural en Colombia. Informe preparado para la Misión de Servicios Públicos.* Bogota, December 2003.

Harbord, D. & N-H. von der Fehr. *Regulation and Incentives for Investment in the Colombian Gas Transport Network.* A report commissioned by CREG, Bogota, 2010.

Harbord, D. *Upstream Issues in Colombian Gas Supply.* A report commissioned by the CREG, Bogota, April 2010.

Mancero Bucheli, G. *Adquisición de Empresas en el Sector Minero y Petrolero Colombiano. Colección de Estudios en Derecho Minero y Energético 4* (Acquisition of Companies in the Colombian Mining and Oil sector. Collection of Studies in Mining and Energy Law 4). Bogotá: Universidad Externado de Colombia, 2012.

Pando, L. *Solución a los Problemas de la Regulación de los Servicios Públicos Domiciliarios.* Thesis, Facultad de Jurisprudencia. Bogotá: Universidad del Rosario, December 1999.

Selected Bibliography

Pando, L. *Regulación y Competencia en gas natural: Una visión crítica del mercado colombiano*, in *Regulación de Energía Eléctrica y Gas: Estudio Jurídico y Económico.* Bogotá: Universidad Externado de Colombia, December 2010.

Poyry Energy Consulting. *Recommendations for Further Development of the Colombian Gas Market.* A report commissioned by the National Hydrocarbon Agency (ANH), Bogota, 2010.

Prosser, T. *Public Service Law: Privatization's Unexpected Offspring.* Law and Contemporary Problems, 63/4, 2000.

Rodríguez, L. *Derecho Administrativo General y Colombiano.* Bogotá: Temis Librería, 1981.

UPME. *Boletín Estadístico de Minas y Energía 1990–2010.*, 2010.

UPME. *La Cadena del Gas Natural en Colombia.* Bogota, 2005.

Vedel, G. *Derecho Administrativo.* Madrid: Aguilar, 1980.

Velandia, M. *Competition Law and consumption.* 2nd ed. Bogota: Universidad Externado de Colombia, 2011.

Articles

Alexander, I., C. Mayer & H. Weeds. 'Regulatory Structure and Risk and Infrastructure Firms. An International Comparison'. *World Bank Policy Research Working Paper No.* 1698 (2004): 1–72.

Asociación Colombiana De Ingeniería De Petróleos. 'Historia del Petróleo en Colombia'. Available at: http://www.alip.org/docs/Historias/breve_historia_petrolera_colombia.pdf.pdf.

Energy Information Administration. 'Country Analysis Briefs: Colombia'. Available at: http://www.eia.gov/cabs/Colombia/pdf.pdf, June 2012.

Frontier Economics. 'Diagnostic of Natural Gas Market Failures in Colombia', Report for the Inter-American Development Bank. Available at: https://www.frontier-economics.com/media/1120/20180118_revision-institucional-del-mercado-de-energia-mayorista-de-colombia_frontier.pdf, 2017.

Macías Gómez & Asociados. 'Legal Analysis'. Available at: http://www.maciasabogados.com/NewsDetail/272/1/BrevesComentariosenTornoalDecreto2820de2010SobreLicenciasAmbientales.

López, E., et al. 'La Economia Petrolera en Colombia'. *Borradores de economía* ('Petroleum Economy in Colombia' *Economy Drafts*). *Bogotá: Banco de la República* No. 692 (2012): 1–102.

Ministerio De Minas Y Energía. 'Memorias al Congreso de la República 2010–2011'. Available at: http://www.upme.gov.co/Upme12/2011/Memorias_Congreso_2010_2011.pdf .

Pipeline, B.I. 'Segundo informe de consultoría para la definición del contrato de vinculación de operadores para las Zonas no Interconectadas'. Available at: http://www.minminas.gov.co/minminas/downloads/UserFiles/File/ENERGIA/sanandres/Informe%20Mecanismos%20Seleccion%20Operadores%20ZNI.pdf.

Proexport. 'Invierta en Colombia'. Available at: http://www.inviertaencolombia.com.co/Adjuntos/062_Brochure%20Invierta%20en%20Colombia-%20Diciembre,%202010.pdf.

Sandoval, A.M. 'Monografía del sector de electricidad y gas colombiano: condiciones actuales y retos futuros'. Available at: https://www.dnp.gov.co/Portals/0/archivos/documentos/DEE/Archivos_Economia/272.pdf.
Statistical Petroleum Report of the Colombian Oil Association. Available at: http://www.acp.com.co/assets/documents/asuntos%20economicos/IEP.xls.
Superintendence of Industry and Commerce. 'What is an Anticompetitive Agreement?'. Available at: http://www.sic.gov.co/es/web/guest/practicas-restrictivas.
The World Fact Book. 'Colombia'. Available at: https://www.cia.gov/library/publications/the-world-factbook/geos/co.htm.
UPME. 'Petroleum Chain'. May 2009.
Universia. 'Población de Colombia'. Available at: http://internacional.universia.net/latinoamerica/datos-paises/colombia/poblacion.htm.
Urbiztondo, S. & J.M. Rojas. 'La Reforma del Sector Eléctrico en Colombia, Breve Análisis y Crítica Constructiva'. Available at: http://www.fiel.org/publicaciones/Documentos/DOC85.pdf, October 2005.
U.S. Energy Information Administration. 'Colombia'. Available at: http://www.eia.gov/countries/country-data.cfm?fips=CO.

Table of Cases

Constitutional Court, Sentence C-447, 9 July 1992.
Constitutional Court, Sentence T-578, 3 November 1992.
Constitutional Court, Sentence No. T-092, 19 February 1993.
Constitutional Court, Sentence SU-039 of 1997.
Constitutional Court, Sentence No. C-796 of 30 October 2014.
Council of State, First Section, Sentence of 6 November 2001.
Council of State, First Section, File 4443, 12 February 1998.
Council of State, Third Section, Sentence of 30 April 2014.
Council of State, Internal No. 000213 of 16 April 2015.
Superintendence of Industry and Commerce, 015 Ruling, 17 March 2011.
Superintendence of Industry and Commerce, Case No. 01425 of 2004.
Supreme Court of Justice, Civil Cassation Chamber, Case No. 6869 of 9 April 2002, MP Ardila.

Legal Opinions

CREG Concept 3-2010-00551 of 2010.
CREG Concept 6587 of 1998.
CREG Document 057 of June 2005.
CREG Document 095 of 2005.
Tax Administration, Revenue Ruling 44126 of 2 May 2008.
Tax Administration, Revenue Ruling 52813 of 20 May 2008.

Selected Bibliography

Index

The numbers here refer to paragraph numbers.

Index

Index

www.ingramcontent.com/pod-product-compliance
Ingram Content Group UK Ltd.
Pitfield, Milton Keynes, MK11 3LW, UK
UKHW020139290926
15471UKWH00003B/592

9 789403 534459